# The Fighting Tigers

World War II Memorial, Ouachita Baptist University, Arkadelphia, Arkansas

# The Fighting Tigers

The Untold Stories behind the Names on the
Ouachita Baptist University WWII Memorial

By William David Downs Jr.

PHOENIX INTERNATIONAL, INC.
Fayetteville
2004

Copyright © 2004 by William David Downs Jr.

All rights reserved
Manufactured in the United States of America

08  07  06  05  04     5  4  3  2  1

Designed by John Coghlan

No part of this publication may be reproduced, stored in a retrieval system, or transmitted in any form or by any means—electronic, mechanical, photocopy, recording, or any other—except for brief quotations in printed reviews, without the prior permission of the publisher.

Inquiries should be addressed to:

Phoenix International, Inc.
1501 Stubblefield Road
Fayetteville, Arkansas 72703
Phone (479) 521-2204
www.phoenixbase.com

**Library of Congress Cataloging-in-Publication Data**

Downs, William David, 1932-
  The Fighting Tigers : the untold stories behind the names on the Ouachita Baptist University WWII memorial / by William David Downs, Jr.
    p. cm.
  ISBN 0-9713470-5-0 (alk. paper)
  1.  World War, 1939-1945—Biography.  2.  Ouachita Baptist University—Biography.  3.  United States—Armed Forces—Biography.  I. Title.

D736.D68 2004
940.54'0092'276749—dc22

2004011035

With everlasting gratitude to the memory of the Fighting Tigers of Ouachita Baptist University and all those others who served so gallantly as members of "The Greatest Generation"

# CONTENTS

| | |
|---|---|
| Foreword by Dr. Andrew Westmoreland | ix |
| Preface by Col. (Ret.) Jack Forgy | xi |
| Introduction | xv |
| | |
| Virgil Benson | 1 |
| Robert Chaney | 6 |
| Merrill Cole | 11 |
| Ralph Croswell | 31 |
| Ecil Douthit | 35 |
| John Duffie | 41 |
| Jarold Duke | 46 |
| Paul Garrett | 54 |
| George Shell Grant | 60 |
|     Sidebar: The American WWII Orphans Network | 66 |
| John Hall | 68 |
| John Halsell | 75 |
| Thomas Royce Johnson | 81 |
|     Sidebar: Coach Lester Bradley | 83 |
| Paul Lambert | 85 |
| William Lawrence | 89 |
|     Sidebar: How Vern Christensen Handled Fear | 98 |
| Ralph Mann | 100 |
|     Sidebar: Cabanatuan Prison Camp | 108 |
| David Matlock | 111 |
| Dan Mathews | 116 |
|     Poem: "The Brother" | 118 |
| Leo Mattox | 122 |
| Clyde McCalman | 126 |
| Francis Norton | 130 |
| William Parsons | 138 |
| Thomas Pool | 145 |
| Curtice Rankin | 150 |
| Thomas Reagan | 159 |
| John Reed | 166 |

| | |
|---|---|
| Wallace Robinson | 170 |
| Carmon Rucker | 181 |
| Gaston Shofner | 186 |
| Joseph Simpson | 190 |
| Edwin Smith | 196 |
| Poem: "For Eddie" | 201 |
| William Stell | 202 |
| Ralph Stockemer | 209 |
| Andrew Thigpen | 219 |
| James Flanagin Turner | 225 |
| William West | 232 |
| Earl Whiteley | 236 |
| | |
| Appendix | 241 |
| Acknowledgments | 249 |
| About Ouachita Baptist University | 253 |
| About the Author | 255 |
| Prayer on World War II Memorial | 257 |
| Index | 259 |

# FOREWORD

World War II had a profound impact on the campus of Ouachita Baptist College. Many students—male and female—postponed their education plans because of the war effort, most of the men due to impending military service. Some faculty and staff members also left for wartime duty of some type. The significantly smaller campus community followed news of the war closely and prayed faithfully for those who were involved. Following VE Day in 1945, a memorial was planned and erected on the campus to pay homage to the memories of the Ouachita graduates and former students who perished in the war.

Today, few members of the Ouachita Baptist University community recognize the names carved in granite on the World War II Memorial or fully understand the sacrifices made by those men so long ago. I am grateful to Dr. William D. Downs Jr., who saw the need to search out the story behind each name and compile this record so an important part of our heritage would not be lost. His painstaking research and thoughtful retelling of these stories provide a fitting tribute to the individuals who gave their all to preserve our freedom and the privilege we enjoy to educate the Ouachita students who came after them.

—Andrew Westmoreland, President
Ouachita Baptist University
August 2003

# PREFACE

Out of a total force of 15,000,000, approximately 406,000 American soldiers died in the service of their country in WWII. Of that number, 77,000 are still missing and by some estimates more than 183,000 orphans were left behind. Those who are fond of making analogies could probably find a small city population or two that would compare. But numbers are still numbers. When one puts names and faces to the numbers it gets up close and personal.

That's what Dr. Bill Downs did—put faces and lives and family histories to numbers. Only thirty-six to be exact, but the thirty-six Fighting Tigers of Ouachita are representative of that generation who gave so much in the fight against tyranny and oppression. Their stories are instructive and worth telling.

As a professional soldier, a WWII researcher, an Arkansan, and a war orphan, I can relate to these men and their fate. As a soldier, I have no illusions about the dirty business of war. As an Arkansan, I understand the underlying strength and inherent obligation to duty that was bred into these men by their forebears, and as a war orphan I understand loss.

But it is as a researcher that I've come to know them best.

During the past few years I investigated the fate of more than three hundred young men who went away and never returned. I did this for the American WWII Orphans Network. We are a group gathered together to honor the memories of our fathers who died in WWII. We do this in many ways: by supporting the WWII Memorial, by reaching out to the children of the fallen in later wars, by helping discover the fate of our own fathers, and by sharing experiences that only a child who was left behind by a long-gone warrior could understand. It was through this work that I learned of Dr. Downs's quest into the fate of the Fighting Tigers of Ouachita and offered to help.

These are much the same as the others I've researched, except that by the nature of where they went to school, there is an underlying common thread of faith. Many looked forward to the ministry, and most could have obtained deferments or become noncombatants. But they chose not to and

THE FIGHTING TIGERS

xi

by so doing, challenged Fate. They died in airplanes over Europe and the Pacific, in the hedgerows of Normandy, in Sicily and Italy, at Guadalcanal and Saipan. One died from neglect, mistreatment, and horrible abuse in the arms of his loving comrades while a prisoner of war. Some died in the final days of the war, shattering the hopes and dreams of those left behind, who came to believe that they would make it through, only to have those dreams destroyed at the last moment. A sniper's bullet, a random artillery round, an engine failure over the vast Pacific—fate forgot the war was almost over. She played no favorites.

Jack Forgy and Bill Downs

The men from Ouachita were young, old, soldier, sailor and marine, married and single, men of God, men of violence. Some died in accidents but most died "while engaging in armed combat against an enemy of the United States" as the criteria for the Purple Heart prescribes.

The men whose stories are told here repose in family plots, national cemeteries, and perfectly manicured overseas cemeteries, perpetually deeded to the United States, by the host nation, in honor of the men who died there. Some remain missing to this day. Perhaps they still rest in their shattered cockpits beneath the ocean or reside in unmarked graves, victims of an enemy who did not have the decency to mark their passing; or they may rest beneath a marker that announces only that they are "known but to God."

As you read their stories, one question may come to haunt you as it did me. Why did they do it? Why did they climb into the bombers and fighters day after day, knowing the odds were heavily against them? Why did the older chaplain go to the front line and place himself in the line of fire? Why did the young marine face his destiny under withering enemy fire at Saipan? What made any of them do what they did?

Some say they did it for their God and country, some say for their buddies. Some say it was pride. Others insist it was fear. Many years ago, my father's regimental commander wrote: "He died a hero's death on the battlefield . . . for the country he loved."

All men who died in war do the same. I am sure that most of them preferred not to die and most probably believed they would not, but they did as many others before and after them. As long as they do, the country is safer but poorer for their loss.

Perhaps my grandmother said it best when writing of her beloved son: "He gave his life for his country, for you, for me, for all."

—Jack O. Forgy
Lt. Col., USA (Ret.)
Warrenton, Virginia
April 2003

# INTRODUCTION

*Trying to build the life of a long-departed warrior is like
trying to eat soft-shell crabs. One does it one sliver at a time.*

—*Jack Forgy, chief researcher for the
American WWII Orphans Network*

Since coming to Ouachita Baptist University in the fall of 1966, I must have passed by the World War II monument on our campus at least once a day, which adds up to thousands of times. And I did so without stopping even once to pay any more than casual attention to the names and the prayer engraved in granite.

That changed two years ago, however, when I noticed that one of the names on the monument was George Shell Grant. Out of curiosity, I asked my good friend Dr. Daniel R. Grant, who served as Ouachita's president from 1970 to 1988, if he was related to the Grant whose name I had seen on the monument.

"He was my brother," Dan replied, and proceeded to tell me about George's life and his death. I was hooked. The interest was already there, of course. My father served in the U.S. Army Air Corps during the war. I served almost four years in the U.S. Air Force during the Korean War and am old enough to remember the Sunday morning when Pearl Harbor was attacked by the Japanese. In addition, I am intensely interested in the causes and results of WWII, an interest that has been further heightened by the recent appearance of such works as *The Greatest Generation* by Tom Brokaw and *Band of Brothers* by Stephen Ambrose. Given all of the above, I was suddenly determined to learn more about the lives and deaths of these thirty-six valiant young men. In the spring of 2001, I applied for and was awarded a faculty research grant to tell their untold stories.

The first step was to check OBU alumni records, which became one of the many experiences that developed in me an ever-greater appreciation of Jack Forgy's admonition concerning attempts to reconstruct the lives of "long-departed warriors." Student records during the war years, as I learned

THE FIGHTING TIGERS

to my surprise, had either been lost or destroyed or had never been created in the first place (*see* Appendix). As I was soon to further discover, much of what little information there was turned out to be inaccurate.

My second experience in this regard came when I learned that a catastrophic fire on July 12, 1973, at the National Personnel Records Center in St. Louis, Missouri, had destroyed about 80 percent of the records of military personnel discharged from November 1, 1912, to January 1, 1960. There were no duplicate records (this was before the widespread use of computer files) or microfilm copies. In short, to this day there is not a complete listing of the records that were lost.

Since no records existed, it became obvious that they would have to be created. For what she did to make this possible, I will be forever grateful to Bettie Duke, assistant director for the OBU Tiger Network. After retrieving a list of the names and addresses of the graduating classes of 1937 through 1945, we sent personalized letters to 648 of our alumni and former students. Enclosed in each letter was a questionnaire (*see* Appendix) containing the names of the thirty-six Ouachitonians who were killed during the war, along with what little information we had on each of these men. The former students were asked to provide any information, memories, and so forth that they might have concerning these names and to return their replies in the stamped, self-addressed envelopes provided with the questionnaires.

Within days, as the responses began coming in, the project became increasingly exciting. Campus mail deliveries each day became an anticipated event as my associate Mac Sisson would yell from his office, "Hey, Bill! You've got some 'old folks' letters!" The responses came by way of letters, telephone calls, and e-mails. "One sliver at a time," as Jack would say, the stories began to gradually come together.

The next major step in the research—that eventually led to the one man who is primarily responsible for the success of this project—was a front-page story by John V. Pennington, a staff writer for the *Hot Springs* (Arkansas) *Sentinel-Record,* that was run in connection with Veterans Day on November 10, 2001 (*see* Appendix). The prominence of the story generated additional feedback but its primary effect was to gain the attention of Jack Forgy, a retired lieutenant colonel who lives in the Washington, D.C., area (Warrenton, Virginia) and the chief researcher for the American WWII Orphans Network. Jack grew up in Hot Springs and Nashville, Arkansas.

The story of what he does was featured on a Tom Brokaw Father's Day Special on NBC a few years ago.

Unaware of my project, Jack was doing some research on a young soldier who had been killed in Normandy. In the process, he came across the name of George Grant, who is buried only a few graves apart and on the same row in Normandy Cemetery as Jack's father, Lt. Col. Percy O. Forgy. While checking the *Sentinel-Record* web site that day, he spotted my name in the front-page story and e-mailed me to ask if I needed some help. It's no surprise that I immediately replied, "Yes." As things turned out, both of us had attended the University of Arkansas at the same time, although we had never met. And our pictures were on the same page of the *Razorback* yearbook in 1956.

The American WWII Orphans Network, Jack said, "is a group gathered together to honor the memories of our fathers who died in WWII. We do this in many ways: by supporting the WWII Memorial, by helping fellow members discover the fate of their fathers and by sharing experiences that only a child who was left behind by a long-gone warrior could understand." In his capacity as a researcher, Jack has investigated the fates of more than two hundred men who gave their lives in the service of their country. His vast knowledge and expertise include access to such invaluable information portals as the American Battle Monuments Commission (ABMC), Missing Aircrew Reports, and the National Archives II, whose holdings include After Action Reports, Journals, Chaplain Reports of Burial, Ships Deck Logs, and more.

The total count on deaths associated with World War II numbers world-wide in the tens of millions. In the United States alone, 405,399 Americans lost their lives and another 78,976 are listed as missing in action on the ABMC web site. The commission's database contains the 172,218 names of those buried in national cemeteries, those missing in action, and those buried or lost at sea. It does not contain the names of the 233,181 Americans returned to the United States for private burial.

Of the thirty-six names on the monument, twenty-eight were killed in action—ten fighting against the Japanese in the Pacific Theater and seventeen fighting against the Germans in the European Theater. Seven others died of noncombat causes, and there was actually one survivor!

For a small college like Ouachita to have lost thirty-five of its graduates or former students in war-related deaths, however, "is remarkable," said

Dan Grant. One reason for the relatively high number, he said, was that the college "had a strong ROTC program producing officers in the reserve. They were called up early and were in action early." In fact, as noted by O. D. Cauby in *The Fighting Men of Arkansas* (Little Rock, Ark: O. D. Cauby, 1946), the reputation of Ouachita's ROTC program had reached the point that it was frequently referred to as "The West Point of the Ozarks."

There is no way to adequately express how helpful Jack Forgy has been in providing documents, many of them previously classified, that would otherwise have been impossible to secure. In the summer of 2002, my wife, Vera, and I had the great pleasure of traveling to Washington, D.C., and visiting with Colonel and Mrs. Forgy in their beautiful country home in Warrenton, Virginia. During that time we also took the opportunity to review an early draft of this research. My gratitude to Jack for his assistance is unbounded.

This same gratitude also extends to Vera, whose love, encouragement, insights, organizational skills, enthusiasm for this project, and—yes—prodding kept me forging ahead. In addition to those already named, I also want to thank my other Ouachita colleagues who have played such an important role in the success of this project: Wendy Richter, assistant professor and archivist; Mac Sisson, director of the OBU news bureau; John Cloud, OBU development officer; and Drs. Deborah Root, Jeff Root, Randall Wight, and Trey Berry. Special thanks also go to my student secretaries, Tiffany Thomas Beck, Jessica Bryant, and particularly Brandi Dodson, whose hard-eyed editing caught errors I had missed. Heartfelt appreciation is extended to those who have been kind enough to read finished drafts before publication: Mac Sisson, Dan Grant, Allen Weatherly, Raouf Halaby, and Drs. John and Billie Bagby.

And certainly I want to express my appreciation to Dr. Andy Westmoreland, the president of Ouachita Baptist University, for his steady encouragement, and to Dr. Dennis Tucker and other members of OBU's Faculty Research Program who made this effort possible in the first place. A word of thanks also goes to Maurice Hitt, director of the Red River Baptist Association in Arkadelphia.

Before ending this introduction to *The Fighting Tigers,* some observations: First, I want readers to know that what began as a faculty research project almost two years ago has developed into a passion, a labor of love to tell the untold stories of these thirty-six brave young men who wanted to live but were also willing to die for their country. For this and other reasons, I have developed a deep emotional bond with each of them. In fact, as I passed by the monument one morning recently, I actually whispered, "Good morning, guys."

Second, the approach that I have used in telling these stories is not offered in the framework of fiction but in most cases as the unembellished words of friends and family members or the dispassionate but sometimes searing accounts contained in War Department reports and other documents. By presenting the stories in this manner, I believe that it will assist the reader in quickly grasping who these men were, how they lived, how they died, and how they served their country.

Third, it has saddened me from time to time to find in a few cases that there is virtually no information on these men. Some of them never married, which means, of course, that there are no surviving widows, children, grandchildren, or other close relatives to provide insights into their lives and deaths. They have simply disappeared in the dark corridors of time. A letter from Dr. Billie Bagby, one of the readers of the manuscript before it was published, captures this sadness most effectively: "To say I enjoyed reading your manuscript is hardly the correct way of putting it," she wrote. "I was deeply moved—the potential of some of [the men] and the loss of such capabilities. Perhaps the saddest ones to read about were those who left no children, nor anyone else to mark their passing anymore. Your book takes care of that."

Fourth, I hope that friends and family members who want to know more about these valiant men will use my research to open additional doors of information. For this reason I have provided serial numbers, which are so essential, along with military units, hometowns, and birth dates. There is surely more "out there" than I have found. I would like to think that as these stories are read, they will ignite a memory, leading the reader suddenly to exclaim, "Oh, yes! Now I remember."

Fifth, I want to provide the former students of Ouachita with a record of how their classmates lived and died to protect America's liberty. At the same time, I want to lead our present and future students to become more aware of the precious heritage left behind by these men. The names on the monument are more than names—they represent young men of strong Christian character who loved life and yearned for the same things that young people yearn for today: a good education, a family, a satisfying career, children, grandchildren, and all the other gifts of an abundant life that can so easily be taken for granted.

It was surely with this in mind that on May 28, 1945, parents, family members, and friends were invited to the unveiling of the campus monument. In a letter of invitation, Dale Cowling, president of the senior class, wrote the following:

> We, the Senior Class of 1945, would like for you to know how deeply our hearts are touched by the supreme price that your son paid for his country.
>
> We are grateful for the influence that his life has had at Ouachita. It was good, much more so than we can say in words, that he came our way and lived with us for a while. Surely heaven is a little brighter today from the radiance of his young manhood.
>
> Because we do appreciate his sacrifice so much, we have sought to memorialize his name on our campus. Also, we think that we are leaving words that he would speak if he could, telling all others who pass by Ouachita that war is horrible and that peace is precious. We are leaving a beautiful monument to those who have paid all. It will be unveiled and dedicated to them on Monday afternoon, May 28th, at 2:30 o'clock. If it is possible, we would like for you, the parents, friends and relatives of these boys, to be the special guests of the Senior Class at that dedication.

The words of the prayer, written by Raymond Rauch, can be found at the end of this book.

In December 2002, I was invited to summarize my research before the entire OBU student body during a weekly chapel program. The attentive silence with which these stories were met was deeply touching. As threats of international terrorism in Afghanistan and Iraq were swirling around us, I shared the words of Lt. Col. Bill Cole, a retired Green Beret and the son of Lt. Merrill Cole, one of the Ouachitonians profiled in this project: "War is an ugly thing, but not the ugliest of things," he wrote, recalling the words of John Stuart Mill. "The decayed and degraded state of moral and patriotic feeling which thinks that nothing is worth fighting for is much worse. A man who has nothing for which he is willing to stand up and fight—

nothing he cares more about than his own personal comfort and safety, is a miserable creature who has no chance of remaining free, unless made and kept so by the exertions and sacrifice of better men than himself."

Sixth, as noted earlier, I served in the U.S. Air Force during the Korean War but never saw action. Consequently, in the process of developing these stories, I had to stop what I was doing from time to time not only because the accounts were so emotionally overwhelming but also because I found myself wondering how I would have reacted had I been under fire. If my platoon leader ordered me to move forward in the midst of a furious battle, would I have overcome my fear and done the right thing? I asked this question recently to Jeral Hampton, Class of 1943, and a successful banker in Russellville, Arkansas, who has served for many years on Ouachita's board of trustees, including three terms as chairman. A platoon leader in World War II, he fought alongside his longtime friend and fellow Ouachita classmate, Johnny Hall, one of the "Fighting Tigers" profiled in this book. Less than a week after Johnny was mortally wounded, Jeral, too, was hit and seriously wounded by German machine-gun fire.

His answer to my question was characteristically straightforward, strengthening, and even contained a good-natured reprimand.

"I guess I am a little amazed at your wondering how you would have functioned under fire," he replied. "You are an American. You have family and friends who are very dear to you. I have no doubt at all that you would have reacted in a way that if you had been a member of my unit you would have acted as Corporal Bryant did when he came to my aid. He did everything possible to remove the enemy and wished me the best with tears in his eyes as I left in the Jeep en route to a medical facility in the rear. You and I are proud to be Americans. We will continue to do everything possible to defend the freedom and life we enjoy."

Question asked, question answered. Thank you, sir!

Seventh, as bits and pieces of information began to accumulate concerning the Fighting Tigers, I became increasingly aware of how so many of these valiant warriors could have avoided the draft by simply requesting ministerial deferment. Yet just as hundreds of thousands of other young Americans did, they chose to risk losing their lives in service to their country. Their deeply rooted Christian faith overcame any fears and strengthened their resolve, as they faced the reality of war and a ferocious enemy.

Finally, to the many people who have responded to my research—their

THE FIGHTING TIGERS

names are listed in the Acknowledgments—I express my deepest gratitude. I cannot begin to say how much it has meant to me to be told repeatedly by family members and friends of these thirty-six Ouachitonians that they appreciate what I am doing to keep memories of the Fighting Tigers alive. To all of you who have expressed such a sentiment, my response is simply this: The pleasure has been all mine.

—William D. Downs Jr.
July 2004

# The Fighting Tigers

# Virgil Benson

Capt. Virgil Benson, B.A., Class of 1941
Hometown: Pine Bluff, Arkansas
Died: March 9, 1945
*0-410527, Third Squadron, Second Combat Cargo Group, U.S. Air Corps*

Capt. Virgil Benson was born on March 26, 1917, to Mr. and Mrs. C. A. Benson in Harrell, Arkansas. After graduating from Pine Bluff High School, Virgil was recruited along with Frank Reed (also killed in action) to play football for the Ouachita College Tigers. Majoring in Bible and minoring in speech, Virgil was a member of the Ministerial Association, the Sigma Alpha Sigma social club, Alpha Psi Omega, the Ouachita Players, and the Student Senate.

## How He Lived

Nicknamed "Nub," he was captain of the football team, a member of the "O" Association, an ROTC cadet captain, and named in *Who's Who in American Colleges and Universities,* and according to the *Ouachitonian* yearbook, he loved to hunt. His marriage to Frances Tow, Class of 1941, of Rogers on February 8, 1940, during his junior year, probably explains the caption under his yearbook photo: "I still believe two can live as cheaply as one."

Thomas Mann, a friend and teammate, reported in a letter that although Virgil "was a good athlete," he was also a "preacher boy" who dropped off the team because "he was afraid it would interfere with his ministerial work. He was very firm in his beliefs." Virgil's name appears in the 125th anniversary edition of the *History of the Pine Bluff First Baptist Church from 1853–1978* as one of "a number of young men of the church who were licensed to begin active Christian service and some of these were ordained." Another classmate, unidentified, remembers Virgil as "a great person and so was his wife. I remember both well. Very few people were married when I attended Ouachita, so they are easy to remember. Virgil and I had the lead

THE FIGHTING TIGERS

Capt. Virgil Benson

parts in the play *The Valiant,* directed by Mrs. Gene Rudolph. Virgil played the part of a prisoner facing execution and I was his younger sister."

Various classmates remember him as an outstanding leader, a nice-looking, confident young man, a very likable fellow, and a fine gentleman.

Virgil Benson in his flight suit in 1943

H. B. "Hunk" Anderson, Class of 1942, of Parkville, Maryland, recalls playing football against Virgil when he was a Pine Bluff Zebra and Hunk was a North Little Rock Wild Cat. "He was a good ball player and exceptional athlete." William C. "Bill" Hargis, Class of 1943, quipped that Virgil was a "great man but had trouble playing football and ministry at the same time!"

### . . . and How He Died

Commissioned in the infantry, Virgil was called into service at Fort Leonard Wood, Missouri, in June 1941 and was later transferred to Fort Benning, Georgia, where he and his wife, Frances Tow Benson (now Barnes), were living when Pearl Harbor was attacked. After transferring to the U.S. Air Corps, he trained for a year in California in 1942, received additional training in Missouri, and later was assigned to Austin, Texas, as a flight instructor.

While in Austin, Virgil and Frances renewed old friendships in 1943 with Bill Walton, the former football coach at Ouachita, who was in the navy. In 1944, Virgil was transferred from Travis Air Force Base in California to Hollandia, New Guinea, where he flew a troop carrier assigned with the task of dropping troops and supplies to American forces in the Philippine Islands.

"On March 9, 1945," Frances wrote, "his plane disappeared with nine men on board during a flight from Hollandia to Biabe, New Guinea. He was declared missing. At the end of the war they declared him dead." The cause of his death was unknown, she said. "It could have been loss of radio contact, or he was shot down." His name is inscribed on the Wall of the Missing in Manila.

After the war, Frances remained in Austin, where she taught piano at the University of Texas. "My parents came and took me back to Rogers where I taught. I went to the University of Arkansas and did some graduate work in piano. There I met Maj. William Barnes, whom I later married in 1947. He was a WWII veteran who had spent 44 months in the Pacific. After the war, he was an assistant football coach at the University of Arkansas, Fayetteville, and later at the University of Central Arkansas in Conway, Arkansas, where he coached until his retirement in 1964." Mrs. Barnes taught music for thirty-four years in the Little Rock, Arkansas, public schools.

She ended her letter, dated less than a month after the September 11, 2001, terrorist attacks on the World Trade Center in New York and the Pentagon in Washington, D.C., with the following observation: "Good luck in your project. It was really a hard time for people of our age who were in the war. Among six close friends who fought in the war, only one survived. He always said he felt guilty. Very sad." Referring to the war in Afghanistan, she said, "I hope we're not having this again."

# Robert Chaney

Maj. Robert Elmo "Modie" Chaney, Class of 1937
Hometown: Brinkley, Arkansas
Died: April 15, 1945
*0351085, Commander, Third Battalion, Thirty-sixth Infantry Regiment, Third Armored Division*

Maj. Robert Elmo Chaney was born January 20, 1914, to Elmo and Laura Hurst Chaney in Brinkley, Arkansas. Nicknamed "Modie," he was a high school all-state halfback in Brinkley, where his father served as mayor and later as a state senator. At Ouachita, he was president of his sophomore class, captain of the football squad in his senior year, a member of the International Club, and a member of the Sons and Daughters Club. A charter member of the Red Shirts (social club) when the fraternity was created in 1934–35, Chaney remained active in the club until his graduation in 1937 with a bachelor of arts in English and history.

A news story of Major Chaney's death reported that in addition to his widow, the former Marsha Hannah, and two children (one of whom he had never seen) in Clarksville, Arkansas, he was survived by his mother; two sisters, Mrs. Frank R. Thurmond and Mrs. Ewell

Major Chaney's senior photo, 1937
*Ouachitonian* yearbook

Thompson of Little Rock, Arkansas; and his half-brother, Carter Chaney of Atlanta, Georgia.

## How He Lived

Red Shirt records reveal that at Ouachita he lettered in football in 1934–37, in track in 1934–35, and in baseball in 1934. Modie was an all-state halfback in 1935–36 and an all-state fullback and team captain in 1937. He was also an outstanding member of the track and field team, generally as a sprinter in the 100- and 220-yard dashes, ran relay races and did the broad jump.

Other memories of Modie Chaney:

> James Walter Brandon, Class of 1937, of Orlando, Florida: "A great athlete and a top ROTC graduate."
>
> Daniel R. Grant of Arkadelphia: "He was a strong, slashing ball carrier in football and an outstanding leader."
>
> Robert W. Smith, of Austin, Texas: "In 1936, Modie Chaney was a senior, and I was a sophomore and we played in the same backfield. I remember him as a great leader on campus in the ROTC program and on the football field. He was always immaculately dressed, courteous, smart and friendly."

In a summary of the 1937 football season, the late W. H. Halliburton, writing for the *Daily Siftings Herald* of Arkadelphia, noted: "The football season of 1936 turned out to be one of the best in Ouachita's history. The Tigers are the toast of the town. Chaney probably was the best fullback of all time at Ouachita. He was smart and a man of fine character. He tore lines to pieces on offense, and his line backing was devastating. We Ouachitonians should be very proud of Elmo 'Modie' Chaney."

Recalling that the football teams Modie played on were among Ouachita's best, Mark Chapel, the Red Shirts' historian, said the 1934 squad was "a Cinderella team that captured the state championship despite numerous key injuries and stiff opposition. The 1936 and 1937 teams played formidable out-of-state opponents (including Notre Dame's B team) and more than held their own."

After graduating from Ouachita in 1937, Modie coached football and

THE FIGHTING TIGERS

taught mathematics from 1937 to 1939 at Warren (Arkansas) High School, where he met and later married Marsha Hannah, a teacher. One of his team members was William C. "Bill" Hargis, a member of the Class of 1943, who played for Modie during his junior and senior years. Robert Newton of Warren recalls that Elmo "came to Warren to coach late in the 1930s. I think Bill Hargis, later a lineman at Ouachita and board member, played for him. He was an outstanding young man. I can see him now walking to church on Sundays carrying his Bible. Then the big war came along."

Jim Shaw recalls an incident during a 1935 football practice that involved a good-natured encounter between Coach Bill Walton and John Floyd, Class of 1934, a six-foot-two all-state tackle, along with his buddy Modie, who was almost as big as Floyd.

Robert Elmo "Modie" Chaney was an All-State fullback and captain of the 1937 Tiger football squad.

"Do you remember last year when Chaney and I led a strike to improve the food in the dining hall and you threatened to whip both of us?" Floyd asked Coach Walton.

After the coach answered, "Yes," Floyd said, "Coach, I don't believe you could have done it."

"No, I probably couldn't," Coach Walton replied, "but it took you almost a year to figure it out."

The Elmo Chaney Athletic Award was set up in the early 1950s, by Mr. and Mrs. Elmo Chaney Sr., in memory of Modie, with instructions that it be given to one of Ouachita's outstanding athletes each year. Scholarship, leadership, sportsmanship, and value to the team were the qualities upon which candidates were judged. The recipient was usually a member of the graduating class.

Hargis, who served in the infantry and was wounded during the invasion of Normandy on June 6, 1944, said, "I had two outstanding football coaches, Elmo Chaney at Warren High School and Bill Walton at Ouachita." He and his wife, the former Betty Callaway, whom he married in 1943, have three children, all Ouachita graduates.

Pointing out that Red Shirts were prominent in ROTC, Mark Chapel said a veterans' fraternity was organized by George Roth, a Red Shirt, in 1945, and that another Red Shirt began the Scabbard & Blade and Pershing Rifle brigades at Ouachita.

## . . . and How He Died

After being commissioned in the ROTC into the infantry (Ouachita was an infantry training unit), Modie was trained at Fort Knox, Kentucky, and Camp Ord, California, and was eventually promoted to the rank of major and assigned as a tank commander of the Third Army Tank Battalion, Thirty-sixth Infantry Regiment, Third Armored Division.

According to unit records, during the "Spearhead" Division's five western campaigns, six separate commanders led the Blitz Doughs of the Thirty-sixth Armored Infantry Regiment. The casualty rate was even more severe in lower echelons. Before the First Battalion reached German soil three months later, it had been commanded by seven officers. In the Second Battalion, the records disclose that fourteen succeeding officers commanded the battalion from Normandy until VE (Victory in Europe) Day. Lt. Col. Carlton P. Russell, wounded in action on August 5, 1944, was the first combat commander of the Third Battalion. Eight other officers succeeded him, with Lt. Col. Paul L. Fowler and Maj. Robert E. Chaney leading for the longest period of time. After surviving the Battle of the Bulge and other actions in France and Germany, Modie Chaney was killed in action at the age of thirty-one at Dessau on April 15, 1945, just ten days before the Spearhead Division fought its last battle of WWII.

Major Chaney was awarded the Silver Star for gallantry and "intrepidy in action" and the Purple Heart on April 15, 1945. No details are given in the citation. "I suspect there were none," Jack Forgy said. "He was one of the longest-serving commanders of the thirty-sixth and he probably received it for extended service above and beyond the call of duty." He is buried at the Netherlands American Cemetery in Margraten.

As reported in *Men of the Thirty-sixth Armored Infantry Regiment,* "The job of the Blitz Doughs was not an enviable one, and yet there was such *esprit de corps* among (the) troops that not one man would have changed places with a tanker. These men were the in-fighters of the division, the soldiers who ensured victory after the cutting edge of the armor had slashed enemy positions. Indeed, in street fighting, the armored Infantry often preceded the tanks. For all the heavy casualties, constant fighting and fatigue, the Blitz Doughs maintained a brilliant reputation for valor."

The Blitz Doughs are said to "trace their immediate history back to Brownsville, Texas, where the unit was activated in July 1916 . . . The new organization did not go overseas in World War I, but saw service on the Mexican border . . . Upon arrival in England, during mid-September 1943, the 36th was billeted at Sutton Veny, Wilshire. With the rest of the division it maneuvered widely over Salisbury Plain, engaged in landing exercises along the British coast and took part in various special training courses . . . In September, the 36th was declared a Combat Infantry Regiment with more than sixty-five percent of its personnel wearing the coveted badge."

Additional information on the Blitz Doughs may be found in the Combat Operations Reports of the Thirty-sixth Infantry Regiment and the Third Armored Division, Records Group 407, National Archives, Washington, D.C.

# Merrill Cole

1st Lt. Jerry Merrill Cole, Class of 1933
Hometown: Harrison, Arkansas
Died: November 29, 1944
*0-305994, Company A, First Battalion, 357th Infantry Regiment, Ninetieth Infantry Division*

Lt. Jerry Merrill Cole was born on October 28, 1908, to Orin and Ida Francis Moore Cole near the Gaither Township in Boone County, Arkansas. After graduating from Valley Springs (Arkansas) High School, he entered Ouachita where he graduated *cum laude* in 1933 with a bachelor of arts degree in religion.

"Never a day passes that I do not remember my dad, his ideas and his devotion to Ouachita," said the late Col. (Ret.) Bill Cole, the oldest of Lieutenant Cole's five children. A totally disabled Green Beret veteran of Vietnam, he retired in Oklahoma where he worked briefly with the late Lt. Gen. Herman Hankins of Arkadelphia before moving to Bentonville, Arkansas.

Lieutenant Cole was an ordained Baptist minister "who didn't have to go to war," Bill Cole said, a fact that led to his realization many years later that several members of his family, including his younger brothers and sisters, misunderstood the circumstances of Merrill's army service. "That inspired me to research and write his biography," he said, which proved to be good therapy. It was also "a wonderful enlightenment for the family members who became aware that their father was in fact a hero," he added.

Two years after Bill's mother's death in 1998, a Cole family reunion was held at Union Church outside Harrison, Arkansas. The reunion included a tour led by Bill Cole of meaningful locations in Boone and Newton counties. "Many friends and relatives in those local areas joined us," he said, and shared family stories. "It is amazing and very satisfying," he said, "to hear the older folk speak of Dad and Ouachita as if they were indeed legendary."

Much of this biography prepared by Colonel Cole was based on material contained in his father's personal effects but some of the most startling information was discovered almost by accident. While Bill was serving at the age of fifteen as an aide in the Little Rock office of Arkansas

1st Lt. Merrill Cole

congressman Brooks Hays, an army sergeant, wearing the patch of the Ninetieth Infantry Division—Lieutenant Cole's unit—on his uniform, came in to the office. Incredibly, when Bill told the sergeant about his father, not only did the sergeant remember him but he also had been with him when he died.

**How He Lived**

Other than occasional entries by the author for the purpose of continuity, the following history of the Cole family was written entirely by

Lt. Col. Bill Cole and published in "Chicken Chatter," the Cole family web site. The following excerpts are used with the family's permission:

> Merrill Cole's family was poor by any standard, growing most of its food in a small garden plot. When Merrill was only a few months old, his mother became ill with the dreaded typhoid fever. After suffering for several days in her home as the doctor fought to save her, she died on September 19, 1909, leaving behind Orin and four small children.

The Orin Cole family, 1912. *Left to right:* Lex, Lonnie, Orin, and Merrill. Cassie is standing in rear.

Despite their poverty and instability, the family rallied to stay together. Bill's sister, Cassie, barely 10 years old, quickly assumed the role of mother, housekeeper, nurse and cook in addition to keeping up her own schooling, frequently taking Merrill to school with her. Their father, seeking work in nearby Harrison, would be gone from home for several days at a time. In his grief he turned to liquor and before long he was addicted.

For several years, Aunt Cassie struggled hard to keep her family together, making do with bare necessities and always unsure of where she could find clothing for the next season. In 1919, she fell in love with Randal Thompson, a young college professor, and the two were married. A short time later, Cassie moved with her husband to Kansas City, Kansas, taking nine-year-old Merrill with her. Soon the Thompsons had two children of their own, Eugene and Martina. All went well for three years and Merrill looked upon Cassie as the only mother he knew and to her children as his own brother and sister. One day, the father failed to come home from work and completely disappeared.

After spending what little money they had, Cassie purchased train tickets to Harrison, and took her family and their scant belongings back to reunite with her father, Orin, and her brothers. However, within a few months, she remarried and moved back to Kansas City, leaving Merrill, not yet eleven, in Harrison with his father.

The ensuing weeks turned out to be a real nightmare for young Merrill, as his father and brothers were gone every day and until late at night. There was no family life and never a prepared meal. Merrill was forced to take care of himself. He found a job shining shoes. Soon he bought his own shoe-shine kit and became self employed. Since he earned a few cents per day, he was perpetually hungry. Often, after working all day at his shoe stand, then playing late in the neighborhood, he would slip into the dark house, remove his overalls and go to bed. Many nights he had nothing to eat at all. He changed his clothes once a week but never knew who washed and provided the clean shirt and overalls.

Merrill had several aunts, uncles and cousins who lived near Harrison whom he had visited at various times. He remembered the big meals served in their homes. Finally, his hunger and fantasy became overwhelming. He knew about where his Aunt Jane Dearing lived and, recalling how well she cooked and fed her family, he decided to pay her a visit. He left a short note to his dad, whom he rarely saw, and set out on foot to try to find the Dearings' house. Uncle George and Aunt Jane Dearing lived in a large two-story house on Crooked Creek, near Union Church about seven miles southwest of Harrison. Along the way Merrill stopped beneath a walnut tree and cracked walnuts to eat for the energy to go on. After two or three hours he arrived at the Dearings' white frame house. Large pails of fresh milk sat cooling in the spring house alongside bowls of freshly churned butter with rocks placed on the container lids to keep them upright. The delicious smell of freshly baked bread sent him hurrying to the open front door.

Aunt Jane received him with open arms. She was a large, bosomy lady with beautiful white hair and a kind, angelic face. She held her dead sister's skinny little boy and vowed he would never again be hungry.

Merrill Cole's formal schooling began at Union Church, about a quarter mile from the Dearings' home, Bill said. Although the school term lasted only three months, that was enough time for Merrill Cole to develop "an insatiable appetite for reading." Later, he enrolled in the training school at Valley Springs, about eight miles away, where he became fascinated with history, geography, and philosophy. "Though (Merrill Cole) was an extremely shy young man," Bill continued, "he enjoyed taking part in debate and drama. During his senior year, he was elected president of his class. In May 1928, he graduated as valedictorian."

## How He Met His Wife, Helen Marie

Because there was very little for students at Valley Springs to do socially, Union Church served as the catalyst for activities for most people of the region. Holidays, birthdays and anniversaries provided some of the endless excuses for a get-together. At Christmas time, the people of the region celebrated a "Christmas tree" at the church. The gathering was always paid a "surprise visit" by Santa who would pass

THE FIGHTING TIGERS

out a number of presents which had been secreted under the tree. Christmas 1928 was especially significant for our family.

On that evening, Santa passed a small gift from Merrill Cole to Helen Marie White. Inside the box was a card which read, "I love you." Until that time, little fourteen-year-old Helen Marie had never dreamed that the handsome eighteen-year-old Merrill had ever noticed her (at least that was her story). At any rate, a healthy romance flourished rapidly as the two young lovers rode the bus to school together, exchanging notes and holding hands all the way, while withstanding the teasing of their friends.

Helen Cole, Merrill Cole's wife

## His Determination to Attend Ouachita Baptist College

Determined to become a Baptist minister, Merrill Cole hoped and prayed that he would be accepted by Ouachita Baptist College. He and Helen planned to marry as soon as she finished school in 1931. When that turned out to be too long to wait, however, they were secretly married in Valley Springs.

A few weeks after [he graduated], Merrill hitchhiked to Arkadelphia to enroll at Ouachita. When the registrar at Ouachita heard Merrill's plan to work his way through college, the registrar laughed at him, insisting that he had to have money for at least one semester in order to apply. Discouraged, Merrill began his trek toward home. On the way, he stopped by Hendrix College where he found a more receptive registrar who assured him that he could enroll in September. While this softened his disappointment, he went on home to get ready for college at Hendrix.

As the time for school grew nearer, Merrill became less certain of his commitment to attend Hendrix. Helen reported that he shut himself up in their bedroom for several hours while he prayed for guidance. Hendrix was a Methodist school and Merrill was an ordained Baptist minister. Finally, Merrill told Helen that he had decided to go back to Ouachita. He felt that the Lord would see that he would get in. When he returned to Ouachita and met the registrar, he was surprised to learn that the President of Ouachita had asked to meet him. Dr. J. R. Grant, the president, listened to Merrill's plan to work his way through school and was very much impressed. He not only directed that Merrill be accepted for enrollment, but also promised Merrill that as long as he remained so highly dedicated, he would see that Merrill was helped to find work.

During the next four years, both men kept their promise. Merrill worked in the cafeteria, worked long hours as a night watchman, and had several other jobs around the campus. Uncle Willie Moore occasionally sent Merrill a small check. On most Sundays, Merrill preached at some small Baptist church in the area around Ouachita.

Merrill grew to love Ouachita and applied himself very intensively to his studies. He learned that the ROTC program would help provide tuition costs, so he enrolled in that program and loved it.

Merrill graduated from Ouachita with highest honors in 1933. Also an honor graduate in ROTC, he led the unit in the parade and was commissioned as second lieutenant in the U.S. Army Reserves. He also received a scholarship to Southern Baptist Seminary in Louisville, Kentucky.

Merrill's achievements, coming from his orphaned background, became legendary in Boone County, Arkansas, as well as at Ouachita College. Surely, with the Lord's blessing, Merrill had earned a chance to pursue his goal to become pastor of his own church. However, it was not to be. The 1930s will always be remembered for the Great Depression and Merrill, graduating from Ouachita in 1933, was right in the middle of the worst part. Also, Billy John, Jerry Merrill Jr., and

Bettelyn Adele had been added to the family, providing Merrill and Helen a great challenge to just survive.

During that time, small churches were not able to pay for a full-time pastor, so Merrill sought out the only job available to him—teaching school. His first job was in Omaha, Arkansas, where he moved his family in 1934. There Carolyn Yvonne was born. Merrill was so desperate for money that he set up a barber shop in downtown Omaha, using nail kegs for chairs. There he offered haircuts for fifteen cents. Business was slow. The family got by on food raised in the garden and small game (rabbits and squirrels) which Merrill hunted nearby. The family cow provided milk and butter but required some commercial feed to supplement her diet of grass and butterheads. When the cow went dry, Merrill decided to sell it for whatever he could get, and buy another one in the fall. In order to do this, he walked the cow twenty miles to the Harrison (Arkansas) stock auction, where he received a few dollars, which helped to get his family through the summer.

Summer time was very critical because with school out, his income stopped . . . that is except for the money he received from the Army Reserve's two-week summer training period.

One day a strange man surprised the small Cole children when he just walked up into the yard. Later they learned that he was their grandpa, Orin Cole, Merrill's father. Orin, who had been in Kansas City with his daughter, Cassie, just decided to come live with Merrill. So without warning, he appeared with a small bundle of belongings. Helen was initially horrified that there would be another mouth to feed, but because he was Merrill's father, she welcomed him into the family.

Merrill Cole's fortunes improved dramatically at the start of the 1936–37 school year, however, when the Valley Springs School Board offered him the job of principal of his alma mater.

He would be also expected to teach English and coach the basketball team, and Helen would teach piano. A completely unexpected break came when Helen's parents, Jeff and Mattie B. White, learned that a native stone house behind the Valley Spring School was for sale.

Jeff offered to make the down payment if the house was suitable.

When Merrill and Helen inspected the property, they simply fell in love with it. They promptly applied for a loan and closed the deal. Monthly payments would be $12.50. Merrill's monthly salary would be $75. Their spirits soared as they considered these developments to be the answer to their prayers.

Four years later, in July 1940, however, as war became more and more imminent, Merrill heard rumors about reserves being mobilized as part of a plan for national preparedness.

Finally, in early 1941, he received official notification about a plan to step up expansion of the active Army. Reserve officers were given an option of volunteering for a limited one- to two-year period of active duty. The alternative was to wait and be called up for an indefinite period. Being an ordained minister, of course, he knew he could request transfer to the Chaplain's Corps and avoid service in his combat branch, the infantry. Moreover, there were provisions for a person with a large family to seek relief from duty. These considerations resulted in many hours of prayer and discussion for Merrill and Helen.

About a year before his death in 2003, Bill was asked to recall details of conversations between his mother and father preceding his father's decision on whether to go on active duty or to remain at home.

I remember quite vividly the prayerful struggle Dad went through with respect to army service. I was eleven years old at the time. Everyone seemed to be aware of the threatening clouds of war in early 1941. Our family would gather around our radio each evening and listen to various newscasters describe the fighting in Ethiopia and China. We heard of Hitler, Mussolini, Chamberlain, and Roosevelt, but, to us, the war was far away. I remember hearing war discussed on "Fibber McGee and Molly" and other popular radio shows. One line was especially impressive to me: "It was Europe, Europe, Europe all through March, but now it's march, march, march all through Europe." This was in April 1941.

Dad received several letters from the Department of the Army concerning his options for service. They were tempting offers. One option involved duty in the Philippines accompanied by family. Dad felt that he had achieved his goal at Valley Springs with the construction of a new school building by the WPA. He believed that he could go on active duty for two years, at Camp Robinson, Arkansas, with the option of returning to Valley Springs—his return was guaranteed by the school board. Our family was in dire need of the money he would receive as an army officer. Dad recalled the years when the extra pay he earned for attending summer training for reserve officers enabled our family to survive.

Since he had attended those training sessions as an infantry officer, he felt that a transfer to the chaplain's branch would be an act of cowardice. He believed that in two years the economy would improve to the point that churches could afford a pastor and he would have an option to pursue his life goal. I remember overhearing discussions he had with Mother and others about the prayerful consideration given to his decision process.

In a second letter, Bill wrote that "being the oldest child, I was fortunate to be able to spend enough time with Dad so as to grasp and understand most of his life values. I vividly recall the great deal of stressful and prayerful thought he gave to accepting active duty as an infantry officer as opposed [to] requesting transfer to the Chaplain Corps." Bill attributed the very strong Christian and family values his parents shared that enabled his mother to face and overcome the challenges of a young widow with five children. "Certainly with the Lord's help," he said, "she succeeded and saw all five of us complete college."

In the end, Merrill's character and strong sense of fairness would not allow him to shirk what he considered to be his duty. He volunteered for active duty. I can vividly recall the anguish he displayed as he made his decision. I'm certain that he never envisioned the intensity and horrors of the great war to come.

In April 1941, he received orders to report on May 28 to Camp Robinson in North Little Rock. But when the Japanese attacked Pearl Harbor on December 7, 1941, Bill Cole said his father turned on the radio to hear an announcement that all military personnel were to return to their bases. Merrill quickly put on his uniform and said goodbye. His first assignment was Umnak, Alaska, where his unit was ordered to occupy and defend the Aleutian Island chain following the Japanese invasion.

Two years later, his regiment boarded a troop transport and returned home. Remembering his dream of being pastor of a large Baptist church, he felt anxious to be separated from the Army as soon as possible to pursue his career goals. After spending some time at home, he received orders to attend officer training at Fort Benning, Georgia, for three months. Because the orders specified that he would then be permanently stationed at Camp Phillips, Kansas, Merrill was delighted with the prospect of spending the duration of the war in Kansas where he could be with his family. Believing that the war would be over soon, he looked forward to at last being on his own and to pursuing a ministerial career.

A week before his scheduled graduation at Fort Benning, however, Merrill received bad news. His orders to Camp Phillips were canceled and he was directed to report to Fort Meade, Maryland, after school to await overseas shipment to a replacement depot in England.

In a particularly poignant remembrance, Bill recalled that when it was time for his father to leave home for the war, "his bags were packed and sitting by the door, ready to be loaded into the car."

The children laughed and played as they waited for their daddy to come out of the bathroom. When he appeared, trench coat slung over one arm, the kids ran to him. He took each one in his strong arms, held them tightly and kissed them goodbye. He asked that they not be taken to the train as it would be too hard for him—he wanted to tell them goodbye at home. I couldn't bear to look into his eyes because I knew they would be full of tears. The kids backed away and watched as they drove away to the railroad station.

Merrill probably had some premonition concerning what lay ahead of him, for as he embraced Helen at the station, he said to her, "Sweetheart, if I don't come back—remember that I want you to remarry. You are too young to go through life as a widow. Just think of me occasionally and remember how much I love you. I don't want you to take the first guy who comes along—but I do want you to find someone who will take good care of you and love you as I have loved

THE FIGHTING TIGERS

you. And you must love him as you have loved me." They embraced one more time, knowing that at the very least it would be a long separation. Merrill boarded the train at the last second and stood waving as it slowly pulled away.

Later, in 1955, "in what must have been the Lord's will," Bill Cole wrote, his mother met and married J. W. Littleton, a man who became "Daddy Lit" to all the children, grandchildren, and great-grandchildren (and "filled the bill," so far as Merrill's prayers were concerned).

Daddy Lit, a devout Presbyterian Elder, supported Mother in maintaining Dad's memory. Mother switched her "formal" allegiance to the Presbytery and soon became the first female Elder in Arkansas. In 1965 she was honored as the Arkansas Merit Mother of the Year due to her involvement in numerous activities. She is buried next to Daddy Littleton in Roselawn Cemetery in Little Rock.

## . . . and How He Died

Continuing his remarkable biography of his family, Bill Cole wrote that soon after his father's arrival in Europe, he was assigned to the Ninetieth Division, nicknamed the "Tough Ombres."

The Division had suffered enormous casualties during the Normandy invasion and after a series of combat failures the unit had been reorganized and assigned to Patton's Third Army under the command of an outstanding West Pointer, Maj. Gen. James Van Fleet. That evening Merrill wrote a lengthy letter to Helen describing much of what he had seen and playfully telling how "the cute French women" waved to him as the truck passed through their village.

The temperature was dropping steadily and on October 21, the ground froze solid and a heavy snow blanketed the area . . . The mission of the 357th was to capture Maizieres, a strategic town on the northern flank. The men of Merrill's company initially followed the tanks to the edge of the town. There the tanks took up firing positions to cover the advance of the Infantry troops into the town. Moments after Merrill signaled his men to advance, he was treated to his first dreaded taste of real combat. German machine-gun fire raked the ground a few feet away, causing all to drop back to the frozen ground.

At that moment, a mortar round slammed into the ground to his right. Startled, Merrill glanced to his right where his radio man had been and saw the youth, lying face down, convulse mightily then lie still. Merrill dove to the man, grasped his shoulder and turned him over.

He was not recognizable. His face was gone. In that nauseating moment as he held the head of his dead radio man and muttered a prayer for his soul, he realized that he must not only lead his men in combat but must also minister to them as his small congregation.

The men soon found themselves battling house to house. . . . The Germans had apparently decided to defend Maizieres to the last man as the fight for the town was tough and bitter. Moving street by street, progress was slow. The GIs used bazookas, grenades and even flame throwers to dislodge the stubborn German defenders. After five days, an intensive artillery barrage was launched to support the weary ground soldiers. That was too much for the enemy. They gave up. Casualties on both sides were high. Company A took charge of 412 German prisoners until they could be evacuated. Merrill was fascinated by how much the young Germans reminded him of young boys back home.

November 1944 found the Allies and German forces locked in mortal combat. Our constant and intense bombing of Germany had so effectively weakened the enemy's ability to support a war on multiple fronts that Hitler and his general staff had become desperate. American and British forces had pushed right up to the German border and were preparing to continue their offensive into the German heartland. Realizing that their only chance to salvage victory was to launch their own counter-offensive aimed at penetrating and dividing allied forces, then drive them back to the sea . . . Hitler launched his attack in the vicinity of the French-Belgian border. The vicious attack, led by elite "Panzer" (armored) divisions, succeeded in penetrating our lines near Bastogne. German forces poured through the rupture and encircled large pockets of American forces.

The most critical pocket of encirclement involved the famous 101st Airborne Division. The resulting desperate effort to save the 101st and to stop the German advance became known as the "Battle of the Bulge." The most critical need for the rescue operation was tanks and other armored units to break through the encircling German forces. Gen. George Patton ordered the armored division of his 3rd Army to turn north and perform that task. Patton declared that he could surprise the Germans because he would continue his drive into Germany using the 90th Division—Merrill's unit. He realized that crossing the Saar River into Germany would be very risky, almost a suicide mission for the 90th. So the order for the next mission came as no surprise for the battle-weary "Tough Ombres" of the 90th. Clearly an assault crossing of the Saar River to penetrate the mighty Siegfried Line would be the 90th's greatest challenge of the war . . .

In the midst of nasty, sub-zero weather, Merrill carefully inspected his forty-two-man unit. Realizing their overwhelming fear and apprehension, he felt a compelling need to minister to their spiritual and emotional needs and gently did so. In his spare time, he wrote a lengthy letter to Helen Marie expressing his love and reflecting on his own feelings and emotions concerning the horrors of war. He declared that, given a choice, he would fight forever to prevent the war from reaching his family.

His last card, addressed to Uncle Willie Moore, said, "I'm still going. Looks like will have turkey for dinner today." On the evening of November 23, 1944, the men of the 90th Division celebrated Thanksgiving with a traditional turkey feast. Late that evening, unable to fall asleep, Merrill sought to find peace with an old companion, his harmonica. Softly he played some old, familiar Ozark Mountain ballads such as "Turkey in the Straw." Then finally some old hymns he loved so much from his days in Union Church. As he put his harmonica away he heard a half-whispered request, "Sir, do 'Amazing Grace' one more time, please." He played it again, louder than before, and sensed that the men of his platoon were silently worshiping together.

That evening the temperature dropped sharply, into the sub-zero range, as the 357th awaited orders to begin its attack. The initial objective would be the German strong point around Hemmersdorf, one of the last remaining enemy positions west of the Saar River. At precisely 1300 hours (1 p.m.) the regiment began its movement toward the Saar River. Stealthily creeping through a forest, the troops reached the village of Tettingen without enemy detection, then halted to await further orders. Shortly after dark, the crossing (of the Saar River) was made swiftly, again without resistance all along the river-crossing sites. The men of the 90th Division expanded its beachhead several hundred yards until they reached the outskirts of Dillingen—and the dreaded Siegfried Line. They stopped and began to dig in.

Later in the morning, Merrill's unit was brought under heavy machine-gun fire from previously undetected pillboxes . . . Around mid-morning, the division was hit by a violent counterattack along their Saar River beachheads. German tanks and armored personnel carriers swarmed through the streets of Dillingen and quickly split the American force into encircled, isolated pockets. Despite the heroic actions by the GI's with their bazookas, the foot soldiers of the 90th were virtually helpless without tank support. Yet they still held out against all odds, beating back thrust after thrust, fighting furiously with every weapon they had.

Merrill's platoon, dug in along the railroad tracks, was effectively pinned down and cut off from other friendly forces. Calling for covering fire, Merrill began to move his men toward a better position. As they approached the new positions they were again pinned down by withering machine-gun fire forcing them to withdraw to cover—crawling inch by inch as German artillery and mortar rounds exploded all around. Sometime after dark they reached a relatively good position which allowed some minimal cover. They settled down for the night.

By this time, the continuous exposure and hardships of winter fighting began to show on everyone. Day by day the men struggled through snowdrifts and frozen ground always clinging to their heavy, yet precious, loads of ammunition and rations. When possible, they sought protection from the weather and constant enemy shelling by digging or scratching into the frozen ground. Blankets were frozen stiff with mud and snow. K-rations were foul tasting and frozen. Water in their canteens froze so that soldiers scooped up a mouthful of snow to quench their thirst.

Shortly after dawn on the 29th, sporadic small-arms fire broke out on the platoon's left flank. Then German artillery came crashing down. Pointing toward a cemetery across the road, Merrill signaled his men to "follow me." As he dashed across the road he felt a tremendous blow to his abdomen which spun him halfway around and slammed him onto the frozen road. The pain was excruciating and he felt the warm blood gushing from his wound. As he writhed and screamed in agony, someone reached his position and dragged him back to cover. There they tore off his clothing to inspect the wound and administered morphine from Merrill's first-aid kit.

He heard the sounds of fighting going on around him as his mind drifted into a confused state of narcotic euphoria. He clung desperately to consciousness as scenes from his life paraded into view. As he weakened, he probably thought of his wife and children. Witnesses reported that he became delirious and incoherent, while calling out various names. The raging battle prevented his evacuation but a member of his platoon remained by his side until he died hours later.

Military records indicate that Lieutenant Cole was the only A Company man killed that day in the attack on Hemmersdorf. However, there were a number of wounded, which indicates some fierce fighting by this unit.

Christmas Day passed rather quietly for the Cole family that year. Although the house was decorated and gifts were exchanged, the mood remained somber. A nauseating combination of hope and fear dominated the scene. This should be the last Christmas without Merrill. Early on the morning of 27 December there was a knock on the door.

A cab driver handed Helen a telegram which she reluctantly opened and read: "The Secretary of War desires me to express his deep regret that your husband First Lieutenant Merrill Cole was killed in action on twenty-nine November in Germany. Confirming letter follows."

The telegram confirmed Mrs. Cole's worst premonitions and fears. She screamed out to the children, "Get up, your Daddy's been killed." As the children rushed in to comfort their grief-stricken mother, Granny Hudson silently slipped into the room and embraced her granddaughter. Granny, although withered and stooped to well under five feet, suddenly loomed as a giant as she began to comfort and minister to all. She felt that this was a divinely ordained moment for her to display her enormous Christian faith.

## A Family of Heroes

After the memorial service at Conway's First Baptist Church, Bill Cole recalled that his mother led her family to an eerily empty house. She was suddenly a thirty-year-old widow with five children to clothe, feed, and educate. She had no income except for the small government "widow's pension," which would not begin to cover basic survival expenses of the family. She was not prepared to do anything except teach piano, and Conway had no need for piano teachers.

Heartbroken and paralyzed with fear, she was near a total emotional breakdown. When she attempted to get up, her knees buckled under her grief and misery. For a few weeks, Granny Hudson functioned in her finest hours—faithfully caring for and ministering to her granddaughter and family. Then one evening, after setting the dinner table, Granny called out to the children, "All right, pin your ears back and dive in." She then went to Helen's bed with a tray of food. In doing so, she slipped on a small throw rug and fell to the floor, breaking her hip. A few days later, Nancy Catherine "Granny" Hudson died from the effects of a broken hip and kidney failure. The shock and reality of Granny Hudson's death forced Helen to get out of bed and face the bitterly harsh reality. Despite having virtually no money and receiving little or no assistance from townspeople, she suddenly realized that without Merrill to help her share her burdens, the responsibility was hers alone. That's when Helen—now called "Granny"—took off the gloves to face life head-on.

In a loving and moving tribute to his mother, Bill Cole said she "grew in stature to become the epitome of Christian strength and faith among the hundreds of friends who adored and respected her. Her indelible and exemplary record of achievement with regards to the children, grandchildren and great-grandchildren clearly shows that the story of her life should be entitled 'Promises Kept.' I am sure that she and Merrill along with Daddy Lit, Mom White and Granny Hudson look down with enormous pride as they survey their wonderful family." Helen Cole died in 1998.

In a letter dated June 1, 2002, in which Bill continued to celebrate the lives of his father and mother, he wrote, "My dad and mother certainly do belong to 'The Greatest Generation.' Their unflinching faith in the Lord coupled with sound Christian teaching has provided clear direction and inspiration to all their descendants. As we consider how his descendants have prospered and achieved, we are sure that God has honored dad's decision and blessed his family beyond his wildest dreams."

"My Son," the inspiring message that follows, was handwritten by Bill's father on the inside cover of Bill's baby book on the night before Merrill Cole left for the war. It remains one of the most profoundly moving reading experiences of my life.

My Son

As I am lying here upon my pillow, tossing uneasily in a vain attempt to sleep, suddenly your tousled hair and laughing face appear transfigured in the room. But this time your dancing blue eyes seem to be challenging me, inquiring about what future lies before you, what dreams are planned, what ambitions will be inspired. My answer to your questioning look is this:

For long years, we shall journey hand in hand. We will follow Goldilocks and Little Red Riding Hood into the woods. We will climb Jack's beanstalk and adventure with Robinson Crusoe. Then we will sit at the campfire of hundreds of people, and lie with the Shepherds of Syrian hills, listening, as each recites the legends of his race.

Gradually, step by step, we shall venture into the halls of knowledge where you shall meet the immortal teachers of man. They will teach you how to live with yourself and others. Sometimes "others" will crowd out the personal pronoun and you will learn the deeper meaning of sacrifice. You will know the high joy of having friends, and greater still of being one. You will be taught the proper attitudes towards your body and how to use and care for it. You will be encouraged to play sports—tennis and golf—to swim, run and enjoy life. History will open the past and show you the kingdoms of the world. You will see man's persistent struggle for light. You will discover that all who wore purple silks were not kings nor all who were persecuted, felons.

Science will teach you to trace the paths of electrons, to analyze compounds, to overcome diseases, and chart a universe of a million whirling galaxies. It will lead you to seek the soul of earth in rock and flower. You will plot the laws of fleeting thoughts and move mountains with figures. The arts will teach you the beauty of line, color and sound. These will be the eyes and ears of your mind to a world essentially invisible. At the same time, you will learn to apply your skill to the world's work. Literature will transport you on its magic carpet to distant (places) and introduce you to strange and beautiful truths.

THE FIGHTING TIGERS

The late Col. (ret.) Bill Cole, a Green Beret veteran, and his wife, Elaine

Philosophy will help you take the long look. It will teach you to think, though no man will be wise enough to tell you what to think. Finally, religion will take your hand and lead you into the temple. There your spirit will be lifted up in worship. Let devout wisdom be the acid by which you test every gem of faith. But above all, find HIM who whispers in the stillness of night, who draws back the curtains for the dawn, and guides the birds in their migrations. Be sure that the essence of your religion is this: to find God and befriend man. Follow that gleam to the new day!!! Gradually you will grow beyond me. The time will come when you will choose your life work and your life companion. You will assume your place of responsibility among new leaders. Then one day you will take your son and show him a still greater day for mankind. By that time we will no longer be walking together. You will have pushed out into a world unknown to me and will be leading a people I shall never see. It will be your day and your generation. Such is my dream for you, my son.

Good night.

Lieutenant Cole is buried with twenty thousand other Americans who died in the war in the American Military Cemetery in Saint-Avold, France. As described by his son, Bill, "The cemetery, situated among peaceful, rolling hills, is only a few kilometers from Dillingen where Merrill was killed. Nearby is the range of hills [that contain] part of the fortifications of the famous French Maginot Line. To the south, in the valley, is the town of Saint-Avold [which] was liberated on 27 November 1944 by advancing American troops from the 80th Division of the Seventh Army." He was awarded the Purple Heart for wounds received which resulted in his death.

American Military Cemetery in Saint-Avold, France, where Merrill Cole is buried. The cemetery is only a few kilometers from Dillingen where he was killed.

# Ralph Croswell

Pfc. Ralph Linder Croswell, former student, 1941–1942
Hometown: Crossett, Arkansas
Died: September 20, 1943
*414794, Company D, First Battalion, Third Marine Regiment, Third Marine Division, USMC*

Pfc. Ralph Linder Croswell was born September 1, 1923, to Mr. and Mrs. Will E. Croswell in Crossett, Arkansas. A 1941 graduate of Crossett High School, he received the Gates Award as the best all-around athlete and was a four-year member of the Crossett High School band. He was also a member of the Ouachita band and became the first Ouachitonian to be killed overseas.

The caption under his photo in the 1944 *Ouachitonian* yearbook's "In Memoriam" section included two quotations: *"I am not afraid of tomorrow, for I have seen yesterday and I love today."* And *"I can do all things through Christ which strengtheneth me"* *(Philippians 4:13).*

Ralph Croswell, freshman section of the *Ouachitonian* yearbook

## How He Lived

Because Ralph was only twenty years old and unmarried when he was killed, no family members have survived who can provide additional details concerning his life. There are a few remembrances, however.

The Honorable Jim Johnson, a former member of the Arkansas Supreme Court who now lives in Conway, Arkansas, was Ralph's classmate

This picture of Pfc. Ralph Croswell in his USMC uniform was published in the 1944 *Ouachitonian* yearbook's "In Memoriam" section.

in Crossett High School and graduated with him in 1941. He remembers Ralph as being "a great center" on the Crossett football team.

Dorothy Hickingbotham of Crossett remembers him not only as an athlete but as "a real nice person from a nice family." His father was employed by the Crossett Company. She and Ralph were freshmen at Ouachita in 1941–1942.

Mrs. Neil Castleberry, also of Crossett, remembers Ralph as "a happy, good-natured young man. His mother was a very gracious lady and I often grieved for her when she lost Ralph. She had several children by her first marriage and had lost her older son several years before. 'Miss Bonnie,' as we called her, had lovely snow-white hair. I went to their home many times . . . and remember the big kitchen with the long table. Her older daughter, Helen, had the most beautiful soprano voice I believe I have ever heard. We were all members of First Baptist Church here and we only lived a few houses from Ralph's family. She also lost Helen as a young mother."

"Ralph was the baby boy from her second marriage to Mr. Croswell," Mrs. Castleberry said. "My husband was in the Coast Guard and I was with him in Port Isabel, Texas, when Ralph was killed. I remember how very hurt everyone was when he was killed. We lost seventeen boys from Crossett. Our Ashley County books lists about one hundred killed in the war but a few of those listed are from surrounding counties."

## . . . and How He Died

Ralph enlisted in the U.S. Marine Corps on August 26, 1942. He trained at San Diego, where he finished the School of Music, becoming a Field Musician First Class. After serving briefly in New Zealand, he took part in the invasion of Guadalcanal in the Solomon Islands in midsummer of 1942. As reported in *New Deal and War* (Vol. 2 of *The Life History of the United States, 1933–1945* [New York: Time-Life Books, 1964]), the invasion took place after the Japanese had been defeated at the Battle of Midway.

"The fighting was fierce," the *Life History* reports:

> Marines . . . faced murderous machine-gun fire; the water literally ran red with their blood. Once ashore, they waded through deep swamps in mud up to their armpits, slept in water-filled foxholes, flushed the Japanese out of dense grass, out of limestone caves, out

of concrete pillboxes. They learned to adapt themselves to a barbaric warfare in which no quarter was given by either side. The worst jungle fighting was the strain of battling an unseen enemy. A Marine would fall, the victim of a hidden sniper. Enemy soldiers would appear suddenly and rush forward screaming, "Marine, you die!" The Japanese would infiltrate by night and induce Americans to expose themselves by whispering from the jungle: "Marine, I'm a Marine. Wounded. Joe, Joe, where are you?"

After a half year of vicious combat in the steaming jungles of the Solomons, the Americans wrested the island of Guadalcanal from the Japanese. Ironically, it was after the island was safely in the hands of American Forces and had become a training and staging area for the invasion of other Pacific Islands that Pfc. Croswell was killed by "friendly fire." As recorded in a U.S.M.C. Casualty Report, "On September 20, 1943, as his Company was running a field problem on the Guadalcanal Mortar Range, a faulty mortar shell fell short of its target, killing Pvt. Croswell."

"Since his death was not caused by enemy action," said Jack Forgy, "Croswell was not entitled to the Purple Heart. However, he probably was entitled to the Asiatic-Pacific Campaign Medal, the American Campaign Medal, and the WWII Victory Medal." Memorial services were on Thursday, September 23, 1943, in the First Baptist Church of Crossett, Arkansas. He was originally buried in the Army, Navy and Marine Cemetery, Henderson Field, Guadalcanal. At his mother's request, however, Private Croswell was permanently interred in the National Cemetery of the Pacific in Hawaii, Section A, Grave 648. His mother was living in Crossett, Arkansas, at the time of his death.

# Ecil Douthit

2nd Lt. Edward Ecil Douthit, Class of 1936
Hometown: Magazine, Arkansas
Died: March 2, 1945
01044499, L Company, Third Battalion, 311th Infantry Regiment, Seventy-eighth Infantry Division

Lt. Edward Ecil Douthit was born May 16, 1912, in Magazine, Arkansas, to George Albert and Ruth M. Douthit (a family member thinks the birth date was June 25).

At the time of his death, War Department records listed his mother's address as 1524 Leland Court, Redding, California. He was one of eight children: Ruby, Thomas, Glynn, Retha, Asa, Opal, and Doyle (who died in infancy, a family member said). Ruby, the oldest of the siblings, was listed at the same California address as her mother.

## How He Lived

Donna Riddle of Magazine, Arkansas, is Ecil's great-niece. As the yearbook adviser at Magazine High School, she had access to a 1932 yearbook, the first ever produced at the school, the same year that Uncle Ecil graduated from high school there. She shared a few of her memories of Ecil.

Ecil Douthit was pictured in the freshman section of the Arkansas Tech (Russellville) 1934 *Agricola* yearbook before he transferred to Ouachita, where he graduated in 1936.

He was the senior class secretary.
His senior-page quote in the yearbook was, "If by being friendly one can make friends, he should never have an enemy."

He played a minor role in his senior class play, John Murray in "High Fliers."

He held the office of sheriff in the Student Council. ("I'm not sure what that means," Donna said, "but the other offices were judge and court clerk, so I guess they had it set up like a county government.")

He was a member of the M Association, "which from the picture appears to have been a lettermen's club," she said.

He played football. The yearbook reported that "Ecil's playing has been outstanding for two years. His place at center will be hard to fill. Ecil always put forth every effort for the betterment of his team." He is also pictured as a member of the basketball and track teams.

"My mother [Gahlia Lee Isaacs of Magazine, Arkansas] remembers that Uncle Ecil did some preaching to help pay his way through college," Donna said, "although she is uncertain what denomination he belonged to, and really believed he was just doing it for the money and had no real religious convictions. She also remembers that he taught some college classes while he was living in California and that J.C. Penney's son was one of his students.

"Uncle Ecil was traveling with the younger Penney through Arkansas on one occasion and brought him by to see the family, and my mother remembers that Uncle Ecil was a little embarrassed because of their impoverished and rough living conditions. My mother remembers that Mr. Penney asked her for a wash basin, and she didn't know what he was talking about."

On another occasion, Donna said, "as Uncle Ecil was passing through, he took my mother to town for a meal, which was a rare treat for her. She was the oldest of his nieces and nephews. She remembers that, not long before he shipped out, he went down to the high school and they let him get up in front of the student body and speak. Family members also recall the time when his older brother was going to throw him a little farewell party before being shipped out, but that when Ecil showed up with a bottle, his brother, who was 'a very religious man,' managed to take it away from him."

Family members are also uncertain whether Ecil was married or if he had children. "Not because I don't remember," one relative said, but because "it was a bit of a mystery at the time." In fact, she added, "Ecil said he really didn't know how many children he might have scattered around the country."

Ecil is said to have called a friend shortly before leaving to go overseas to announce that he had gotten married, not because he wanted to but because he was about to be sued for breach of promise. His wife contacted his mother after he was killed to say that she was a lawyer from New York and believed she was entitled to his insurance.

"My mother remembers that [Ecil's wife] mentioned something about having worked hard to get her name up on her office door," Donna said, "but apparently Uncle Ecil hadn't put her name on any of his paperwork, because my great-grandmother got the insurance money."

Noting the troubled relationship that existed between the Douthit siblings and their father, who was said to be physically abusive, Donna wrote that "the family took [Ecil's father] to the state hospital twice, but he beat them home both times." Eventually, the brothers and sisters forced him to leave town. "Mom says that he died in a boarding house in Memphis when he was sixty-three."

On the other hand, Donna said, "the brothers' and sisters' relationship with their mother was one of respect. She was a very religious woman, so I'm sure that she didn't approve of many of Ecil's activities during his young adulthood." Eventually, Donna said, Mrs. Isaacs moved to California to live with her oldest child, Ruby. Ecil may have been living in California at about the same time, "although he was not noted for staying in close touch with his family."

Little is known about Ecil's college days. But after reading a news story in the *Booneville Democrat* reporting the search for information on Lieutenant Douthit, one of his distant relatives contacted Mrs. Isaacs by telephone to remind her that Ecil attended a college in Ames, Iowa, and Arkansas Tech in Russellville before he decided to head for Arkadelphia. What happened, Mrs. Isaacs said, was that Ecil had intended to do "farm work" to help pay his expenses while at Arkansas Tech. But after deciding that there had to be an easier way to make money, Ecil "stuck a Bible under his arm and transferred to Ouachita" to study for the ministry. He graduated in 1936 with a bachelor of arts degree.

At Tech, he served in Battery D of the 206th Coast Artillery, Arkansas National Guard, with his freshman classmate, Dale Sandlin, now ninety, of Freeport, Texas, who sent photos from the 1934 *Agricola* yearbook. Ecil and Dale were also members of the Arkansas Tech YMCA. Ecil was in charge of "athletics" in the 1932–33 cabinet and of "religious" in the 1933–34 cabinet.

As far as his Ouachita experience is concerned, Ray Langley of Tulsa, Oklahoma, Class of 1937, said in an e-mail message that he and Ecil "were roommates for a short time, and I am ashamed to say that I remember very little about him. Our room was above the Conservatory *(it burned down the next year with all I had!).* I did not even know he was from Magazine. Since I lived in Booneville for five years, some twenty miles from Magazine, we would have had something to talk about.

"He was about 5'10"—I suppose, what we used to call a 'raw bone'-built sort. He liked to run, though I don't remember that he was on the running team. Early on he invited me to go to the track with him, which I did. We started. After ten yards, he was twenty or more ahead of me. I dropped out. No more running for me! We evidently did not talk much, each going his own way. He must have been a senior, intent on graduating, and [we] just did not have much time together except for the night. That is the one other thing I remember about him—he slept in the nude. I asked him why he did that. He said, 'It's warmer that way!'"

"Bill, I am eighty-seven and memories fade," Ray Langley said. "Honestly, I never thought of Ecil again after we roomed together until I found he was killed in the war. I am sorry."

## . . . and How He Died

An Operational Report describing events on March 2, 1945, contains a Regimental Casualty List announcing Lieutenant Douthit's death and company assignment:

> Records show that the Regiment was involved in the bloody battles to seize and cross the Roer River. By 1 March the Regiment was between the Roer and the Rhine. They continued the attack all through the night to enlarge their Roer River bridgehead. The Battalion entered Hausen, encountering heavy enemy resistance in the form of small arms, automatic weapons, mortar and artillery fire. Heavy casualties resulted from this action as well as from the house-to-house fighting, which continued in the town until 1700 when it

was completely cleared. At the end of the period, 3rd Battalion had assembled in the town and was preparing to continue the attack south.

The Regimental Objective was the town of Heinbach with all three Battalions involved. Lt. Douthit's battalion, the Third, had the mission of cutting the road running East of Heinbach. Two pillboxes were encountered and reduced along the way. The Regiment continued the attack all during the night to extend and enlarge this Roer River bridgehead in the division zone. Snow flurries during the morning hours did in no way hinder the advance, and the Regimental Command Post moved to Hausen . . . to facilitate close control of the situation. The Third Battalion started its drive at 1000 (10 a.m.) cutting the road running east of Heinbach. Company I reduced two pillboxes at 1230 and by 1510 the mission of the 3rd Battalion was accomplished. The high ground 1,200 yards east of Heinbach was secured.

"There is no specific mention of Lieutenant Douthit's fate in these records," says Jack Forgy, "but we can assume he fell sometime between 1000 and 1230 when the fighting was at its worst." (SOURCE: *After-Action Report, 311th Infantry Regiment, for the period 1 March 1945 through 31 March 1945.*)

## Awards

Lieutenant Douthit was awarded the Combat Infantryman's Badge (CIB) effective March 1, 1945, "for exemplary conduct in action against the enemy." "The date indicates he was a new arrival, as this medal is usually awarded after twenty-four hours of combat," said Jack Forgy. By virtue of his award of the CIB, he would have been eligible for award of the Bronze Star Medal for Meritorious Service, the American Campaign Medal, the European-African-Middleastern Campaign Medal with one Bronze Battle Star, the WWII Victory Medal, and the Purple Heart.

Burial arrangements were made by the War Department with his mother, Ruth M. Douthit. She had requested that he be buried in the Flanders Field Cemetery in Belgium but was told by the War Department's Memorial Division that this would not be possible since the cemetery had been established earlier as a World War I cemetery and that there was "no additional grave space for those who gave their lives in this last war." Lieutenant Douthit is buried in Plot E, Row 5, Grave 53 at the Henri-Chapelle American Cemetery in Belgium.

# John Duffie

Maj. John McDonald Duffie, former student, 1917–1919
Hometown: Hope, Arkansas
Died: July 17, 1989
*0243335, First Battalion, 275th Infantry Regiment, Seventieth Infantry Division*

Surely the most surprising discovery made during this project was to learn that even though Maj. John McDonald Duffie's name is engraved on Ouachita's WWII monument, he survived the war! The account of what actually happened makes for one of the more interesting untold stories of the "Fighting Tigers."

## How He Lived

Major Duffie was born on August 18, 1900, to Jerome and Anna McDonald Duffie. Beyond that, little is known about his high school and college career other than that he played football at Hope High School and later at Ouachita. Two years later, he began his career in the army. In the 1919 *Ouachitonian* yearbook's "Record of Football Men," "Duf" Duffie, a guard, was listed at five-feet, nine inches and 170 pounds. His "worst habit," which wasn't explained, was "Hoping."

His son, Richard Duffie, Class of 1956, said no one in his family ever knew how his dad's name was selected as part of the Ouachita monument. "I suppose that since the Department of War had for several months listed him as missing in action," he said, "someone assumed he was killed. My mother never received any communication stating that he was KIA, only MIA."

Major Duffie's military career began as a member of the Hope National Guard unit, Company A, 153rd Infantry Regiment, which he joined "sometime in the 1930s." Although he was known throughout his adult life as "Mac," he was called "Cap'n Mac" when he served many years before the war as the unit's company commander. In 1940 the unit was activated and sent to Seward, Alaska (Fort Richardson), and remained there until 1942.

Maj. John Duffie, who actually survived the war, spent several months as a prisoner of war in Germany before negotiating the surrender of his German captors as Allied forces approached the prison camp. Because he was thought to be dead, his name was inscribed on Ouachita's WWII monument.

Formerly called the Students Army Training Corps, Ouachita's ROTC program was established in 1918. In this photo of the noncommissioned officers that appeared in the 1919 *Ouachitonian* yearbook, Sgt. John Duffie is at the right end of the second row from the bottom.

John Duffie *(top row, left)*, age eighteen, with the varsity football squad of 1918, coached by Morley Jennings

In a letter dated in March 2002, Richard said that later in 1942, Mac's unit was transferred to Camp Adair, Oregon, "to become part of a newly formed division, the 70th, whose nickname was the Trailblazers."

In 1944, the Seventieth was moved to Fort Leonard Wood, Missouri, for further training before embarking to Europe. The same year, the Seventieth sailed for Europe and Mac was aboard the SS *West Point* liberty ship. They debarked in Marseilles, France, and went into combat as part of General Patch's Seventh Army moving out of Southern France toward southwestern Germany.

During the movement, several major battles were fought with the one at Philippsbourg, France, being the most costly in terms of casualties.

The following is a word-for-word account by Richard Duffie of what happened next:

> Mac was part of the first Battalion, 275th Infantry Regiment and was serving as the executive officer for the battalion. As the 275th advanced toward the German Siegfried defensive line, Mac went to the furthermost forward line to try to get the 275th moving forward anew. While at this line, the Germans launched a counterattack, which was preceded by artillery fire. [Mac] was moderately wounded by this fire in the left hand, arm and shoulder with minor wounds to both legs. The 275th was ordered to withdraw and regroup but since Mac was wounded and unable to move with any speed, he ordered his radio operator to pull back without him.
>
> As he was attempting to crawl back to friendly positions, he was surrounded and captured by the German Infantry. The date was Feb. 21, 1945, which was the day he was to be promoted to Lieutenant Colonel and become C.O. of the 275th. His captors marched him to their lines where he received first aid for his wounds. He was then taken to a German army hospital, where the shrapnel he had received was removed. When he awoke from the surgery he found the removed shrapnel bound up in a small sack and tied around his neck for a souvenir. After a few hospitalized days he was marched to a prisoner of war camp near Rottweilder, Germany, near the Swiss border. During his confinement, he was well treated with the exception of not [being] given enough food.
>
> Early on April 27, 1945, the prisoners could hear the sounds of

war nearing their camp. Mac, being the senior officer, approached the German camp commander about surrendering and placing all German troops in the camp in the hands of the prisoners. His arguments were that the camp would soon be overrun by the allies and an early surrender would save lives on both sides.

Incredibly, the German commander agreed and surrendered the camp to Major Duffie and the other allied prisoners of war. "Mac, along with the British NCO, then moved toward the advancing allies," Richard said, "and made contact with French forces." From the POW camp, Mac was sent to a Paris hospital for evaluation of his old wounds and later to Newport News, Virginia, and another brief hospital evaluation.

After being sent to Fort Chaffee, Arkansas, where he was discharged, he returned to Hope where he and his brother, Jerome Duffie, were co-owners of Duffie's Hardware Store. Major Duffie died in 1989.

# Jarold Duke

Pfc. Jarold Duke, former student, 1935–1936
Hometown: Strong, Arkansas
Died: July 12, 1943
32204854, Company C, 180th Infantry Regiment, Forty-fifth Division Artillery, Thirty-eighth Infantry Training Battalion

Pfc. Jarold Duke was born March 20, 1916, to Harold Morgan and Sula Ida Brillhart Duke of Little Rock and Strong. Jarold was a member of the Strong Methodist Church during the early years. A graduate of Strong (Union County) High School, he attended college for two years, the first at Louisiana Tech in Ruston and the second at Ouachita Baptist College. His name appears on a memorial marker in El Dorado, the county seat, along with the names of others who were killed in the war.

Jarold Duke

### How He Lived

In a letter dated May 13, 2002, his brother John Harold Duke, eighty, of Arlington, Texas, wrote that Jarold was in "the upper part of his class" at Union County High School, citing his report card showing A's for biology, English, and basic arithmetic and a B+ in Democracy. Jarold was also listed as "Class Pessimist" in "Class Night Exercises" on a high school program dated May 15, 1934.
Asked what that could mean, Harold replied, "Maybe it was because we were always full of mischief" or that the two brothers were known for enjoying a good argument.

During his junior year, Jarold's name also appears on the program for "Acceptance of Will." The commencement address that night was delivered by Dr. J. R. Grant, who was president of Ouachita at that time. While a student in high school, he worked at Star Drug Store in Strong, Arkansas. "While at Ouachita," his brother said, "Jarold worked in a local restaurant."

After leaving Ouachita, Jarold and a friend hitchhiked to the Chicago World's Fair, later moving on to New York City where he managed Bick's Food Shop, a fast-food restaurant on 102 West 86th Street in New York City.

He worked there for more than six years before he was drafted into service out of New York City, where he had registered for the draft on October 16, 1940.

He is described on his draft registration card as being five feet, eight inches tall, 135 pounds, with blue eyes and brown hair. The only defect noted in his examination was an "ingrown toe nail removed from the right large toe, 1939."

Jarold Duke

## From Brillhart Family History

Sula and Morgan were married (1908) in a buggy near Strong, Arkansas, a scene they reenacted at Little Rock when they celebrated their Golden Wedding Anniversary in 1958.

"In his teen years, (Jarold) was always doing something to better himself," his brother recalls. "Magazine route, worked in a drug store. He wasn't an outside person although he liked it. But he put his time to other things. He and a friend were school custodians in high school. He worked his way through the years he was in school."

Why the trip to the Chicago World's Fair with a school friend? "I have no idea," Harold said. After hitchhiking to Chicago "to save money," Harold added, "they took a train a few days later to New York City where they stayed with Jarold's friend's family. I guess that he took the first job he could get in those days. . . . As far as I know, he started as a dishwasher ('counterman,' according to the Selective Service Questionnaire), stayed with the company until he went in service, eventually becoming manager. He had a girlfriend but I don't know of any plans. I feel like they would have married if he had made it back. The last letter that I had from him he was in Africa at the staging area getting ready for the invasion of Italy."

Harold was also unaware of what his brother's plans may have been for the future. "He had a chance to go to Navy Officer Candidate School before he was called up. He also turned down a cooking job after he was inducted. He had a middle name but would not use it as an initial. In high school years, he took violin but didn't follow up. I still have the violin, which had belonged to our father."

In an undated telegram from New York City to his mother on Mother's Day, Jarold wrote, "Greetings to my mother. For every mile that separates us on this your special day I send a hundred wishes for your happiness." In another letter, also undated but written between 1938 and 1940, from Jarold to his "mother and all," he writes, "I got your Monday's letter yesterday. Glad to hear all the news. Wish I could go fishing with all of you. Bud must be practically married taking his girl on trips with the family. I had a date with a new girl Saturday night and again last night (Wednesday). She is very nice." In a postscript to the letter to his mother, Jarold announced jubilantly: "I got my raise last week. $18 per week now. I made $21.50 last week because I worked an extra day."

## . . . and How He Died

Documents from the National Archives reported that

> The convoy carrying Private Duke left Oran Harbor in North Africa on July 5, 1943, and proceeded toward the object of the invasion, the southern coast of Sicily. On 9 July, the sea, which had been calm,

THE FIGHTING TIGERS

arose in swells and became very rough. A stiff wind blew, subsiding only slightly by 3:50 a.m. on 10 July, when debarkation via cargo nets and landing barges was in progress . . . For some reason that is not understood, the coxswains of the landing craft guided them almost everywhere except to the correct beaches.

As a result, instead of being landed on relatively compact beaches a few hundred yards east of the valley of the Acate River, the Regimental Combat Team (RCT) [an Infantry regiment reinforced with artillery, tanks and other combat support elements] was scattered over a beach front of 13 miles. This played havoc with the carefully worked out plan of the RCT . . . It is likely that only the heavy naval bombardment which preceded the landing precluded much heavier losses to RCT troops than did occur during the initial stages of the landing.

Initial objectives called for the First Battalion, 189th Infantry, to take the town of Biscari, which lies about eight miles inland by noon, 10 July . . . the commanding officer of the First Battalion gathered what he could of his organization together and drove inland from the beaches. Elements of this Battalion, decimated in strength by the faulty landings, passed Sicilian Highway Number 115 and were within three miles of Biscari when they were struck by a well-organized German force, consisting of what was estimated to be about two Infantry companies reinforced by a platoon of Mark VI tanks.

These troops were from the Hermann Goering Division with which the First Division was contending to the left of the RCT. They were well equipped with artillery mortars and automatic weapons. An undetermined number of their Italian allies were in the neighborhood of this operation. They constituted little more than a first-class annoyance. Doubtless, however, some of the casualties received from sniper fire by the RCT came from this source . . . At 4 p.m. on 11 July, an attack was launched by the RCT, which failed to break the deadlock which existed since the First Battalion had been repulsed across Highway No. 115. At 2230, American paratroopers landed in the Regimental Area.

On 12 July [the day on which Jarold Duke was killed], the German forces began a withdrawal and upon orders of the Commanding General, 45th Infantry Division, pursuit immediately began. A lively action was had near Biscari. It was during this battle that Duke lost his life. Jarold was mortally wounded during heavy fighting in a fence row in Gela, Sicily. Because of heavy fire, his comrades were unable to pull him to safety before he died the same day on July 12, 1943. At 2000 (8 p.m.) the town fell. On 13 July, the advance toward Biscari Airport began. On 14 July, as a result of a direct attack by the First Battalion and a single envelopment by the Third, this airport fell.

Letter from his regimental commander to Jarold's mother dated October 3, 1943:

My dear Mrs. Duke:

By the time you receive this letter the War Department will have informed you of the very regrettable death of your son, Jarold. I realize that there is little that I may say by way of condolence that will lift the burden of sorrow which must lie heavy upon your heart. It should, however, be a comforting thought to contemplate that your son gave his life for his country on the field of battle.

He died that those back home might have a better and a safer world in which to live. The loss of your son has been felt keenly in this regiment as he was an excellent soldier. I can only assure you that I and the others of my command will dedicate their every effort toward ultimate victory, so that your son's death may not have been without a solemn purpose. May God's Divine Guidance be with you in this time of tribulation.

With deepest sympathy,

F. E. Cookson, Colonel, 180th Infantry, Commanding

Mrs. Duke's reply to Colonel Cookson's letter clearly reveals the depth of her anguish:

Dear Mr. Cookson:

Your letter of October 3rd received Thursday, December 23rd. I appreciated your letter very much. One month & ten days after Jarold was wounded, I got my 1st message he was seriously wounded. No more news. As hard as I tried to get a message until 3 weeks later. The

THE FIGHTING TIGERS

2nd message came, stating he was dead. God in Heaven only knows how heart breaking it is for me to give him up. He was always such a good boy in every respect. I had the utmost faith, that he would come thru all-right & be back to me.

If you can answer any of the following questions, I would appreciate it so much. There is so much I would like to know about his life after leaving the States, especially after he was wounded.

How many days was he in combat duty before being wounded? How long did he live after being wounded? What part of body wounded caused his death? Was he conscious at any time before he died? If so, do you know if he left a message with anyone, for me? Will I ever get it? Do you know if he was buried? Where? I haven't got his personnel (sic) things yet. Do you know how soon they might be sent out? If you can tell me please tell me. You don't know how much I will appreciate it. God speed the day for the war to end & all who are left, to be back with their loved ones.

> Your friend,
> Jarold's Mother

In response to what evidently was a second letter later sent to the War Department by Mrs. Duke requesting more information on her son's death, she received the following reply dated October 16, 1943, from Lt. Errin O. McDaniels, Company B, 189th Infantry:

My dear Mrs. Duke:

In reference to your letter of September 29, 1943, requesting information on the death of your son, Jarold, I'm sorry I can be of such little help at the present time. Later, possibly after the war, I will be more than glad to give you all the details. Now all I can say in answering your question is:

1. He was in the firing line when killed.
2. He was not acting as a sniper.
3. He was not killed outright—he was given first aid but could not be evacuated to a hospital.
4. I know exactly where he is buried, but that information should be furnished you by the War Dept.

In Memorial Day Services for the Forty-fifth Infantry Division at Königsplatz in Munich, Germany, on May 30, 1945, Maj. Gen. Robert T. Frederick paid tribute to his troops for "a job well done." He noted in his message that the victory had "cost the lives of many of your comrades, and it is to honor and remember them that we are here. To these men and to the families and homes from which they come, we all owe an undying gratitude. These men have made their own glory by their deeds. It is for us to see that they shall be eternally memorialized by the perpetuation of the ideals and principles for which they fought and fell." (SOURCE: *The History of the 180th Infantry*.)

The dedication of the memorial at Königsplatz included this statement: "From the beaches of Sicily to the birth-place of the Nazi party in Munich, Germany, has been a long and circuitous way. It has been an (sic) historical one, with high points that shall be forever remembered—Salerno, Volturno, Venafro, Anzio, Rome, Southern France, Vosges, Saar, Rhine, Bavaria. Not everyone who started on that July day in 1943 made the whole conquest which we have completed now in some units, not many made it. They made another conquest; they were the sacrifice. To these our comrades is this day and this occasion dedicated and of those names to be remembered, their names shall stand above all." The Memorial Day program concluded with a "minute of silent tribute," volleys and the playing of "Taps." The benediction was given by Chaplain Andrew J. Pollack, Catholic chaplain, Forty-fifth Division Artillery.

In a last letter to the quartermaster general dated August 13, 1944, from Strong, Arkansas, in which Mrs. Duke expressed gratitude for being told "where her son was buried, the ceremony, is all a measure of comfort. However," she adds, "it doesn't heal our broken hearts, our grief is beyond words."

Mrs. Duke then wonders "why the date of our son's death has never been told me. I have [written and] asked about it several times. The War Department has told me he was wounded July 12, 1943, which resulted in his death. I would like to know if possible the exact date of his death. As yet I haven't received our son's [personal] things. In due time maybe I will get them. It has been over a year since his death. Seems a long time to wait. Sincerely yours, Mrs. Sula Duke."

The reply on December 30, 1944, from an administrative assistant with the Army Effects Bureau to Mrs. Duke must have been devastating:

It is with regret that I tell you the Army Effects Bureau has received information indicating that no effects of Private Duke were recovered. Knowing that any possessions of your son would be of immeasurable value to you, I sincerely wish it were possible to give you a more favorable report.

Pfc. Jarold Duke was temporarily buried at Pasteum American Cemetery in Mount Soprano, Italy. In a Western Union telegram dated July 2, 1948, Jarold's father was asked to "instruct funeral director to accept remains at railroad station upon arrival . . . Remains will be accompanied by military escort." The funeral was held at the Strong Cemetery by the Reverend W. E. Jackson, chaplain of the Roy Kinard American Legion Post of El Dorado, Arkansas. The Strong and El Dorado American Legion posts participated in the military graveside service.

# Paul Garrett

1st Lt. Paul Beverly Garrett, former student, 1932–1933
Hometown: Okolona, Arkansas
Died: December 24, 1944
*01182117, Battery B, 423rd Armored Field Artillery Battalion, Tenth Armored Division*

## How He Lived

Lt. Paul Beverly Garrett was born on September 6, 1914, to George W. and Theenie Garrett in Okolona. His father was a state senator who later served as Clark County school superintendent and his mother taught first grade. A graduate of Okolona High School, he attended Ouachita College in 1932–33. For seven years before volunteering for service in the army in August 1942, he was postmaster at Okolona.

The *Southern Standard* (Clark County, Arkansas) weekly newspaper reported on January 18, 1945, that he had one sister, Matilda, and two brothers, George M. Garrett in Boston, Massachusetts, and Rufus Garrett, "in government work in Panama."

Betty Young of Arkadelphia, one of Paul's distant relatives, remembers that the family lived on a farm—cows, horses, a pond, and so forth. "My memories are numerous and most pleasant of times spent there on holidays and throughout the year," she said. One of his classmates, Paul Roberson, said that since Okolona was such a small school district, most of the students were bussed in from about a fifteen-mile radius.

Another childhood friend, Ken Phelps of Arkadelphia, remembers Garrett as "a tall nice-looking young man. Paul followed my dad as postmaster at Okolona in the mid-thirties. I do remember him sitting on the old wooden bench in front of my dad's store with the town folk, mostly men, I guess. I also remember that Paul would show off by opening a bottle of Coca-Cola with his teeth. That was when it came in small bottles. Lots of young people today don't remember them.

"One time when he came home on leave, he brought an ocelot, a feral cat native to Panama. Beverly Garrett (Paul's nephew) and I would hold the

1st Lt. Paul Garrett

The 1932 Okolona (Arkansas) High School Bears basketball team. Paul Garrett, the tallest player on the team, is second from left on the back row.

cat in our lap making sure that he didn't bring blood when he would grab our hand. He was not mean so we never got into trouble with him, as I remember. He left the cat with the Garretts when he went back to duty and they later gave him to the zoo in Little Rock."

### ...and How He Died

After receiving military training at Camp Chaffee, Arkansas, and at Fort Sill, Oklahoma, Paul received his commission in the Armored Field Artillery in May 1943. According to undated newspaper clippings, Lieutenant Garrett, who was unmarried, "went overseas in September 1944 on a volunteer mission and was serving as a reconnaissance officer for General [George] Patton's 'Tigers' at the time of his death. The Tigers, a part of the 10th Armored Division of the 3rd Army, were the first to enter Germany and had received a special commendation for the number of towns, prisoners and equipment they had captured."

The citation, issued December 3, 1944, from the headquarters of the Tenth Armored Division, signed by Maj. Gen. W. H. H. Morris Jr., commanding officer, proclaimed:

Tigers of the Tenth: Your accomplishments against the enemy have earned high praise from our corps and Army commanders. During the first three weeks of fighting you have liberated one hundred square miles of France, and occupied fifty square miles of German territory. Many of the hometown papers have already announced the Tigers as the first of General Patton's divisions to enter Germany.

You have seized 64 towns, captured over 2,000 prisoners of war, and repulsed 11 counter-attacks. Enemy personnel and material you destroyed in substantial quantities. All of this has been done at a minimum cost to yourselves in lives lost and vehicles destroyed.

Lieutenant Garrett received two awards posthumously in 1944 for gallantry, the Oak-Leaf Cluster for action taken on December 21, and the Silver Star for actions taken on December 24, 1944, the day he died.

## The Citation for the Silver Star

For gallantry in action in Luxembourg, on 24 December 1944. Lt. Garrett, a reconnaissance officer, was attached to a combat team to provide artillery support in an attack on Moesdorf, Luxembourg. Placing himself at the head of the attacking force to ensure adequate artillery support, he received a mortal wound shortly after the attack began. Despite his serious condition and the severe pain and shock from his wounds, Lieutenant Garrett, tenaciously clinging to consciousness, directed his radio assistants to return a shell report to his battalion and instructed them on how to maintain artillery support until relief arrived. The outstanding devotion to duty, initiative and courage displayed by Lieutenant Garrett, in the face of an extremely critical situation, reflects great credit upon himself and are in keeping with the high traditions of the United States Army.

## The Citation for the Oak-Leaf Cluster to the Silver Star

For gallantry in action in Luxembourg, on 21 December 1944. Lieutenant Garrett distinguished himself while acting as a forward artillery observer during an Infantry attack upon the enemy-occupied town of Waldbillig, Luxembourg. Shortly after the attack upon the enemy began, Lieutenant Garrett abandoned his forward observation post and, carrying his radio, advanced on foot with the forward Infantry elements in order to more effectively direct supporting artillery fire. When the advance was pinned down by terrific enemy mortar and machine-gun fire, Lieutenant Garrett established himself in an exposed position amid flying shrapnel and machine-gun bullets and effectively adjusted artillery concentrations on the enemy positions until his radio was demolished by a shell fragment. His intrepid action enabled the Infantry to prosecute the attack to a successful conclusion. The audacity, initiative and calm devotion to duty displayed under fire by Lieutenant Garrett reflect great credit upon himself and the military service.

In addition to the Silver Star, the Oak-Leaf Cluster to the Silver Star, and the Purple Heart, Lieutenant Garrett was also said to be entitled to the European-African-Middle Eastern Theater Service Ribbon with one bronze campaign star for participation in the Rhineland campaign. The awarding of the Silver Star and the Oak-Leaf Cluster to the Silver Star indicates the second award of the same decoration.

Upon being notified that her youngest son had been killed in action, his mother, Theenie, sank into a deep depression from which she never recovered. Originally buried in the U.S. Military Cemetery in Grand Failly, France, Paul's body was returned three years later to Arkadelphia by the Missouri Pacific Railway at 12:30 P.M. on December 17, 1948, for final burial in the Baptist Cemetery in Okolona.

A marble memorial, erected near the gravesite by American Legion Post 33 of Okolona, lists thirteen men from the rural, relatively remote Okolona School District who were killed in WWII. In addition to Paul Garrett, their names included Hosea Clark Jr., J. F. Clark, Loyd F. Cox, Felix W. Gathright, Edsel Malone, Dick Nichols, James O. Nichols, Leighton Osborn, Richard Shackelford, Bert Spradlin, Sidney E. Watson, and William Stewart.

Paul Roberson recalled that Loyd Cox, one of those thirteen men from this tiny community who was killed in the war, died during the Battle of Midway in the Pacific. "He was very popular when he was in school with us and was the first person from Clark County to die in the war. It could have been the first war death in the state, but I'm not sure. I do remember that when a message reached J. O. Kelly, the superintendent of the Okolona School District, that Loyd had been killed, we were all so saddened that school was dismissed for the rest of the day."

# George Shell Grant

Maj. George Shell Grant, Class of 1939
Hometown: Arkadelphia, Arkansas
Died: June 6, 1944
O-351088, Third Battalion, 506th Parachute Infantry Regiment, 101st Airborne Division

Maj. George Shell Grant was born on December 7, 1915, in Little Rock to Dr. and Mrs. J. R. Grant when his father was state supervisor of rural education with the Arkansas Department of Education. George was the middle child of five children: two brothers, Richard and Daniel; and two sisters, Harriet and Elizabeth. Daniel, the youngest, would become president of Ouachita in 1970.

George attended grades five through eleven in the public schools of Russellville where his father served as president of Arkansas Tech University from 1926 until 1932. In 1933, Dr. J. R. Grant moved his family to Arkadelphia where he served as president of Ouachita until 1949, a tumultuous period that included both the Great Depression and World War II. George graduated from Arkadelphia High School with honors and later graduated *magna cum laude* from Ouachita in 1937 with a bachelor of science degree in mathematics. While at Ouachita, he was cadet captain of the ROTC and a member of the Sigma Alpha Sigma social club, the Pi Kappa Tau scholarship society, and the Mathematics Honor Society. George also played football and was assistant manager of the team.

George Grant, Class of 1937

He and his wife, the former Melba Smith of Hot Springs, whom he married while they were both students at Ouachita, had two children, George Shell Grant Jr. and Judith Grant-Botter, also of Hot Springs. Judith recalled during a recent conversation that her mother and father were both born on December 7, 1915, but that George was two hours older than Melba.

THE FIGHTING TIGERS

George Grant *(back row, left)* poses with his family in Russellville, Arkansas, during a family gathering, Christmas 1935. Family members included his father, Dr. J. R. Grant, and a brother, Richard Grant. *Second row:* Harriet Grant, a sister; Mrs. J. R. Grant, his mother; and Elizabeth Grant, his second sister. Daniel R. Grant, George's youngest brother, is seated in front.

"He wouldn't let her forget that," she said, still amused by the memory.

## How He Lived

The following remembrance of George Grant was written by his brother Daniel in 2001:

> We moved to Arkadelphia in 1932 where George finished his senior year in Arkadelphia High School and then went on to Ouachita. He loved all sports *(football, basketball, track, tennis, golf and wrestling)*, and competed fiercely with his one-year-older brother Richard, much to the consternation of his mother and father, who had to separate them and make peace, not infrequently. Richard was already a student at the University of Arkansas when we moved to Arkadelphia, so I began to receive more attention from George.
>
> George taught me to play tennis, starting me out with the correct "handshake" grip on the racket for the forehand, and showed me how to put just a little top spin on the ball. He started me out hitting practice balls against the west side of the president's home, which had a lot of smooth brick space, with strong warnings to avoid the one window that kept it from being a perfect tennis practice wall. That's probably when control became an important part of my tennis game.
>
> George liked to sing, as did all members of our family, and Mother and Daddy encouraged him with some formal voice instruction, along with earlier band training on the trombone. He was a pretty good baritone soloist and high school quartet member, although I always thought he went flat just a little when he belted out *Invictus* with great enthusiasm. That particular theme, "I am the master of my fate," seemed to have a pretty strong influence on his life, although his Christian conviction ultimately prevailed.
>
> George excelled in math and the sciences at Ouachita, and had a strong interest in being an inventor. Even during his college days I can recall he tried out several ideas on the other members of the family, including a four-wheel cart whose back wheels would turn when the front wheels turned, and a flat compass that could be stored in the math textbook much more easily than the traditional one. He had a strong attraction to modern gadgets and he loved to give Christmas gifts that were new and unique and would cause the other members

of the family to "oo" and "ah," such as an unusual lemon juicer or a double-decker waffle iron.

George's first job after graduating from Ouachita was to coach and teach at Piggott (Arkansas) High School for two years. He coached "seven-man football," which was a new experiment for small high schools.

His next football coaching job was in Fordyce, Arkansas, where their first child, George Shell Grant Jr., was born. After a year and a half, he moved his family to a Kansas City, Kansas high school where he served as professor of military science and tactics.

He liked R.O.T.C., which was a two-year requirement at Ouachita, and took the additional two years of Advanced R.O.T.C., leading to a lieutenant's commission in the Army Reserve when he graduated in 1937.

Not long after the Pearl Harbor attack, George's Army Reserve unit was called up. Dr. Wayne Ward (Class of 1943) credits George Grant as the major factor in his decision to bypass the University of Arkansas for Ouachita. Although George had been given the option of remaining in Kansas City to teach ROTC rather than go into battle, Ward said, George told his dad, "Somebody has to go and I will do it." He volunteered for paratroop service in August 1942 *(because advancement would be faster and paratroopers received fifty dollars more pay per month)* and trained at Toccoa, Georgia, Fort Benning, Georgia, and Camp Mackall, North Carolina. He was promoted to captain in April 1942 and to major in January 1943.

Continuing his memories of his brother, Dan Grant wrote: "Not long after that training was completed, he was ordered to England where he trained with the 101st Airborne Division for the D-Day invasion of Europe at Normandy. As I recall, their second child, Judy, was born while he was in England and he never saw her before his death.

"Before leaving for England, George gave his watch to Daddy, explaining that it had a 'stretch band' that was not suitable for parachute jumps because it could come off in mid-air. Daddy always cherished the watch and frequently told friends the story about it, including that George wanted him to have something for a remembrance in case he did not return."

Dr. Andrew Hall, Dan Grant's brother-in-law, recalls how his wife,

Harriet Grant Hall, had intended to respond before her death in September 2002 on the influence of her brother George. "I heard her say, 'He taught me to swim, play tennis and many other things.' She also delighted in telling the story about when George was football coach at Fordyce. Her dad, Dr. J. R. Grant, pulled into a filling station and innocently inquired as to who the coach was.

"'Was he a good one?' he asked. He 'cased' the town about his own son."

## . . . and How He Died

As reported in *D-Day with the Screaming Eagles* by George E. Koskimaki, 101st Airborne Division Association, Major Grant served as the executive officer of the Third Battalion of the 506th Parachute Infantry Regiment, commanded by Lt. Col. Robert Wolverton. The unit had been given the assignment of capturing the two wooden bridges across the Douve River to the northeast of Carentan. The (paratroopers) were also to seize the high ground overlooking the bridge positions on the east bank near Brevands. This was to be a meeting point for the Allied forces advancing from the Utah and Omaha beaches.

As the plane carried Grant's men to the assigned drop zone, Staff Sgt. William Pauli, who was the message-center chief for the 3rd Battalion at the time, described what happened next. "Col. Wolverton was in the door and grumbling as he knew we were not on our Drop Zone. It was a shock to see how light it was, with the enemy flares illuminating the countryside . . . All the occupants of (the) plane were destined to be killed or captured as the men were dropped over (St. Come-de-Mont) half mile southwest of Drop Zone "D" in fields heavily fortified by German troops who had been preparing a defense line in the area. Col. Wolverton . . . was killed on the drop.

As the paratroopers approached the area from the west in their low-flying troop carrier planes—most of the D-Day jumps (were) made from about 400 feet—and from planes that failed to slow to the normal drop speed . . . the Germans lighted a house which had been doused with kerosene. The holocaust illuminated the entire area . . . On the ground, a small group of (American) pathfinders *(paratroopers dropped earlier to assist in directing the troop carriers to their assigned*

Maj. George S. Grant in battle dress (from Currahee scrapbook).
Grant's tombstone in the American Cemetery at Coleville-sur-Mer, Normandy.

*drop zones*) watched helplessly as the silently-dropping men—including Major Grant and his commander, Lt. Col. Wolverton—were picked off by machine gun and rifle fire as they entered the circle of light.

Of the 800 men in the Third Battalion, only 117 reached the objective, the bridges across the Douve River. Although the bridges were later knocked out by American planes, the Germans were unable to use them to bring up troops toward Utah Beach.

"I have the bitter-sweet memory," says Dan Grant, "of being with my father and mother at the Siloam Springs (Arkansas) Baptist Assembly where Daddy was teaching a seminar on 'The Christian Home' when news was received of George's being killed in action on that first day of the Normandy invasion. We were standing under a beautiful tree at the time and, after having a time of family prayer, my father and mother made the decision to stay at Siloam Springs and finish the week before returning to Arkadelphia. More than a half-century later I still have people tell me what a strong Christian testimony it was to stay and finish that seminar in spite of the sad news.

Major Grant is buried with many of his fellow soldiers in the American veterans' cemetery at Cherbourg, France.

### Sidebar: The American WWII Orphans Network

In her response to my request for additional information on her father, Maj. George S. Grant, Judith Grant-Botter asked that some mention be made of the American WWII Orphans Network, an organization of the sons and daughters of Americans killed and missing in World War II. It was founded in 1991 by Ann Bennett Mix, daughter of Sydney Bennett, who was killed in Italy.

An organizational profile on the web site states that "More than a million fathers served in World War II. Leaving their wives and children, they traveled overseas, where many paid the highest price in service to their country. Some are still there, buried in foreign cemeteries. Others are still missing or were never recovered. Many are memorialized on the Wall of the Missing, examples of which may be found at a number of overseas cemeteries and in home town cemeteries across the USA."

"By checking Veterans Administration statistics on benefits paid to war orphans," Bennett said, "I learned there had to be at least 183,000 children who were left fatherless as the result of WWII! I knew with greater surety that we needed to find each other, form a network all our own, and find out how to locate information about our fathers!"

The network services include:

- Locating and registering all American WWII orphans and their fathers.
- Holding local, regional, and national gatherings.
Maintaining on-line communication with WWII orphans from all over the world.
- Directing orphans to sources of information about their fathers from military and government records and locating war buddies, family, and friends of their fathers.
- Helping family and friends locate the families of men who were killed in WWII.
- Welcoming family and associate memberships from those other than sons and daughters, from sponsoring individuals and organizations, from veterans groups, members of the media, and other interested parties.

Responses from those who were orphaned during WWII provide poignant evidence of the organization's value:

> My father was just a name among a row of crosses on the edge of the town cemetery. I can't recall anyone speaking of the men those crosses represented as individuals. They were always addressed collectively. The "Great Silence" was not just a thing my mother subscribed to, the whole war-weary town developed the same habit. Now that the "code of silence" is broken, I can deal with my grief openly and help others face their hidden hurt and abandonment. Ann, thank you for your dedication, genuine caring and love in helping us all toward completion and appreciation of our precious gift of life defended so dearly by our fathers.
> —Brenda K.

> I have reflected that when I was born in July of 1943, my father was already stationed overseas. We never lived on the same continent. Our lives overlapped one another's for only fourteen months; the first fourteen months of my life and the last fourteen months of his. While flying on a mission, he was killed in France on September 11, 1944. There are no memories of him for me to cherish, no hopes of ever seeing him in this life, but he remains a beloved part of my life which though gone is always held dear. How good it is to know that he and the other fathers will be remembered as we, the children come forward and join together.
> —Anne O.

Further information on the American WWII Orphans Network and how to receive a newsletter may be found on the organization's web site: www.west.net/~awon/awover.shtml.

# John Hall

2nd Lt. John Milton Hall, Class of 1943
Hometown: Arkadelphia, Arkansas
Died: July 4, 1944
O-525225, 331st Infantry, Eighty-third Infantry Division

**How He Lived**

Lt. John Milton Hall was born on June 15, 1921, to R. C. and Hattie Jordan Hall in Arkadelphia, Arkansas. Johnny attended Arkadelphia High School, where he was a four-letter athlete. At Ouachita College, he was a member of the Sigma Alpha Sigma social club, serving as vice president and a member of the Rifle Club, the Math Honor Society, and the tennis team (he was the state singles champion during his freshman year); as a senior, he was ROTC cadet captain of Company A and a member of the "O" Association. The caption under his yearbook picture: "His mien distinguished any crowd." Johnny was also the seventeenth member of his family to graduate from Ouachita.

Dan Grant, a lifelong tennis player, says he tried to pattern his forehand swing after that of Johnny, who was two years ahead of him at Arkadelphia High

Johnny Hall, 1943 senior class photo

THE FIGHTING TIGERS

School and Ouachita. "He once advised me in ROTC on how to answer tough questions on a test— Always say 'It depends upon the terrain.'"

On November 16, 1943, Johnny married Ellen Frances Johnson, Class of 1943, from Pine Bluff, who later attended the Pasadena (California) School of Theater. At the time of their marriage, Ellen was an English instructor at Lake Village (Arkansas) High School. After Johnny's death, Ellen married James Kelley of Warren, Arkansas. Their son, Jim Kelley, Class of 1971, who was president of the OBU Student Senate in 1970–71, now serves as president of BancorpSouth in Tupelo, Mississippi. Mrs. Ellen Hall Kelley died in September 1990.

## . . . and How He Died

Jeral Hampton, Class of 1943, of Clarksville, Arkansas, a classmate, one of Johnny's closest friends, and a former member and chairman of the OBU Board of Trustees, provided the following account of his friendship with Johnny that followed them to the beaches of Normandy:

> Lt. John Milton (Johnny) Hall and I entered Ouachita Baptist College in 1939 and graduated in 1943. Johnny and I had many classes together at Ouachita, and entered Officer Candidate Training at Fort Benning, Georgia, as graduates of the Ouachita R.O.T.C. We were also members of the Sigma Alpha Sigma social club at Ouachita.
>
> The spelling of Hall and Hampton placed us in adjoining beds in Officer Candidate School at Fort Benning, Georgia, which made our friendship even stronger. It was most unusual for buddies to be assigned to the same military unit, but Johnny and I were assigned to the 83rd Infantry Division upon graduating from O.C.S. and were also assigned to the same company with Johnny as platoon leader of the Second Platoon and I as platoon leader of the Third Platoon.
>
> While stationed at Camp Breckinridge, Kentucky, we married Ouachita girls and lived for a short period in a small town in Kentucky. In the spring of 1944, our division moved to England in preparation for the invasion of France.
>
> In June 1944, our division replaced the 101st Airborne Division in Normandy, and on July 4, 1944, joined with other American troops in the offensive as we attempted to move the Germans out of

Lt. John Milton Hall

Johnny Hall *(right)* with his brother, Harry, and their mother, Hattie Hall

France. About mid-day on July 4, Johnny and I crawled to each other so as to plan for our hopeful movement forward (our platoons were side by side in the attack). A very short time later, I received a message that Johnny had been killed by a direct German mortar shell. During the same period of time, I lost about half of my platoon by death or being wounded.

Needless to say, this was one of the big shocks of my life. Johnny was one of the best friends I have ever had. We played together, we studied and attended classes together, we fought for our country together. He was a great Ouachitonian and a great American.

Following Johnny's death, Jeral Hampton said,

> On July 4 our Division continued to move forward in the Normandy hedge rows of France. These hedge rows and sunken roads made it difficult to use any type of motorized vehicle such as the

Newlyweds: 2nd Lt. Jeral Hampton with his wife, Betty Lou Standfill Hampton, on their wedding day, February 17, 1944. Jeral was later promoted to captain during the war and retired as a lieutenant colonel after twenty-two years of service spanning World War II and the Korean conflict. Between the two wars, he served in the National Guard. Mrs. Hampton died on December 7, 2003.

armored tanks. Therefore, we as foot soldiers led in the attack. On July 12, we were pinned down by enemy fire. I thought it wise to take a look at our situation to the front and to our right. Taking Corporal Bryant with me, we started our reconnaissance. We were moving down a sunken roadway when we were fired upon. We did the usual thing of trying to protect ourselves but I was hit by machine gun fire.

When Johnny Hall was killed by enemy fire I was shocked and hurt. When I was wounded, I was angry and anxious to fight back. We were able to find the position of the enemy machine gun, threw caution to the wind and destroyed both the gun and personnel.

Members of my unit quickly came to our location, gave me first aid and I was transported by jeep to the rear area for treatment.

Jeral Hampton, 2004: At the age of eighty-two, Jeral is chairman of the board and CEO of First Western Bancshares, the holding company that owns First Western Bank in Booneville, Arkansas.

Leaving the men of my unit was tough. We had been together for several months, we trusted and depended on one another. But my wounds required treatment to the extent that I was shipped to a hospital in England.

## But That Is Not the End of the Story . . .

Jordan Hall Williams, Johnny's daughter, who was born after he was killed in action, lives in Fayetteville, Arkansas, where her husband, Miller Williams, is a professor of English at the University of Arkansas and a widely acclaimed poet. In a telephone interview on July 28, 2002, Jordan told me that while living in Rome in 1978, she and her husband traveled to the Normandy American Cemetery at St. Laurent-sur-Mer, where Johnny is buried. After visiting the grave, they stopped at a "McDonalds-type" fast-food restaurant where they struck up a conversation with some fellow Americans, including a middle-aged lady who asked Jordan whose grave she had visited. When Jordan told her it was her father's, John Milton Hall, the woman burst into tears. Identifying herself as a U.S. Army nurse during the invasion, she said Johnny had died in her arms on July 4, 1944, at the St. Lo hospital.

Johnny Hall is buried in Plot D, Row 2, Grave 10, Normandy American Cemetery, St. Laurent-sur-Mer, France. His awards include the European-African-Middle East Area Campaign Medal with Bronze Star, the American Theater Medal, the Combat Infantry Medal, and the Purple Heart.

# John Halsell

2nd Lt. John Calvin Halsell, Class of 1939
Hometown: Little Rock, Arkansas
Died: August 23, 1944
O-691093, Eleventh Bomb Squadron, 341st Bomb Group (M)

**How He Lived**

Lt. John Calvin Halsell, the youngest of three brothers, was born on December 8, 1917, to William Calvin and Marie Annette Marbury Halsell in Bradley, Arkansas. Soon after his birth, his family moved to Little Rock and later to Arkadelphia. After graduating from Arkadelphia High School, he attended Ouachita in 1938 and 1939, where he was a cheerleader.

His sister-in-law, Mary Elizabeth Halsell, Class of 1943, of Princeton, West Virginia, said that before "J.C." enlisted in the Army Air Corps, he "had surrendered to preach. He had preached two times in his daddy's church." His three brothers were all Ouachita graduates—Col. Aubrey C. Halsell, USAF, chaplain in WWII and the Korean War; Comdr. William Howard Halsell, U.S. Navy; and Dr. Thomas E. Halsell, Mary's husband, a missionary to Brazil, who during WWII was preparing to be a chaplain.

John C. Halsell, freshman, Class of 1939

Howard Halsell was Ouachita's Baptist Student Union director before moving to New Mexico and then to Nashville, Tennessee, with the Baptist Sunday School Board. Aubrey was

Lt. John Calvin Halsell was reported missing in action on August 23, 1944. He was flying the "Hump" in China with Gen. Claire Chennault's squadron when his plane went down.

a longtime pastor in Memphis after serving as army chaplain. Tommy was for many years the executive director of West Virginia Baptist Convention.

Mrs. Halsell remembers J.C. as being "very jovial," having a good sense of humor and being liked by everyone. After enlisting on April 27, 1941, he received his pilot training in San Antonio, Texas, and at Fort Ord, California. During this time, he became engaged to Juanita Jordan of Batesville, who was a senior at Ouachita. He entered her picture in a contest at Fort Ord and she became the Sweetheart of the Air Corps there.

## ... and How He Died

The pilot of a B-25, Lieutenant Halsell was stationed in South China at Jueilin. In a letter dated November 28, 2001, Mrs. Halsell wrote that her brother "had completed over 50 missions bombing the Japanese, and was due for R&R in Hawaii, but the Japanese were coming into South China and the Americans were evacuating so he went on one more mission and did not return."

While John Halsell was in pilot training in California, he became engaged to Juanita Jordan of Batesville during her senior year at Ouachita. When John entered her picture in a beauty contest, she was selected as the Sweetheart of Camp Roberts's "Keep 'em Happy Club."

What is known about Lieutenant Halsell's fate is contained in a Missing Air Crew Report on his final mission: "(The) pilot of a B-25 took off at 0600 on a low-level bombing mission on 8-23-44 from Leiyang, China.

THE FIGHTING TIGERS

Radio transmission indicated that when the plane with its five-member crew 'had some trouble, (Lt. Halsell) said he'd see others later.' The plane's position, when last contacted, was 10 minutes east of Lingling, the weather was overcast at 1500 feet in the vicinity of Lingling lowering to 400 feet at target, with widespread rain. Last radio transmission at 0714 [two miles southwest of Anjan]."

In response to two sections on an Individual Report of Downed Aircraft questionnaire—(1) "Bail-out, crash, forced-landing, shot down or missing"; and (2) "Any other known circumstances surrounding the incident, condition of crew when ship abandoned, if known"—the laconic reply was "Unknown."

Additional information on the circumstances surrounding Lieutenant Halsell's death is contained in a letter written to his mother by Capt. Theodore J. Michel, commanding officer of the Eleventh Bombardment Squadron, that was found in Lieutenant Halsell's AG 201 [personal] file.

> On the morning of August 23, 1944, John was flying on a low-level mission against enemy ground forces about 20 miles southeast of Hengyang, China. The plane in which he was flying first pilot had successfully completed its mission and was returning to its home base when the formation became separated by bad weather. The last contact that he had with them was by radio when John called in that he would meet the others at the home base.

The letter concluded with an assurance that he would notify her "as we get any definite information."

The search party found a burned Mitchell B-25H twelve miles east of Leiyang but no bodies were found. In an American Graves Registration Service report dated February 27, 1947, "Investigation made by Search and Recovery Team No. Six, 9 April 1946 at Leiyang [although 'not made on the actual ground'] netted no results." After adding that the search was made with the help of Chinese search teams, the report concluded, "How thoroughly the job was done is open to conjecture."

According to a second Casualty Clearance and Case Review, it was reported that a plane had burned at the Chu Tah village, but no remains had been found. The team proceeded to the scene of the crash where "they found some indication that there had been a fire. However, the ground was covered with new undergrowth, and a thorough search of an area of several hundred feet revealed nothing, neither human remains nor parts of the aircraft."

Upon receipt of a Graves Registration Report signed by the village chief of Chu Tah, Huang Chia-hsing, stating that "there were no American War Dead or graves in this village," the U.S. Search and Recovery Team recommended that the case be closed.

His sister-in-law, Mary Elizabeth Halsell, and others have expressed the possibility that rather than being killed by enemy action, Lieutenant Halsell may have crashed into a mountainside since he was "flying the hump" for Gen. Claire Chennault.

According to Mary Elizabeth,

> He was reported missing in action on August 23, 1944. The family never heard more. My husband, Thomas E. Halsell, and I visited Kueilin in 1990. There are many tall mountain peaks and pinnacles in that area. The Lijiang River is near the city. There is always mist and clouds over those mountains so we think that if he were not shot down by the Japanese he probably hit one of those mountain peaks on his return.

She said that airplanes had no radar at that time. His family never heard any more information. He was declared missing for one year, then declared by the government to be dead.

In a Statement of Investigation dated March 15, 1949, it was said that:

> In the event that the aircraft crashed in the vicinity of Anjen where it was last seen, it might have crashed into a mountainside. In the immediate vicinity of Anjen, the terrain is hilly with elevations of approximately 600 feet above sea level, while within a radius of about thirty miles to the south and southeast there are mountains of about 1,500 to 3,000 feet. If the radio transmissions were substantiated as originating from the aircraft and was attempting to follow the valley in the Kewilin-Lingling-Hengryand area, it could have crashed in a mountainside since the valley is flanked on both sides by mountains.

THE FIGHTING TIGERS

However, the natives in this area were friendly to Americans, and had there been a crash, it could not have gone unobserved.

His sister-in-law said Lieutenant Halsell's mother "took a large portion of the insurance after his death—I think it was $10,000—and helped build a wing onto the Baptist hospital in Kueilin. Later the Communists took over and made a medical school of that building and built a big new hospital."

A carton containing Lieutenant Halsell's "effects" was sent by the Quartermaster Department to his mother, with instructions to return the property to Lieutenant Halsell, should he be found alive. Among the effects were a pen knife, a pair of earrings, two pilot's wings, the silver bars of a first lieutenant, and a check for $91, "which represents funds belonging to him." In a letter accepting responsibility for the property, his mother wrote that she would "be only too glad to return [the property] to him when he returns." Noting that her son had "no wife and no children," she added, "He made his home with us before entering service April 27, 1941."

The case was closed on February 18, 1946, however, when Lieutenant Halsell was declared dead. His name is inscribed on the Wall of the Missing at the Manila American Cemetery. His military awards include the Air Medal and the Purple Heart.

# Thomas Royce Johnson

Sgt. Thomas Royce Johnson, former student, 1941–1943
Hometown: Nashville, Arkansas
Died: May 14, 1945
*38479496, Company K, Third Battalion, 103rd Infantry, Forty-third Infantry Division*

## How He Lived

Sgt. Thomas Royce Johnson was born on December 5, 1923, to Thomas Henry and Blanche Tolleson Johnson in Amity, Arkansas. Although he spent his childhood in Texarkana, Texas, he graduated from Nashville (Arkansas) High School, where he was chosen guard on the nonconference all-state football team of 1940. When his family moved from Nashville to Texarkana, Arkansas, in 1941, "Tommy" worked for Gieb-LaRoche-Dahl-Chapell, architect-engineers, a contractor at Red River Ordnance Depot, during summer vacation. He attended Ouachita from 1941 to 1943 before being inducted into the army. Sergeant Johnson was a member of the First Baptist Church of Arkadelphia. He was killed in action at the age of twenty-one.

Thomas Royce Johnson, freshman, 1942 *Ouachitonian* yearbook

The report of his death in the *Texarkana Gazette*, June 14, 1945, stated that he was survived by "his parents, one brother, Sgt. John Charles Johnson, who was stationed with the 12th Corps in Regensburg, Germany; four sisters, Miss Nina Johnson, El Dorado, Arkansas, Mrs. Maude Sue Doyle and Misses Anne and Elizabeth Johnson, all of Texarkana, Arkansas; his grandparents, Mr. and Mrs. V. J. Tolleson, of Kirby, Ark.; two aunts, Mrs. Theodocia Tucker, Hot Springs, Arkansas, and Ms. Ruby Sue Blish, Kirby, Arkansas; three uncles, Hubert

Johnson, Vancouver, Washington; Jeff W. Tolleson, Lake Village, Arkansas, and Carl Tolleson, Kirby, Arkansas; two nephews, James Thomas Doyle and Charles E. Doyle III, of Texarkana, Arkansas.

"He is also survived by one sister-in-law, Mrs. Jerry Meador Johnson of Texarkana, and one brother-in-law, Lt. Charles E. Doyle, stationed at Camp Rucker, Alabama, after serving two and one-half years in Alaska."

Mrs. Elizabeth Johnson Carroll, the youngest of his brothers and sisters, who was fifteen years old when Sergeant Johnson was killed, now lives in Texarkana, Texas. In a telephone interview on December 28, 2001, she said her brother was not married at the time of his death. "I am the youngest of six. All others are deceased." In a later interview (January 9, 2002), she said her brother had been engaged to Mary Atchley of Arkadelphia, who, after his death, mailed her engagement ring back to the Johnson family.

Archie Lyons, a childhood friend who lives in Nashville, Arkansas, recalled in a letter dated January 15, 2002, that "Tommy delivered the *Arkansas Gazette* for about five years in Nashville. He did it on a bicycle, which kept him in good shape for football. He was a guard and linebacker on the 1939 and 1940 teams. We finished school in 1941. He went to Ouachita, I'm sure, on scholarship. I don't know how long he stayed before joining the Army. . . . Tommy was a good person and was a good friend of mine."

Mrs. Mary D. Ponder Nelson, also of Nashville, Arkansas, who once dated Johnson, said in a letter dated February 13, 2002, that

> Tommy or "Shorty," as he was known to his schoolmates at Nashville High School, was a very popular young man. He was co-captain on Mr. Lester Bradley's football team in 1941. It was a great team and Mr. Bradley was a noted football and basketball coach during that era. I was very aware of this because I played on the basketball team during 1940, 1941 and ending in 1942.
>
> Mr. Bradley was fond of Tommy and allowed him to be chosen for our mascot, so he was able to go with us on our tournaments, trips, and bus trips. This made me happy, too, as Tommy and I were dating those last years. I lost contact with him after he went to Ouachita and I began dating others and eventually married a young man who lived in Saratoga, Arkansas.

## . . . and How He Died

After being inducted into the army at Camp Wolters, Texas, on August 6, 1943, Sergeant Johnson received his basic training at Fort McClellan, Alabama. In November 1944, Sergeant Johnson was sent first to New Guinea and then to Luzon, where during a fierce battle in the Ipo Dam area northeast of Manila he was mortally wounded on May 11 when a Japanese hand grenade exploded on his abdomen.

His parents received a telegram on May 30, 1945, notifying them that their son had been wounded, but his sister said in an interview early in 2002 that he died three days later "of an infection caused by the wound."

After being temporarily buried in Manila 2 American Cemetery, Sergeant Johnson's body was returned to Texas for burial after the war "in our family plot at Hillcrest Cemetery in Texarkana, Texas," Mrs. Carroll said.


## Sidebar: Coach Lester Bradley

By Jack O. Forgy, Lt. Col. USA (Ret.), Nashville High School, Class of 1952

Coach Lester Bradley was a legendary high school coach in southwest Arkansas. He had a reputation as a great coach with a volcanic temper and a man who could field great football teams. He coached football and basketball and by the mid-1940s was also principal of Nashville High School which he ruled with an iron hand. Of course in those days, one had to be tough to be a coach or a principal. Many of the students had to help plant and get crops in so it took them longer to get through school—they were bigger and tougher than most. It took a tough coach to field a good team and run a high school.

He also taught math classes. Unlike some coaches who were also teachers, Lester Bradley knew his subject matter well and anyone who took his courses came away well prepared for further study at the college level, and in life for that matter.

I recall my first day in his tenth-grade geometry class. He insisted we show up with protractor and ruler. I had the protractor, but not the ruler, so of course he called on me to draw a straight line. Since I was already shaking in my boots, my line was about as straight as a black snake. He said to me, "Forgy, if that's the way you draw straight lines in life, its going to take you a lot longer than anybody else to get where you are going." Needless to say I always had protractor and ruler after that.

Stories about his volcanic temperament were legendary and usually on public display on game nights. At home games, cane-bottomed chairs were put out on the sidelines for the coaching staff. Coach never sat down and in the course of a game he would take any frustrations that he had (and there were many) out on the cane-bottom chairs, sometimes totally destroying them. I wonder how much of the equipment budget went for new chairs?

Coach also had firm rules about student behavior. For the student body, there was no smoking on campus. For his athletes, there was also no smoking, period. He used a hickory paddle to enforce the rules, often entering the men's room unannounced and administering a few whacks here and there. He used to say of the transgressors, "I would have gotten more of you but the smoke was too thick to see who you were!"

Legend further has it that if he saw one of his players smoking on Main Street he would stop his car, grab his paddle and administer summary punishment on the spot.

Years later I was living in the Washington, D.C., area when Vince Lombardi became coach of the Washington Redskins. Coach Lombardi always reminded me of Coach Bradley. All too frequently they are remembered for their temperaments, but they were both highly intelligent men, supremely confident in their abilities, who had an amazing knack for getting the most from their athletes and hated to lose.

I expect that any student of Lester Bradley who was called into the service of the nation couldn't help feeling the same way and acquit himself accordingly. Besides, I suspect that if word got back to Coach that a man wasn't doing his best, the man would never want to come home and face Coach again.

# Paul Lambert

Pfc. Paul Brantley Lambert, former student, 1942–1943
Hometown: Memphis, Tennessee
Died: December 16, 1944
*38599666, 132nd Infantry Regiment, U.S. Army*

## How He Lived

Pfc. Paul Brantley Lambert was born on March 8, 1925, to Ollie D. and Lola M. Lambert, in Forrest City, Arkansas. He attended Ouachita College and later Memphis State College. A ministerial student, he directed the choir at Harvey's Chapel Church near Hot Springs, Arkansas. He was a member of Bellevue Baptist Church in Memphis. In the news report of his death, his survivors were listed as his parents, two sisters, Mrs. Milton W. Blair Jr. of Memphis, Tennessee, and Mrs. Henry Mills of Wilton, Arkansas; and a brother, Lawrence "Larry" Fletcher Lambert also of Memphis, Tennessee.

Pfc. Paul Brantley Lambert

Larry Lambert, who was in the process of moving from Memphis to Lexington, Tennessee, when contacted in late September 2003, said that because he was only twelve when his older brother Paul was drafted, "I didn't know him very well but I never heard anything but good revelation about my brother. Paul was a good and even-tempered man," he said. "His goals, as I hear them, were to administer Christianity through the church with music, prayer, and devotion to God."

H. Frank Dearing, Class of 1943, who was Paul's roommate in the summer term of 1943, writes that they both were drafted into the army in the fall of 1943, Frank into the Chaplains Corps and Paul into the infantry. "In the fall of 1944," he said, "I wrote Paul a letter. It came back with a note saying Paul had been killed in action. He was a likable young man, and I think he played the piano. We got along well, and I was hurt to find that he had died in action in Europe."

Another classmate, Mrs. C. H. Seaton (formerly Mary Jernigan) in Little Rock, said that while she was a freshman and Paul was a sophomore, she and Paul had dated the summer before he went to Memphis State.

Mrs. Seaton said she visited him at Camp Fanin, Texas, in February 1944. "Even though our bus had broken down and we were late," she said, "he and a buddy met me at the station." Paul later visited her in Hayti, Missouri. Remembering him as a "nice guy," she said he served as music director at Harvey's Chapel, between Hot Springs and Mountain Pine in southwest Arkansas, where he would go on weekends and lead the music.

In a V-mail letter to Mary dated October 1, 1944 (that "came in a little envelope from the War and Navy Departments after he died," she said), Paul wrote:

> Well, I am settled a little so I can write. I am now in the Intelligence Section of Battalion Headquarters and we take care of prisoners that are brought back from the front. My work at Ouachita helped me to secure this job. Mary, I dreamed of you last night and it was very pleasant. We were together in Brazil doing missionary work and we were very happy. Hope you will have great success at Ouachita for our Lord. Mary, I sure do miss you very much and I hate that things turned out for me like they did, but I want you to know that I have the deepest and sincerest love for you. Love
>
> Yours in Christ,
> Paul

In his last letter to Mary from somewhere in France, this one dated November 29, 1944, less than a month before his death, he wrote:

I received your letter and picture and sure was glad to get them. The picture of you is very good, and you look lovely. Sure wish I could be with you now. The picture brought back old memories, which are very pleasant. The freshman initiation must have been some fun. You didn't have to take it, did you? Coming in the summer you miss it. So! You like the organ. Maybe some day the Lord will give you a position playing in a large church. Does Pro [Mitchell]* still hit or pinch himself when you make a mistake? I use (*sic*) to get so tickled at him, because he was always slapping himself when I was in his class. Ha. Oh! You have the music box [an antique musical powder box she still has that plays "Ava Maria"] at Ouachita? Glad to hear Aurice is better. [He sang in her church—FBC—when he visited her in Hayti, Missouri.] Tell everyone hello for me. . . . I am getting along fine. It has been raining today again. This weather is awful. We're now on a rest period and we sure need it. Larry, my small brother, is learning to play the piano and accordion. Hope he does better than me. Ha. Will close for tonight. Write one of your (wee) soldiers soon.

Yours in Christ,
Paul

*[Dr. Livingston Harvey "Pro" Mitchell was director of the Music Conservatory at Ouachita from 1909 until 1949. Mitchell, for whom Mitchell Auditorium was named in 1942, was the first non-Baptist member of the faculty. A Presbyterian, he was described by Baptist historian James Sterling Rogers as "a true Christian with a beautiful spirit." (From *Once in a Hundred Years: A Pictorial History of Ouachita Baptist University*, by Michael E. Arrington and William D. Downs Jr.)]

During the 2002 interview, Mrs. Seaton pointed out that since Paul was a ministerial student, had he remained at Ouachita, he probably would not have been drafted. Mary and her future husband, C. H. Seaton, did not date until after Paul's death. Mr. and Mrs. Seaton were married fifty-four years before Mr. Seaton's death in May 2001.

## . . . and How He Died

An undated obituary published in the *Memphis Commercial Appeal* reported that "Pfc. Paul B. Lambert, nineteen-year-old son of Mr. and Mrs. O. D. Lambert, 727 Trigg [in Memphis], previously reported missing in action in Germany, December 16, 1944, has been reported killed in action on that date. He had been on combat duty since June." Frank Dearing said Paul's death, at the age of nineteen, occurred "in action leading up to the Battle of the Bulge." Specific information on circumstances surrounding his death had not been found at the time of publication. According to the Report of Death document from the War Department dated February 23, 1945: "The individual named in this report of death is held by the War Department to have been in a missing in action status from 16 December 1944 until such absence was terminated on 17 February 1945, when evidence considered sufficient to establish the fact of death was received by the Secretary of War from a commander in the European Area."

In an anguished letter to the War Department dated December 10, 1945, almost a year after he was reported missing and later declared dead, Mrs. Lambert wrote:

> This letter is to acknowledge the message that our son is missing in action . . . needless to say we are stunned but hoping for a definite word as to his whereabouts. Would you advise me to continue my letters to him? Could the Red Cross help me in locating him, or am I helpless, and must just wait? If there is anything or person that could help me, please inform me. Can I obtain his personal effects? Who shall I write to?
>
> Respectfully, his mother, Mrs. Lola M. Lambert

There is no record of a reply. Pfc. Paul Lambert was temporarily buried at Hamm Cemetery, Luxembourg, and then returned to the Memphis National Cemetery after the war. At the request of his mother, who was listed as his next of kin, his body was returned to the Memphis National Cemetery three years after the war. Final burial was handled by Brantley Funeral Home in Olive Branch, Mississippi, on August 4, 1948.

# William Lawrence

Capt. William C. Lawrence, former student, 1935–1937
Hometown: Little Rock, Arkansas
Died: September 14, 1944
*0-804692, 831st Bomb Squadron, 485th Bomb Group, U.S. Air Corps*

## How He Lived

Capt. William C. "Billy" Lawrence was born October 20, 1918, to the Reverend and Mrs. Roland W. Lawrence of 3421 High Street, Little Rock, Arkansas. After graduating Little Rock High School (now Little Rock Central High School) in 1935, he entered Ouachita College the following fall. Captain Lawrence later transferred to George Washington University in Washington, D.C., where he majored in music.

Before enlisting in the Army Air Corps in 1942, he was employed by the Bureau of Statistics in Washington. As reported in the September 28, 1944, edition of the *Arkansas Gazette*, "Captain Lawrence had been reported missing in action over Poland since September 11 but was later declared to have been killed in action."

"He has two sisters," the *Gazette* story reported, "Mrs. William Vail of Seattle, Washington, and Mrs. Mike Dillon, whose husband is a corporal in the Army in Italy. His father, Reverend R. W. Lawrence, is a Baptist evangelist in Arkansas." According to War Department records, however, Captain Lawrence was also survived by his mother, Mrs. Clara C. Lawrence. His father was not included in the list of survivors.

William C. Lawrence, sophomore, 1937 *Ouachitonian* yearbook

Captain Lawrence's Hell's Angel crew. *Front row, left to right:* Homer Disheroon, copilot; William Lawrence, pilot; Arthur Wichmann, navigator; Patsy Campolieta, bombardier. *Back row:* Arthur Nitsche, tail gunner; Joe Lawson, nose gunner; Vernon Christensen, top gunner; Richard Garner, radio operator; Everett MacDonald. Photo taken during the summer of 1944 at Venosa. Lawrence's crew was one of the original crews assigned to the 485th Bomb Group. Lawrence, Nitsche, and MacDonald were killed when their plane was shot down over Oswiecim (Auschwitz), Poland, on September 13, 1944.

485th Bomb Squadron Reunion, Little Rock, Arkansas, September 2003. *Pictured left to right:* Lt. Col. (Ret.) Dan Sjodin, squadron commander; Jerry Whiting, a retired law enforcement officer from California whose father was a tail gunner in the 485th; Tech. Sgt. (Ret.) Vernon Christensen, top turret gunner and one of Captain Lawrence's original crew members; Bill Downs Jr., author.

Two of Bill Lawrence's flight mates—Lt. Col. (Ret.) Dan Sjodin, eighty-four, his commanding officer, and Tech. Sgt. (Ret.) Vern Christensen, eighty-three—were among those present for the national reunion of the 485th Bomb Squadron held in Little Rock, Arkansas, on September 17, 2003.

Colonel Sjodin (pronounced *zhoh-DEEN)* said Lawrence was "a handsome guy, and when he sat down to the piano, you would know right away that this guy knew what he was playing. He could play anything on the piano. A great addition to our squadron. He was also one of the best formation flyers in the squadron," Sjodin added.

He continued, "These pilots could tuck in on each side of me and fly just as tight formation as you would want. The tight formations were important for two reasons: By flying in a tight formation, our bomb pattern is going to wipe out the target. Two, because we all drop off the lead bombardier. When he drops, we drop."

Lawrence is further remembered as always being ready to fly on a mission and as a pilot who "filled his position perfectly," Colonel Sjodin said. "He was the best combat bomber pilot you could ever ask for. A combat pilot who can go ahead and fly an airplane. He would fly any mission and he would take his position and fly it perfectly. He would go through the flak so thick it looked like you could get out and walk on it. But that didn't hinder Bill Lawrence. He would stay in position and fly his plane right through it. I could not ask for a better combat pilot than Bill Lawrence. He died a hero. He tried to get out but couldn't."

Tech. Sgt. Vern Christensen, who was one of Captain Lawrence's original crew members and who stayed with him through their fiftieth—and last—mission, recalls Lawrence's flight skills in his book, *By God, We Made It!* published in 2002. During a training flight on how to land the cumbersome B-24 bombers, "Lawrence was the pilot and Homer Disheroon was the co-pilot. It was Disheroon's turn to land the plane," Vern wrote, noting that the copilot "was fresh out of flying school and he came down and hugged the runway to make this landing and he hit the runway too hard and busted the wheels off the airplane."

"Well, I'll tell you there was hell to pay for a minute," Vern continued, "but Lawrence was a more experienced pilot and he got the plane back up in the air and he had the rest of the crew bail out. Then Lawrence and Disheroon brought the plane back in without wheels on it and skidded it on its belly. The experience was too much for the mechanic-gunner, who said he refused to fly anymore. Nobody was forced to fly because to have somebody up there who couldn't cope with it and be scared, they wouldn't want him up there, because it naturally would be a lot worse during combat. So he was taken off the crew and two days later, I was put on that plane [as a mechanic-gunner, the M.O.S. for which he had been trained]. And that was the crew I was to be with through thick and thin for a long to time to come."

After completing their training in Fairmont, Nebraska, Captain Lawrence's squadron was transferred to Venosa, Italy, via Florida, Puerto Rico, and Brazil, followed by a twelve-hour flight across the Atlantic that led them through "the damnedest storm you ever did see," Vern recalled. "The plane would fall 2,000 feet in a second. It just literally bounced." Most of the crew members were sick, including Bill Lawrence, the pilot.

But despite the ferocity of the storm, Vern said, "we never worried about it because Bill Lawrence was at the controls."

In Venosa, the crew built a sand-block chapel and Bill Lawrence supplied the music. "He was a fantastic musician," Vern said. "He could play anything, anytime, anyplace. His sister was a fantastic singer and sang in New York City."

The first mission for Lawrence's crew was in northern Italy to support ground troops. Flying in their assigned B-24, which they nicknamed *Hell's Angel*, their plane received a direct hit "between No. 3 engine and the fuselage, right where the top turret was and that's where I was. We didn't know we had been hit hard until we got back and here was this hole so big you could crawl through. I thought, 'Holy Samoley, how in the hell is a man ever going to get fifty missions in when they treat you like this on the first one?'"

One of Sergeant Christensen's favorite Bill Lawrence stories concerns what happened during one of the crew's days off. "We sometimes took the plane for a little vacation—how this could be, I don't know—but I remember one time Lawrence was flying the plane and we went down to Bari, on the Adriatic, to go swimming and we flew along the beach first and here is this boat with two old Italians in it sitting there fishing. We couldn't let that go, of course, so Lawrence (who was twenty-two or twenty-three years old at the time) just dove down on them with that plane and gave them a buzz job. We could see those two guys, one went out one side of the boat and the other guy out of the other side, right into the water. We pulled up and the prop wash really blasted them and they came out of the water, shaking their fists. We really thought it was something. I don't suppose those poor old Italians did, but we did. We did our swimming and went back to the base."

## . . . and How He Died

So far as the next forty-eight missions were concerned, "Some were bad, and some not so bad," Vern wrote in *By God, We Made It!* Targets included the Ploesti Oil Refineries in Rumania but the worst were over Munich, Germany, and Vienna and Weiner-Neustadt in Austria.

After the crew had finished its forty-ninth mission, Vern remembers thinking that at last he was about to go home. "It was September 13, 1944.

We went to briefing that morning, the last one. When they pulled the shade down with the map on it that showed where we were going, we saw that the target was a synthetic rubber plant connected to the prison camp Oswiecim (Auschwitz), Poland. A 'milk run, thank God!' There was a standing rule on your last and 50th mission. If it was a tough one, you had the option to sit it out and wait for the next one. I don't think anybody ever did that, regardless of where the mission was. We bombed it and I'll be doggone if we didn't get hit over the target or close to it." He remembers coming out of his turret and on to the flight deck where he discovered to his horror that his parachute was on backwards and had crimped his oxygen hose. "A crew member helped me turn my parachute around and booted me out at an altitude of 24,000 feet. But when I looked back I saw Lawrence and 1st Lt. Matthew W. Hall, the co-pilot, standing up out of the cockpit waiting to go out. And that was the last I saw of Bill Lawrence."

Vern was the only member of the original crew to parachute safely. The other crew members were replacements. "Polish people said they saw the plane burst into flame. It went down about fifteen miles further on. Just before it hit the ground, four parachutes came out, but too late. The first crew member wasn't dead but a German soldier came around and killed him with his rifle butt. But Lawrence and Hall didn't get out. They burned up in the cockpit when it crashed. There were eleven people working in the field. A little girl, later identified as Mary Opalinski, tried to help but her clothes caught on fire and she later died from her burns."

"The people were forced to dig the graves," Vern said. "When the German soldiers stripped the bodies, the Polish people objected. The Germans refused to stop, however, saying their people needed the clothes more than the dead American airmen. Lawrence, his copilot, and four enlisted men were buried in a common grave. The bodies, exhumed in 1947, were identified through dental records." (At this point, Sergeant Christensen lost his composure and began to sob.) "By golly," he managed to choke, "it's hard to talk about it now—after sixty years, if you can believe it."

I could.


In describing the bombing mission on September 14, 1944, during which Captain Lawrence was killed, a Missing Air Crew Report provides a chillingly graphic account of the events leading up to his death:

At 0635 hours, twenty-eight (28) B-24 "Liberators" took off (from Venosa Air Force Base in Italy) to bomb the Oswiecim (Auschwitz) Synthetic Oil and Rubber Plant in Poland. The 1st attack unit was led by Lt. Col. Herblin, Deputy Gp CO and the 2nd attack unit was led by Captain Vern E. Bryson, 829th Flt. Cmdr. Also, two spare aircraft took off. The Group assembled into Wing formation. Thirty (30) P-38's joined the formation at 0930 hours and at 1025 hours, thirty P-51's joined the formation. The two spare aircraft left the formation at 1253 hours. The two spare aircraft returned to base plus six aircraft returned prior to bombing: 486, 536, 495, 416, 819, and 474.

Twenty-two aircraft were over the target at 1121 hours and twenty aircraft dropped fifty tons of 500-lb. RX bombs from 24,000 feet. The bomb run was begun with the aid of PFF as the target was obscured by smoke and clouds. The bombing results were poor with the main bomb pattern 3.5 miles west of the briefed MPI. There were three strikes in the marshaling yard, damaging at least five wagons. Also, there were ten strikes in probable barracks area, damaging several buildings. No enemy aircraft were seen. Intense, accurate and heavy flak was encountered over the target for three minutes.

An eyewitness to the crash, S/Sgt. Wade Allen Jr., reported that after Captain Lawrence's B-24 (Aircraft 51139) was hit by flak between the No. 3 and No. 4 engines about thirty seconds after bombs were away, fire started as the plane went into a slow spin. "Two men got out and then the plane began tearing apart. I saw the plane hit the ground and explode." The MACR stated that "five chutes were seen to open before the aircraft disappeared at 1126 hours."

In a Casualty Questionnaire contained in the MACR, a survivor of the crash said that before he jumped, he believed Captain Lawrence and several other crew members were standing in the bomb bay preparing to jump when the plane went into an uncontrollable spin and crashed. Apparently they were pinned in the aircraft by centrifugal force and died in the crash.

THE FIGHTING TIGERS

Polish eyewitnesses on the ground provided grim accounts of what occurred after Captain Lawrence's plane crashed:

**Marja Skrzynska, Marja Gajosowna, Janina Skrzynska:**

On 13 September 1944 *(sic)* while the German front was moving into our village, there was a plane crash. We saw the burning plane and were so overwhelmed with the sight of the dropping flyer that one of us, not heeding the dangers in the area of the dropping plane, which was cracking and burning in the air, ran to the rescue of the flyer in the hope of saving his life. However, it was too late—the flyer was already dead.

Within a few seconds the Germans arrived and one of them was about to hit the flyer with his gun, but did not go through with the blow when he saw that he was dead. They chased away the crowd of people which had gathered to see the accident, after which they busied themselves with the dead. This happened around 1100 in the forenoon. On the following day at seven in the evening the fliers were already buried. We felt it was our duty to put wreaths and flowers on the grave. Seeing that, the German guards, which were placed by the grave side, did not spare us with their most brutal and insulting language. They forbade us to pray for the souls of the dead when we tried to do that kneeling at the grave, nor did they permit us to put wreaths and flowers on it.

The following day a German soldier caught us by the grave. He addressed us in German in the crudest manner, but we could not understand what he said. When he saw that, he began speaking in Polish, telling us that the Americans were our enemies who were wronging innocent civilians and Polish children. He kept shouting at us and was pulling out the wreaths. In the end he said that should he ever see us here again he would take us all into the concentration camp in Oswiecim (the infamous Auschwitz). On the third day, the Germans came back to the grave, threw off all the wreaths and flowers that were on it and started trampling them with their feet.

When we saw that, we made up our minds to put the wreaths and flowers back on the grave and we carefully stole ourselves through to the cemetery through fields and woods and when we reached the grave we suddenly saw a German car drive up from out of the woods. We were horror stricken, but it was too late for us to turn back or to run away. The Germans called us and spoke to us in German and Polish and asked us whether we could understand them, to which we shook our heads and said, "No." They began using a sign language imitating the way we prayed, laughed and made fun of us.

In the end they left in their car without doing us any harm. Even though they tried to scare us off, we were not afraid of them and put the wreaths and flowers back on the grave.

**Antoni Rams:**

On 13 September I noticed a plane which was burning in the air. I also saw how two fliers without their parachutes were dropping to the earth. They fell on the territory of Ligota near the town of Zygodowice. When I reached the place where one the fliers had fallen, I saw that he was . . . not yet dead because his body was still jerking.

Shortly a German sergeant by the name of Sikora arrived and upon seeing that the flyer was not yet dead, hit him in the head with the butt of his gun, while at the same time pulling out the flyer's billfold from his pocket. He also unfastened his watch from his wrist and took it as booty, after which he went over to the other flyer who fell nearby, about 200 meters from the first flyer . . .

On the following day, 14 September 1944, I buried the two fliers together with four other fliers, their comrades. All of them were stripped by the Germans. Four I buried with their shirts and shorts on and the other two were completely naked. All of their belongings were taken by the German Military. And as to Sikora's fate, he was killed during the Soviet offensive and is buried in the woods of Ligota.

After the end of the cold war, said Sgt. Vern Christensen, the villagers in Zygodowice erected a monument in memory of Captain Lawrence's crew who died on September 13, 1944. "A small group of Polish citizens gathered at the site to solemnly express their gratitude after so many years for the sacrifice of the Americans who had come to attack their Nazi oppressors."

At the request of his family, Captain Lawrence is buried in the Ardennes

American Cemetery in Belgium. His awards included the Distinguished Flying Cross, the Air Medal, two Oak-Leaf Clusters, and the Purple Heart.

## Sidebar: How Vern Christensen Handled Fear

Fascinated by Vern Christensen's harrowing story of surviving fifty missions, I asked him how he had handled fear. Without embellishment, this was his reply:

> During the months we made these missions you kinda get used to seeing your wingman blow up. And of course, you don't think it will happen to you. And the day it did, I couldn't believe it. In fact, I said it later, "I can't believe I'm hanging in a parachute. That they would do this to a man on his last and fiftieth mission." And then I thought of that doggone yellow telegram that my mother would get. I don't really remember praying. If I didn't I should have but it would have been an opportune time to do it.
>
> I got down close to the ground and I saw these Germans standing around plus about fifteen to twenty Polish people who I know they would have gladly helped me if they could have, but of course the German guards were there, being that close to Auschwitz. But fear— you kinda get used to it. I'm no different from anyone else, believe me. But remember you're young. You're eighteen, twenty, twenty-one years old and you're tough and you're strong. That part I could do again but I couldn't do that terrible forced march [to the prison camp] again.
>
> After we were interrogated, we were taken to prison camps. In that prison, we didn't get much food. But when the Russians were coming from the east and the Yanks were coming from the west, we were going to be bottled up. The Germans wanted to run off and leave us in that camp and let the Russians take us. But they had orders not to leave the prisoners but to take them with them and not leave any stragglers. This went on during the winter.
>
> It was tough. There was snow and there were no hotels or cafes to eat in, I can tell you that, because [the German soldiers] didn't have much food themselves. So we scrounged. Once in a while, we were given a ration of potatoes, sleeping outside or in barns or in barnyards.

But we were liberated on April 26, 1945, by the 104th Timberwolf Division. We were sitting in a barnyard popping lice because we were all so lousy. And this jeep drove in with a major and a sergeant and a driver and they took our guards prisoners and we had to walk another eighteen kilometers into the city of Bitterfeld, Germany.

"When we were sitting in that barnyard and that jeep drove in," Vern said, as he began to sob again, "I put my arm around my buddy, Norman, from Casper, Wyoming, and cried, 'Norman, by God, we made it!'"

# Ralph Mann

1st Lt. Ralph Carlton Mann, former student, 1932–1935
Hometown: Judsonia, Arkansas
Died: September 5, 1942
0-5919, USMC Unit: Company F, Second Battalion, Fourth Marine Regiment, Philippine Division

**How He Lived**

Lt. Ralph Carlton Mann was born on October 26, 1915, to Ralph C. and Winnie Mann. Ralph was a graduate of Searcy (Arkansas) High School, where he was a straight-A student and "a good athlete," a classmate remembers. He attended Ouachita from 1932 to 1935, where he lettered in football, basketball, baseball, and track. As a basketball player, he made the all-state team in 1935. He was a member of the "O" Association, the Spanish Club, and "a number of other organizations," said his brother, Thomas Mann, Class of 1939. Dan Grant remembers him as being an "outstanding student leader." He was also a charter member of the Red Shirts social club when the fraternity was founded in 1934–35.

At the end of his junior year, Ralph left Ouachita to enter the U.S. Naval Academy, where he graduated in 1939. In the Annapolis yearbook for that year, he was described as "a combination of a scholar and an athlete":

Ralph Mann, sophomore, 1933 *Ouachitonian* yearbook

> Ralph is the ideal type of man one seldom meets. Starting Plebe year in what promised to be a brilliant athletic career, he was stopped for a time by injuries; but doggedly persistent, he succeeded in overcoming his reverses. Youngster year found him handling left field on the varsity nine. By steadily upholding his good record in studies and

at the same time being a versatile player on the diamond, he has shown himself to be an all-around man. His conversation, forceful and interesting, makes him a pleasant companion, and his Southern accent immediately identifies him. Determination will carry him far in life, and the Navy will find his varied capabilities valuable when he wears his commission star.

After transferring to the U.S. Marine Corps as a second lieutenant, Lieutenant Mann's first assignment was the Fourth Marine Regiment in Tiensien, China. While stationed there, he met his future wife, Jessie Catherine Brown, the daughter of an American official in the consul's office in Shanghai. Her father had been a riverboat pilot on the Yangtze River before the war and held a commission as a lieutenant commander in the U.S. Naval Reserve.

In a handwritten letter dated March 15, 2002, Joseph Dupont, a fellow marine, remembers Ralph Mann as the unit's six-man football coach, but added that Mann "was a better baseball player than a basketball player." Capt. Austin Shofner called him "the best outfielder the Naval Academy ever had." Although officers and enlisted men didn't mix, this was not Lieutenant Mann's style. "He was a regular guy," Shofner said. "He and Col. Jack Hawkins [a fellow graduate of the U.S. Naval Academy] were from the same breed—military academy people. The men loved them. We would have followed them into any machine-gun nest."

As the threat of Japanese military aggression became increasingly imminent, the Fourth Marine Regiment and the embassy personnel—including Jessie and her family—were ordered to the Philippines, where she worked for the U.S. Consulate. On December 5, 1941, just two days before the attack on Pearl Harbor, she and Ralph married.

Lieutenant Mann and another young lieutenant were placed in charge of a forty-three-marine rear guard that was ordered to provide security for the U.S. Field Headquarters in Bataan. "After a valiant yet futile battle against the Japanese forces on both Bataan and Corregidor, however," Colonel Hawkins wrote, "the last elements of the 4th Regiment surrendered to the Japanese on Corregidor on April 9, 1942." Captured on Bataan, Lieutenant Mann participated in the Bataan death march, eventually arriving at the Cabanatuan prison camp "in extremely poor health." Hawkins described Cabanatuan as "the most infamous of all the Japanese

1st Lt. Ralph Carlton Mann, U.S. Naval Academy yearbook, 1939

POW camps. From June 1942 until January 1943, men were dying the rate of 30–50 per day from starvation, illness and brutality."

His wife, Jessie, her sister, and her parents were interned in the Santo Tomas University prison in Manila. Jessie was later chosen for a prisoner exchange and was sent home (in what Hawkins described as *"a harrowing voyage"*) on the *Gripsholm*, a neutral Swedish transport ship used for this purpose. Her father, however, was less fortunate. He was placed on a Japanese "Hell Ship" to be sent to Korea but lost his life when the ship was torpedoed and sunk by the U.S. Navy. Thomas Mann, a retired lieutenant colonel who served for thirty years in the army, said, he "was fortunate enough to be in the liberating forces and visited with Jessie's sister and mother within two hours after they were liberated."

"Jessie Mann, who died in 2001, later remarried [becoming Catherine Brown Mann Marten] but maintained her contact with the marines," Colonel Hawkins said, "frequently attending their reunions."

## . . . and How He Died

In reply to a letter from Ralph's widow, who had requested information about her husband and what had happened to him in the Philippines, Colonel Hawkins recalled his first meeting with the young couple in Shanghai shortly before the marines left for their new assignment in the Philippines.

> I remember visiting you and Ralph at your apartment and seeing the beautiful oriental rugs you had bought. I had bought rugs, too, which soon were to be abandoned along with all my other belongings on the dock at Olongapa when the bombs began to fall.
>
> You asked about Ralph at the Academy. I did not know him well in those days, for we were in different battalions, lived in different wings of Bancroft Hall, attended different classes and were not thrown together in other activities. I remember him as a star player on the Academy baseball team and learned first hand later in Shanghai what an exceptional player he was when we played ball there together. I got to know him well at the Basic School in Philadelphia and we served together in the 2nd Battalion, 4th Marines in Shanghai and the Philippines.

Soon after the war began, Lieutenant Mann was assigned to a marine guard detachment in the headquarters of the U.S. Army Forces Far East (USAFFE) in Bataan. It was from Mike Dobervich, second in command and Hawkins's former housemate in Shanghai, that he learned what Ralph Mann experienced after the fall of Bataan in early April 1942.

His reply to Mrs. Mann pulled no punches:

> I know you have read accounts of the Death March, and I can assure you, having talked with numerous survivors, that it was as horrible as the worst you have read. Our men were forced to march

about 100 miles in the blistering tropical heat without food or potable water. The Japanese provided neither.

Crazed with thirst, men would drink from any ditch they could find, and as a result, practically all of them fell victim to dysentery. Scores dropped out unable to continue. These were bayoneted or shot. The death toll among the American and Filipino prisoners on the march and after arrival at Camp O'Donnell was horrendous—literally tens of thousands. Mike told me that so many died after reaching the camp that the weakened survivors were unable to bury them. Bodies were everywhere. The Japanese gave little food and water and no medical assistance whatsoever.

While this was taking place, I was on Corregidor where we had established defense of the beaches. The 4th Marines had been given that responsibility by the Army. When Bataan fell, I had little hope that I would ever see Ralph and Mike again. We held out for another month there before the Japanese, suffering heavy casualties at the hands of the 4th Marines, seized a beachhead on the island and General Wainwright decided that further resistance was useless. Our food supplies on Corregidor were almost exhausted.

After about two weeks crowded into a barbed-wire enclosure on Corregidor with pitifully little food or water, the 12,000 captives were moved in increments to Billibid Prison in Manila and thence by rail and marching to Prisoner-of-War Camp No. 1 about fifteen miles east of Cabanatuan, Nueva Ecija. I was to spend the next five months there.

I will try to portray for you what life was like at this camp where Ralph spent his last days. You will see why he had no chance to recover from the killing ordeal of the Death March.

Camp No. 1, Cabanatuan, was under construction for the expanding Philippine Army when the project was halted due to the beginning of hostilities. Critically necessary parts of the military camp such as kitchen, mess halls, latrines, showers and medical facilities had not been constructed. The water supply system based on wells was only in the first stage of development and there were only a few spigots in the entire camp. What had been built was long rows of rectangular, thatched-roof huts about 50 feet long, with nipa palm siding. Inside, there was a floor of bamboo strips at ground level, and above the floor on both sides where shelf-like sleeping bays, also of bamboo. The large, tropical-style windows on both sides of the huts

THE FIGHTING TIGERS

had nipa palm shutters, but there was no screening to keep out mosquitoes, flies and other insects. There was no furniture of any kind. The primitive state of the camp was not improved upon by the Japanese.

In describing the camp's condition, he said the prisoners slept on a bamboo floor using "a blanket or shelter half for bedding if we were lucky enough to have such items. The Japanese provided no bedding, no clothing, no toilet articles, no soap, no eating utensils, plates, cups, buckets, cookware—none of the ordinary things that civilized people use in their daily lives. We stood in long lines to fill our canteens at the few available spigots. We had to live with whatever clothing and equipment we had with us when captured. The Japanese gave us absolutely nothing."

Hawkins further describes the horrible conditions:

> Bathing in the usual sense was impossible. All we could do was sponge off with water from a canteen. When it rained, many of us went outside naked and let the rain wash us. I spent a lot of time standing in the rain. This inability to bathe presented a difficult problem for the multitudes of us who had dysentery and for those who tried to take care of them.
>
> Sanitary facilities consisted of open slit trenches. These produced swarms of flies. Our food at Cabanatuan consisted of rice three times a day boiled in large iron cauldrons over wood fires. At times there was not enough water to wash the rice before cooking and it was wormy. We called this our "protein." There was no salt. Occasionally, we had "soup" which was a greenish water made from boiling *camolte* (sweet potato) vines. We passed in line to get our serving of rice and sat on the ground or on the floor of our hut to eat it. Those who had no mess kit ate from tin cans discarded by the Japanese guards.
>
> There were Army doctors among us, but they had no medicines or medical supplies of any kind . . . The Japanese provided none of this and even refused to allow the Manila Red Cross to deliver vaccine when a diphtheria epidemic swept through the camp. Under these conditions, the prisoners were stricken with all sorts of diseases, including scurvy, beri beri, pellagra, malaria, dysentery and tropical ulcers.
>
> One depressing element of our lives at Cabanatuan was boredom. We had nothing to do and nowhere to go. We talked about the war,

but all we could do was speculate, since we had no news at all of the outside world. We did not even know the extent of the damage inflicted upon Pearl Harbor, for this had not been revealed to us by the American high command in the Philippines for reasons of morale. We talked a great deal about food, what we liked best, what we were going to eat in San Francisco. Food was on our minds all the time. A rice diet leads to that. We could not read to pass the time, for there was nothing to read.

Some of us played cards with imaginary funds running up huge poker debts "payable in San Francisco." We talked about our chances of ever getting out of the place. No one thought they were very good. We just tried to survive one day at time and hoped for the best.

I remember only one beautiful thing about Cabanatuan—the sunsets, the equal of which I had never seen.

Not long after my arrival at Cabanatuan, the Japanese began to bring in large numbers of survivors from Bataan and Camp O'Donnell. The appearance of these men was shocking. The best way to describe them is to refer to the pictures we all have seen of the pitiful survivors of the Nazi extermination camps such as Buchenwald and Auschwitz. Our people looked like that.

I scanned every arriving truck in hope of seeing Ralph and Mike. And I first found Mike. To my surprise, he was in relatively good physical condition and he told me that he owed this to the fact that early in the Death March he had been pulled out of line by Japanese guards and made to drive a truck to Camp O'Donnell. Most Japanese soldiers of the time did not know how to drive. He fortuitously had escaped the killing week-long march without food or water.

## Lieutenant Mann Arrives in Camp Cabanatuan

Not much later, Colonel Hawkins said, Ralph Mann arrived in poor physical condition like many others that he had seen: "Extremely emaciated, pale, jaundiced and barely able to walk. I feared for his life when I saw him." He was placed in a nearby tent, which housed marine and army personnel. Meanwhile, survivors of the Bataan Death March continued to die at a rate of thirty to fifty every day.

Hawkins remembers that terrible scene,

waking in the morning and seeing the bodies of those who had crawled out of their huts during the night to die in the open air, or had died in the hut and been carried outside by the living. Although Ralph's fellow Marine officers did all they could to care for him, there was little they could do other than bring him rice and water.

Mike and I visited him often and tried to cheer him up. He was too sick to do much talking, but we did talk about the things we all talked about as mentioned before. He spoke of you and worried about your safety. We said that you would have diplomatic immunity. This thought comforted him. Ralph knew and we knew that he was going to die.

During Colonel Hawkins's five months in the prison camp, he said, about three thousand American GIs had died, most of them American servicemen who had experienced the Death March. In concluding his letter to Lieutenant Mann's widow, he wrote:

> They were buried unceremoniously in mass graves scooped out by the Japanese with bulldozers outside the barbed-wire fence. When Ralph died on Sept. 5, 1942, his classmates, acting through the American camp commander, obtained permission from the Japanese to bury Ralph ourselves in an individual grave. Four of us, Mike Dobervich, Carter Simpson, Al Moffett and I, placed his body on a window shutter from one of the huts and carried him on our shoulders to the burial ground where we reverently laid him to rest with his identification tags in a glass bottle.
>
> Jessie, I know this is painful for you to read, but I believe that you want to know, and deserved to know, how it really was. Ralph was stricken beyond recovery by the Death March as were thousands of others. Coming from this into a place like Camp No. 1, Cabanatuan, he had no chance at all. Ralph was a good, brave and honorable man. I was proud to have him as a true friend and brother Marine.

As pointed out by Jack Forgy, however, the reported causes of Ralph Mann's death are "inconsistent." One report states that he died of malaria, while another states that he died of dietary deficiency (which, according to Forgy, means that "the Japs starved him to death").

Lieutenant Mann's military awards included the Purple Heart, the POW Medal, the Asiatic Campaign Medal, the Marine Corps Combat Action Ribbon, the American Campaign Medal, the American Defense Medal, the Asiatic-Pacific Campaign Medal, the Philippine Defense Medal, and the WWII Victory Medal.

Lieutenant Mann was buried by his fellow POWs in the Camp 31 Cemetery. After the war, he was reburied in Grave 2962, Row 21, Plot 3 in the U.S. Army Forces Cemetery, Manila #2, Luzon, Philippine Islands. At the direction of his family, his body was returned to the United States for final burial in Evergreen Cemetery in Judsonia, Arkansas.

## Epilogue to Ralph Mann's Story

After escaping from the Japanese prison camp in Davao in the Philippines, Jack Hawkins, then a twenty-eight-year-old lieutenant colonel, returned to the United States. He later returned to the Pacific with the First Marine Division, which at the time was preparing for the Okinawa invasions on the islands of Pavuvu, Banika, and Guadalcanal.

"It was a revelation and a joy for me to witness the great power of the United States crashing down on the enemy like a mighty hammer," he said, recalling the Okinawa invasion. "This was certainly nothing like the Philippines where bombs and shells were constantly raining down on us for five months. Now we were raining it down on them . . . I remembered my fellow prisoners of war in the Philippines and what the Japanese had done to them as we slowly but inexorably destroyed the 130,000 Japanese defending force almost to the last man. I felt great pride and satisfaction in this great victory after knowing the humiliation of defeat in the Philippines."

## Sidebar: Cabanatuan Prison Camp

The following is an excerpt pertaining to the Cabanatuan Prison Camp as described in *Ghost Soldiers,* a nonfiction account "of World War II's Greatest Rescue Mission," by Hampton Sides (New York: Anchor Books, 1991).

> Essentially, [Cabanatuan] was an extermination camp—extermination not in the Nazi sense of the word, not according to a cold master plan, but through a kind of malign neglect. The first comman-

dant of the camp, Shigeji Mori, a calm, impenetrable man in his late fifties who was said to have run a bicycle shop in Manila before the war, seemed either unaware of or uninterested in the death rate. In some ways he was the direct opposite of Captain Tsuneyoshi, he was a rabid American-hater at Camp O'Donnell. Mori had a dignified facade, an air of quiet precision. He wore black-rimmed glasses and kept his clothes immaculate. His neat black hair was filamented in gray along his temples, and he spoke in a carefully modulated voice. He usually used an interpreter, although he spoke tolerably good English. Colonel Mori was neither stupid nor baldly mean-spirited, but he seemed impervious to the horror that he left in his wake. He once remarked, "The prisoners are sick because they need more exercise."

For reasons that were never apparent, basic medicines that could have readily saved legions of lives, medicines like quinine, emetine and sulfa tablets, were never made available. Five hundred and three men died at Cabanatuan in June 1942, another 786 in July 1942. As summer dragged into fall, the toll began to level off. The graveyard details buried tens instead of fifties each week. Finally, on December 15, 1942, Cabanatuan reached a gratifying benchmark: its first "zero-death day."

Colonel Mori preferred to rule the camp as a single organism. To an extreme degree, the welfare of the one and the many rose and fell together. It was a managerial philosophy predicated on certain social hallmarks of Japanese culture, and typical of the Japanese Army at that time. This same rule of mass punishment applied to escapes. Col. Mori grouped the prisoners at Cabanatuan into units of ten. These ten were generally prisoners who slept close to one another in the same barracks and often worked on the same detail. The men were supposed to get together frequently and discuss the futility of escape . . . At all times, each prisoner was keenly attentive to the whereabouts of his nine brothers and for good reason. If a single American attempted to break out, all nine of his comrades would be executed along with the culprit.

The deterrent was highly successful. Very few people even considered escape, let alone attempted it. Most of the escapes were undertaken by people who were out of their heads with malaria, or out of their heads for some other reason. They almost invariably ended up getting caught—and promptly shot. Camp memories are a little fuzzy on the subject, but it is generally agreed that while many prisoners were executed either singly or in small groups, the blood-brothers concept was carried out only twice.

One of the occasions was in June 1942 on a bridge-repairing detail that had left the premises of Cabanatuan. During the night a prisoner escaped. In the morning the guards flew into an apoplectic rage. The nine men in the escapee's shooting squad were forced to dig a large hole and stand at the end to await execution. As it happened, there were two actual siblings in the work crew, the Betts brothers; Edwin Betts, the older of the Betts boys, was forced to watch as his younger brother, Ross, lined up with the condemned. Then the nine were all shot. Their bodies crumpled in the common grave. Edwin Betts returned to his work.

# David Matlock

Pfc. David Neil Matlock, former student, 1942–1943
Hometown: Arkadelphia, Arkansas
Died: January 15, 1945
*38517615, 357th Infantry Regiment, Ninetieth Infantry Division*

## How He Lived

Pfc. David Neil Matlock was born on February 13, 1925, in Arkadelphia, Arkansas, to Mr. and Mrs. W. T. "Tom" Matlock. Neil graduated from Arkadelphia High School and attended Ouachita where he was a star athlete in 1942–43.

His father, Tom Matlock, was sheriff of Clark County (Arkansas). Neil had three brothers, all in military service at the time of his death: Capt. Owen Matlock, who served with him in Patton's Third Army; Capt. Hallie Matlock, stationed on Adak, Aleutians; and Pvt. John Dayton Matlock in Belgium. Both Owen and Hallie were Ouachitonians. Neil also had two sisters: Madge Matlock Fowler (former student 1937–38) and Merle Matlock McClain, both of Arkadelphia, Arkansas.

Neil was married to Mary Margaret Stueart in May 1942 and they had one son, Neil Stueart. Both Neil Jr. and his wife, Mary Nancy Salter Matlock, are Ouachita graduates. The Matlocks have two sons and two grandsons.

Remembering his friendship with the Matlock brothers, Dan Grant said Neil was known as "Little Sody" and Owen was known as "Big Sody," because they both sold "Sody Pop" at athletic events. A classmate, W. N. "Wink" Bledsoe, of Tyler, Texas, remembers Neil as being "big like Big Sody," who also played football for Ouachita. His sister, Merle, "was a genius," Bledsoe added, "and I was in class with her in Arkadelphia. Madge was also a brain."

In seeking to remember the brief time they had together, Pfc. Neil Matlock's widow, Mary Stueart Daniel, who lives in Hot Springs, said, "I had a lot of letters in an old trunk at my mother and father's house. My second husband worked for an oil company and we lived all over the country. My

Pfc. David Neil Matlock

mother had her handyman throw out the trunk and its contents. All I can remember is that Neil was a mortar man until the Battle of the Bulge at which time a machine gunner was killed and he replaced this man. He was a machine gunner at the time of his death."

Neil entered the army on November 6, 1943, and trained at Camp Wolters, Texas, and Camp Robinson, Arkansas. He was sent overseas in February 1944, serving in England, France, and Germany. His military honors included the EAME Theater Medal with three Bronze Stars, the Oak-Leaf Cluster, the Good Conduct Medal, and two Purple Hearts.

How he earned his first Purple Heart is reported in an undated newspaper clipping thought to have appeared in the *Daily Siftings Herald* of Arkadelphia:

Neil Matlock holding his son, Neil Stueart, in 1943

> Pvt. David N. ("Little Sody") Matlock, aged 19, son of Sheriff-nominee and Mrs. W. T. Matlock of Arkadelphia, has received a Purple Heart and has become a hero among his former football teammates of Arkadelphia High School after being wounded in France. In the battle of St. Lo, he was struck in the right shoulder by a piece of German shrapnel. However, he lifted a more badly wounded soldier on his left shoulder and carried him a mile and a half to safety.

Private Matlock's wound was dressed and he was transferred from one hospital to another until going to England via an LST. Four of the five members of (his) mortar squad were wounded in the St. Lo engagement. The French "treated us pretty well," he said, while the Germans "aren't such tough fighters. They are either old men or young kids."

### . . . and How He Died

Neil was killed in action in Luxembourg during the Battle of the Bulge on January 15, 1945. In his obituary, it was reported that Neil was with Patton's Army. He was in the invasion and was wounded soon after D-Day and was hospitalized in England. After recovering from his wounds he was returned to combat service.

One of the most poignant stories to come out of this effort to tell the untold stories of these thirty-six Ouachitonians was recorded by his brother, Dayton, in a letter to Hallie and Owen. For reasons that will become obvious after the story is read, I have chosen to call it "The Reunion." In a letter written on January 1, 1974, Dayton recalls receiving two letters after Neil's death, one dated Christmas Eve, 1944, and another dated January 13, 1945, expressing hope that the three brothers—he, Neil, and Owen—could get together for a family reunion. "Both of these letters were received after his death," said Dayton, "so his plans to see me didn't materialize, *but I did see him about the nineteenth or twentieth of January.*"

Dayton explains:

> A day or so before this occurrence, my tank received a direct hit from artillery on the turret, knocked out the electrical system and traversing mechanism, which made a trip back to ordnance (about 50 miles) necessary for repair.
>
> The roads were iced over and traveling by tank was slow. There was another tank from my company that had to have repairs. I was driving one, and one of my best buddies . . . drove the other, when we hit a hill that took quite a bit of maneuvering to climb. Halfway up we stalled and had to pull over to let a convoy of trucks make an attempt at getting over. His friend had gotten off his tank, climbed on mine and we were watching the trucks slide back and forth up the hill. Some were loaded with ammunition, gasoline and other supplies,

some with Infantrymen on their way back for a few days of rest and others with the dead, on their way to Graves Registration.

One of the trucks near the top of the hill stalled and a truck even with my tank stopped and I looked in the bed to see what it was hauling. One soldier was lying on his back in the middle of the bed and I thought he was taking a nap until looking closer I realized he was dead and recognized him. Jumping off the tank and heading toward the truck I think my remark was, "My God, that's my brother." The line started moving before I could get on the truck and I had to get out of the way.

[My brother Neil] could have been on one of a thousand other trucks that day, Dayton recalls. They could have sent one of a hundred other men from my company to drive the tank I was in. Any other truck in the convoy could have stopped in the line in front of me. There could have been several men in the truck instead of just Neil by himself and then I wouldn't have even noticed him among the others, but none of those "could have been's" were. He was in that particular truck, I was in that particular tank directly in line with the point where the truck stopped and all the other odds considered leaves only one conclusion three decades later in my mind today—this meeting was meant to be, regardless of the odds.

Dayton and his brother had reunited after all. Neil Matlock is buried in the American Cemetery in Luxembourg.

Just three months after Neil's death, Dayton was wounded in action in April 1945 in Germany. A heavy-tank driver, Corporal Matlock was with General Hodges's First Army. In a story published in the *Texarkana* (Arkansas) *Gazette*, Private First Class Dayton Matlock wrote that his tank had been destroyed by a German shell "and that he was wounded in the hips but was making a satisfactory recovery in a hospital. It was the second tank destroyed under Corporal Matlock. He later received commendation for a device he constructed that increased the speed of fire of tanks to a great extent. Dayton "was clever with tools and mechanical apparatus," his father said.

# Dan Mathews

Lt. Dan Joseph Mathews, former student, 1939–1940
Hometown: Little Rock, Arkansas
Died: July 26, 1943
207-418-16, AAF Training Command, Fifth Squadron, U.S. Army Air Force

**How He Lived**

Lt. Dan Joseph Mathews was born on October 7, 1922, in Little Rock to Mr. and Mrs. George A. Mathews. He graduated from Little Rock High School in May 1939 and was a member of the Immanuel Baptist Church. Alice Gardner Meek of Southern Pines, North Carolina, who dated Dan during their high school years until his National Guard unit based in Arkadelphia was mobilized, said Dan entered Ouachita in the fall of 1939 with a major in biology and planning a medical career.

Air Cadet Dan Joseph Mathews was to have received his wings and commission as a second lieutenant the day after he was killed during a training flight.

His unit, Company H, was activated on December 20, 1940, and sent to Camp Robinson in North Little Rock, where it was mobilized with the 153rd Infantry of the National Guard into the regular army in January 1941. After several months of training, he was sent as a corporal in August 1941 to Juneau, Alaska. From there he was transferred to the Army Air Force in the fall of 1942 and sent to Santa Ana, California, to begin his primary flight training. In a story announcing his death, the *Arkansas Gazette* (July 28, 1943) noted that "while taking his basic training, he was voted the best athlete in his class."

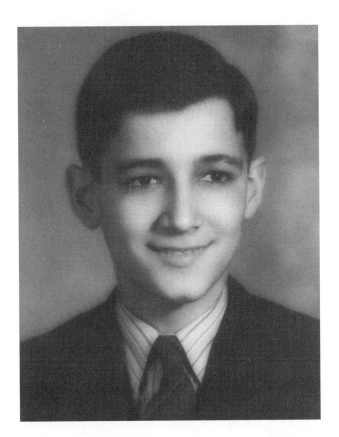

This high-school graduation photo of Dan Joseph Mathews was the inspiration to his sister, June Mathews Stuckey, when she wrote the poem, "The Brother."

Emily Kathryn Michael, who grew up with Dan, said she considered him to be a good friend. "He was a brilliant young fellow in his studies and a wit who kept his friends laughing. Everyone who knew him liked him. I still haven't gotten over his death."

Dan had three sisters, June Mathews Stuckey, Class of 1947, of Lafayette, Indiana; Jarine Mathews May, Class of 1938 or 1939, who now lives in Baton Rouge, Louisiana; and, Cherry Virginia Mathews Smith (Class of 1945), who died in 1996. Jarine is the widow of the late William "W. L." May, a navy veteran and a Ouachita graduate who died in 1967.

## ... and How He Died

Aviation Cadet Mathews, twenty, was killed on July 26, 1943, while flying a P-40E during a training flight out of Luke Air Force Base, in Phoenix, Arizona. The account of the crash was recorded in a U.S. Army Air Force Report of Aircraft Accident, dated July 26, 1943:

> **Description of Accident:** He had logged 256 hours and 45 minutes of flying time in the P-40 at the time of his death. Cadet Mathews made a satisfactory take-off at about 0915 on 26 July 1943. He had radio contact with the control [tower] at that time, but there was no radio communication with him afterwards. A witness, living two miles from the scene of the crash, saw the plane just prior to the accident and reported that the plane was seen flying very high then descending "in an uncontrollable dive" with one wing high, almost on its side. While descending, the plane continued its forward movement, at the same angle, until it crashed.
>
> At no time did the witness see the plane spin. The engine was audible while it was descending and the only unusual thing observed was an occasional "miss" in the engine, as though it were idling. The plane exploded when it crashed, proving fatal to the pilot and a total loss of aircraft. The responsibility of the accident remains undetermined, and the cause unknown.

Headquarters Flight Control Command dated July 27, 1943: "The accident occurred at approximately 10:30 a.m. 20 miles southeast of Luke Field, Phoenix, Arizona. 'Possibility of material failure.'"

In an announcement of his death published in the July 28, 1943, issue of the *Arkansas Gazette,* it was reported that "Cadet Mathews was scheduled to receive his wings and commission as second lieutenant today. He had planned to spend a leave at home before reporting back for P-40 fighter-pilot training, for which he had volunteered."

The Brother
By June Mathews Stuckey

After your plane
Crashed in Arizona,
The casket arrived
Sealed and guarded
By a young lieutenant;
At your funeral
An old man said:
There's nothing
In that casket;
It's too light.

In the August heat
I stood in white pique,
Sixteen years old,
Trying hard not
To hear things I wished
Were never said.

From the piano
Your graduation picture
Smiled irrelevantly down
On neighbors and
Country kin
Drawn by the exhilaration
Of death.
Before that
We were children,
Teasing for sweets,
Elbowing in church,
Playing elaborate tricks:
One evening when I was
In the house alone,
You pulled the light
Switch on the back porch,

Making the house instantly
A black cave;
Below my window,
A flashlight under your chin
You made grotesque faces and
Called to me.
What were your hands,
Your voice like?

After your funeral
We went to the country cemetery,
Forty miles over gravel road
To add you
To neat rectangles
Of great-grandparents
And grandparents:
The Jacksons, the Crows;
We felt that day
Like a frame
From which the picture
Had slipped.
Summer trips to the cemetery
Are now picnics
With visits to the country
For icy Cokes.
Nieces and nephews
You never dreamed of
Wade in the creek,
Go leaping over graves,
Weave in and out
The tombstone,
Tracing letters on stained marble
Where dusty cedars make little shade.

A thousand miles away now,
I think of you seldom,
Never with grief;

I disturb
The dust of twenty years
To become one of the old women
Who keep calendars;
You have become the picture
Smiling irrelevantly from the piano;
And we, having crossed over something,
Rest in comfort and peace.

"The Brother" was written by June Mathews Stuckey in memory of her brother, Lt. Dan Joseph Mathews, and published in *Southern Poetry Review,* North Carolina State University at Raleigh, North Carolina, Spring 1974.

# Leo Mattox

Lt. Leo Winfred Mattox, Class of 1943
Hometown: Shawnee, Oklahoma
Died: September 26, 1944
0-5252288, 144th Division, U.S. Army

**How He Lived**

Lt. Leo Winfred Mattox was born on January 26, 1917, to Robie Lester and Bernice King Mattox, in Poteau, Oklahoma, and he attended high school in Shawnee, Oklahoma. Gifted in math and aiming for a career in government, family members said, he had enrolled at Ouachita in 1939 after attending business school in Memphis. He graduated twelfth in his class of one hundred at Ouachita in 1939 *magna cum laude* with a bachelor of science in mathematics and a bachelor of arts in economics.

Winfred had a younger brother, Harrell King Mattox, who was killed during the Japanese attack on Pearl Harbor, and a sister, Norma Jean "Neanie" Mattox Kramer, Tulsa, Oklahoma, who nicknamed her brother "Fit." Mrs. Kramer said recently that she didn't know how her mother lived through the loss of both of her sons during the war.

Winfred went through high school in Shawnee with his future wife, Thelma Wallace (now Thelma Hamilton), the daughter of Dr. L. T. and Jessie Leigh Iler Wallace. Dr. Wallace, who was at one time professor of Greek and religion at Oklahoma Baptist University, had come to Ouachita in 1939.

Leo Winfred Mattox, Class of 1943

Still in their caps and gowns as members of the Ouachita Class of 1943, Lt. Leo Winfred Mattox and his wife, Thelma Wallace Mattox, pose for a graduation photo that includes their one-year-old son, William Harrell Mattox. "Billy" is named for his two uncles: William Wallace, Thelma's brother, also a 1943 Ouachita graduate, and Harrell King Mattox, who was killed at Pearl Harbor on December 7, 1941.

Bill Wallace, Class of 1948, Thelma's brother, and Winfred were "great friends," Thelma said, "and shared a house while they were students at Ouachita."

Thelma and Fit were married on August 29, 1941, in a ceremony performed by her father in the Shawnee First Baptist Church.

More than six decades later, Thelma remembers Winfred as being "very happy" and as having a positive attitude and loving his family. His sister, Neanie, "almost worshiped him," Thelma said. Neanie still talks of Winfred's warmth and keen intelligence and how he worked at his father's Blue Front grocery store in Shawnee, "the largest in town."

Winfred and Thelma had one son, William Harrell Mattox, who graduated from Ouachita in 1966 with a B.A. in accounting. For the past twenty-five years, he has been associated with the Pulaski County Special School District, where he served as assistant director of accounting and auditing. He and his wife, Margie, and his mother live in North Little Rock. They have one son and two grandchildren. At the time of Winfred's death, Thelma was expecting a daughter, Sherry Kay, who was born January 7, 1945, three months after his death. Sherry lives with her husband, Elvis Dunn, in North Little Rock, Arkansas. They have one son and three grandchildren.

### ... and How He Died

"Because his brother had already been killed at Pearl Harbor, Winfred could probably have received a deferment, but he couldn't live with that," his sister said. So after his graduation in June 1943, he enlisted in the army and was sent to Fort Benning, Georgia, for officer's training. He was later stationed in Camp Fannin, Texas; Fort Lewis, Washington; and Camp Phillips in Salina, Kansas.

Before being shipped overseas, Lieutenant Mattox's unit was being trained at Camp Phillips in the use of flamethrowers. Although his unit realized that the flamethrowers were faulty and had made their superior officers aware of the problem, Fit and his fellow officers were told to continue with their practice. Several of the flamethrowers exploded, including his own. One officer was killed immediately but Winfred succeeded in smothering the flames that had engulfed him by rolling around on the grass. Forty-eight days later, however, on September 26,

1944, Winfred died in O'Reilly General Hospital in Springfield, Missouri, as the result of severe toxemia caused by the third-degree burns on his thighs and legs.

Capt. Luther Suiter, a Presbyterian minister, led a brief prayer service at the Herman Lohmeyer Funeral Home in Springfield, Missouri. Lieutenant Mattox's body was then shipped to Shawnee, Oklahoma, where his funeral was held at the First Baptist Church on September 29, 1944. Burial was in the Resthaven Memorial Park in Shawnee.

# Clyde McCalman

Pfc. Clyde Vernon McCalman, former student, 1941–1943
Hometown: Bradley, Arkansas
Died: March 17, 1945
*38662508, Ninth Division, Sixtieth Infantry*

## How He Lived

Pfc. Clyde Vernon McCalman was born on June 13, 1923, in Bradley, Arkansas, to R. O. and Gertrude Cupp McCalman. He attended Ouachita from fall 1941 to fall 1943 and was a member of the Beta Beta social club, ROTC, the Symphonic Choir, the Ministerial Association, and the *Signal* student newspaper staff. His roommate was Wayne Ward, who later became Distinguished Professor at Southern Baptist Seminary in Louisville, Kentucky. Next to the youngest of four boys in the McCalman family, Clyde had three brothers: Marvin McCalman, who lives in Walnut Hill, Arkansas; the late Byrd McCalman of Bradley, Arkansas; and Glynn McCalman, Class of 1950, of Hammond, Louisiana, who served as a missionary to Brazil but later returned to be a Baptist pastor in Little Rock, Arkansas.

A ministerial student, Clyde Vernon served as pastor of churches at Biscoe and DeValls Bluff (Arkansas). He is remembered by Marjorie Allen Bishop, Class of 1942 (and Glynn McCalman's sister-in-law), as "a wonderful young fellow and one of my younger brother's very best friends." She and her older sister, Janet, traveled to DeValls Bluff in the summer of 1943 to teach classes in a Training Union study course Clyde was conducting for a week. The church in Biscoe, she said, "was in a cotton field and was also used by other denominations. It seems his services were held in the afternoon on Sundays, but I'm not sure about this. We knew him well. He often spent the night at our house. His home then was at least two miles south of Walnut Hill. Clyde could play an accordion and he loved music."

Glynn, Clyde's brother, wrote that "Older Ouachitonians will recall that the upstairs of the Student Union Building on campus was devoted to daily

Clyde Vernon McCalman, former student, 1941 to 1943, was a ministerial student and is remembered for his "good bass voice" and as the driver of the choir bus.

'vespers,' where a large number of students gathered each day for brief music and a student-led 'devotional' immediately after the evening meal. After Clyde's death the area was dedicated to his memory, and remained so for several years."

"Clyde was universally respected in his home community in and around Bradley as an 'All-American boy,'" Glynn continued. "He was handsome, athletic, much involved in local church activities, with a good sense of humor and popular among his peers.

"At Ouachita he was a ministerial student, active in several religious activities. He loved participation in the college choir, offering a good bass voice and serving as driver of the choir bus.

"He was selected as 'King' at Siloam Springs Baptist Assembly one year, and participated as a 'summer field worker' sponsored by the Arkansas Baptist State Convention. He particularly enjoyed his work with youth and adults in the Ozark mountains in the summer. He especially enjoyed his work on the *Ouachitonian*, serving as its business manager in 1944."

In a recent letter, Mrs. Bishop remembered "the McCalmans, their cousins here (in Bradley), as well as cousins from Louisiana were all such good friends. We were all outdoors—playing, riding horses, swimming, a 'community' bunch, very carefree. As his brother Glynn said, Clyde had a good sense of humor. But he also had a serious side to him. Clyde and my brother Josiah 'Buddy' were on the same basketball team. It was after games that Clyde often spent the night with us."

Although Clyde never married, Majorie said she was "almost sure" that the girl he was dating at the time of his death was Kathleen Jolley of Jonesboro, Arkansas. "I know she visited in his home here before he went overseas, and she also came down to see his parents after he died."

Virginia Queen remembers the special friendship she enjoyed with Clyde, especially as they worked together as members of the Ouachita choir. "We spent many weekends singing in the churches throughout Arkansas," she said. There were the "sing-a-longs" on the bus rides and Clyde, in his deep bass voice, singing "Give the world a smile each day." She also remembers how his death affected her. "I saw him when he came by for his last visit to Ouachita," she said. "We sat outside the library and he talked about what he would be facing. He was very solemn and apprehensive."

## . . . and How He Died

Clyde "was loved very much in Biscoe and DeValls Bluff where he preached. Although he could have used his status as a ministerial student as a basis for deferment from active duty, he enlisted in the army because he felt he could better relate to the fellows after the war who had been in the service," Mrs. Bishop said.

An additional incentive to enlist came when his good friend and double cousin, R. Harland Bird of Bradley, Arkansas, was killed in a bombing attack on German forces in Europe, said Glynn. Clyde enlisted in the army on March 17, 1944, and was killed in Europe on the same day one year later, on March 17, 1945, "a short while before the war in Europe would end," his brother said.

Mrs. Bishop said Clyde frequently wrote to her brother, Josiah, once telling him about holding Sunday services in the field. Toward the end, he wrote of almost all the boys in his company having been killed. "I remember he sounded so tired and sad," she said.

Dan Grant, one of Clyde's closest friends at Ouachita, has similar memories of his relationship with Clyde. "We pledged Beta Beta together and were in the choir together. He was my campaign manager for 'King of Siloam Springs Baptist Assembly' in the summer of 1943. I received letters from him as the war grew more and more brutal in the European invasion. Then the letters stopped coming. Later word came of his death in action. Clyde's early letters were full of humor—he was a fun-loving person. But he began describing the trauma of carrying his wounded and dead buddies and the letters turned grim."

After being buried temporarily at Henri-Chapelle in Belgium, Pfc. Clyde McCalman's body was returned to Arkansas for final burial in the Walnut Hill Cemetery near Bradley. Walnut Hill is one of Arkansas's oldest communities. It was the home of James Sevier Conway, the state's first governor. Land for the Governor Conway State Park at Walnut Hill was donated by Clyde's uncle and aunt, J. Willie and Mariah McCalman of Bradley.

# Francis Norton

Capt. Francis Allen Norton, Class of 1929
Hometown: Washington, D.C.
Died: June 15, 1944
*SN O-14440, Headquarters and Service Co., Twenty-fifth Marine Regiment, Fourth Marine Division, USMC*

**How He Lived**

Capt. Francis Allen Norton was born in Sunnyside Plantation, Lake Village, Arkansas, on January 1, 1906, to Dr. and Mrs. Marion and Elizabeth Norton. He attended Greenville and Columbia Military academies and Ouachita College, where he was described as "a brilliant student, engaging in many extra-curricular activities." At Ouachita, Allen was a member of the military band, the Glee Club, and the Dramatic Club, and he was a cheerleader. The caption under his yearbook picture read: *"To love one maiden only, cleave to her and worship her by years of noble deeds."*

After his father's death in 1918 and his mother's marriage to T. D. McCallum, also a Ouachita graduate, the family moved to Arkadelphia in the late 1920s. The move was made, said one of his relatives, so "his five children—two boys and three girls—could go to school." Allen's sisters, Sara Warner (Nowlin) and Mildred Carter Norton (who never married), were freshmen at Ouachita in 1926–27.

Allen Norton, freshman, 1929
*Ouachitonian* yearbook

Following his graduation from OBC in 1929, Allen and his brother,

Capt. Francis Allen Norton

Madison, moved to Washington, D.C. Allen entered George Washington University to pursue a law degree. He did additional study at National Law University, where he was affiliated with the Sigma Chi fraternity and later with the Congressional Country Club. It was also during this time that he married the former Virginia Beal of Washington.

"He was crazy about the Washington Redskins, and often had players in his home," said Floy Pope, his sister who lives in Camden. "Allen loved everybody and everybody loved him. His keen black eyes made him one of the favorites during his years at Ouachita."

After serving briefly with the Universal Credit Company, he held an administrative post with the Office of Price Administration, a position he held until he volunteered as a first lieutenant in the Marine Corps on October 15, 1942. He received his training at Quantico and at the Marine Corps Training Center at Camp Lejeune, North Carolina. After being promoted to captain on March 15, 1943, Allen was sent to Camp Pendleton, California, in September 1943, and then overseas as the adjutant of his unit.

Katherine Hobgood of Arkadelphia, a niece, said, "I can't think of anyone who would have been more pleased to have him remembered than his sisters, all of whom are deceased. . . . A fine family . . . [When they heard of his death] it killed them all."

Glimpses of the close relationship he enjoyed with his sisters is evident in a letter to Isabel, his "little sister" in Camden, Arkansas, concerning the birth of her son, Norton A. Pope, on March 13, 1937, who is now a surgeon in Little Rock.

> Isabel, honey, you sweet child. Seems only yesterday since I made you give back to Peter Kincannon a nickel he had given you for an ice cream cone. And how I had to go with you to the skating rink because you were too little to go alone. And to think, instead of a doll you have a real, honest-to-goodness baby. I can't get used to the idea but I think it's grand. Unless I break two legs we're coming to see him, and of course, you, this summer.
>
> You sweet thing, I know you're happy and I'll bet the house isn't big enough to hold Crawford's [their father's] chest. I'll also bet Miss Lizzie [their mother] is struttin' her stuff. Granma Lizzie now. Tell

Floy [his dad's sister, who never married] not to lay too much of a claim on him. Ginny says she refuses to be left out in the division of the loot. We are all so proud of him—and you—and Crawford. Take care of him—Love to the little rascal and all. Allen.

In a letter that same year to "Miss Lizzie," his mother, on the occasion of the birth of Norton, her first grandchild, he wrote,

Hi Granma—How does it feel? Just like you're starting all over I guess. Well, your Washington folks may not always be a disappointment to you [referring to the fact that he and his wife, Ginny, were still childless]. You know how it is. "The last shall be first" or "and a little child shall lead them" or some such appropriate business.

We are really so happy over little "Norton Allen Pope." I hope he'll grow up to be able to write his own name the same way twice. That's more than Uncle Al can do. I'll bet you're proud and happy. I know you've been terribly worried about your own baby [Isabel] and I can't blame you. She'll make a splendid mother and will be so happy. And Crawford Pope [Norton's father, Isabel's husband] is so fine, from all I hear. Wish I knew him better.

Floy's [Dr. Pope's aunt] letter sounded as if she had borne half the burden and I guess all the Popes and Nortons feel the same way. If love and sympathy and hope are any help, Isabel must have had an easy time of it. Our hearts are full for you all. Your son, Allen

In a V-mail sent just eight days before he was killed, Allen told his sister, Carter, that he was being sent to the South Pacific.

Hi, Sis,

If you don't know it already your brother is on his way to the Mariannas Islands to help Tojo out—Plumb out. I know we'll go through and that will mean getting this thing over and getting back to all the things we love. These Marines are wonderful and you can tell Miss Lizzie [his mother] they won't let any thing happen to her boy. The invasion in Europe should be a big step toward getting things buttoned up. I think of you all many times a day and I love you. It's families like you who make fellows like me want to keep things for you as they should be. Love, Allen

## . . . and How He Died

Details concerning Captain Norton's death by enemy gunfire while he was coming ashore during the assault of Saipan on June 15, 1944, were provided in a letter from M/Sgt. C. J. Hoebreck to Allen's widow, Ginny (Virginia). The letter is dated July 17, 1944.

Dear Ginny:

You well know how I sympathize with you in your bereavement. I cannot find words to express adequately my feelings in the loss of your husband and my very good friend—the Captain. Difficult as it will be, I am sure you will force yourself to carry on bravely, as he did himself and as he would have wanted you to. It may be some slight consolation to you if I tell you what I know of the Captain's death.

He came in with his staff in the early afternoon of D-Day. At the time that he and his staff came in, the Japs were shelling the beach with mortar fire. With no thought of his personal risk, he hastened forward to find the command post where he was to take up his battle duties. He advanced about half a mile inland when he was struck by a piece of shrapnel from Jap artillery. One of our chief corpsmen rushed to his position but the Captain was beyond all human aid, unconscious, and died a few minutes later in the corpsman's arms. He never knew what hit him so there was no suffering. The word of his death passed hurriedly through the regiment and it was a shock to all his good friends who were legion. Many of the men considered the Captain the most popular and best-liked officer in the outfit.

Ginny, I do not know if you fully realize just how busy he had been the past seven months. His duties kept him busy every day and many nights with maneuvers and packing plus the usual administrative work that goes with an adjutant's job. He thought of you constantly, I know, because we have talked about you many and many times. The Captain was the first officer to be buried in the Fourth Marine Division cemetery on Saipan. Captain Robinson saw to the

During a respite from the fighting in the South Pacific, Allen Norton relaxes with his fellow marines. He was killed going ashore during the assault on Saipan.

details personally. . . . It also may be of consolation to you if you try to remember—his death and the death of many others—made possible the taking of this island which is bound to shorten the war and spare the lives of many men. . . . With my kindest regards, C. J. Hoebreck, M.Sgt.

The depth of Ginny's loss is reflected in her letter dated August 17, 1944, to Isabel, Allen's "little sister."

Thank you for your sweet letter. Yes, your brother was a wonderful person—and we had two beautiful years together for which I am most grateful. And it's some comfort to know those years were as happy for him as they were for me. It just doesn't seem possible—though you know it is—that it is so. He was so alive and loved life so—and we all know he gave a lot of happiness to this grim old world. You're a lot like him, you know. I'm doing all right, I guess. I manage to get through one day and the next and so on. Let me hear from you when you can find the time. Love to you all, Ginny

Originally buried in the Fourth Marine Division Cemetery on Saipan, Captain Norton was later permanently interred in the National Cemetery of the Pacific section N, Grave 1432 in Honolulu.

An undated newspaper report on his death listed his survivors as three sisters, Mrs. Jack Nowlin and Miss Mildred Carter Norton, Arkadelphia, Arkansas, and Mrs. Crawford Pope, Camden, Arkansas; and a brother, Madison M. Norton, of Washington, D.C.

**The Significance of the Battle of Saipan**
Called "the decisive battle of the Pacific offensive" by Lt. Gen. Holland M. Smith, commander of the Fifth Amphibious Corps, USMC, the victory "opened the way to the home (Japanese mainland) islands." Japanese general Saito said at the time that "the fate of the empire will be decided in this one action." Agreeing, a Japanese admiral observed, "Our war was lost with the loss of Saipan." As if to illustrate the truth of these statements, four months later one hundred B-29 bombers were taking off from Saipan for bombing missions over Tokyo.

"The bloody battle resulted in the deaths of 23,811 Japanese "with uncounted thousands of others charred by flamethrowers and sealed forever in their caves. Only 736 prisoners of war were taken, and of these, 438 were Koreans. American casualties numbered 3,225 killed in action, 13,061 wounded in action, and 326 missing in action." (SOURCE: Capt. John C. Chapin, USMC (Ret.), *Breaching the Marianas: The Battle for Saipan* [Washington, D.C.: Marine Corps Historical Center, 1994].)

# William Parsons

Lt. William Reed Parsons Jr., Class of 1939
Hometown: Washington, Arkansas
Died: March 4, 1945
*SN 0-388384, Third Army, Eighth Infantry Regiment, Fourth Infantry Division*

## How He Lived

Lt. William Reed Parsons Jr. was born on December 26, 1918, to Mr. and Mrs. W. R. Parsons in Old Washington, Arkansas. His mother died when he was born during the flu epidemic of 1918, the worst epidemic the United States has ever known. (In 1918–1919, America was ravaged by an influenza epidemic that sickened about 20,000,000 Americans and killed more than 500,000—more than all the wars of the twentieth century combined.) After graduating from Louann (Arkansas) High School in 1935, Bill entered Ouachita where he studied for the ministry and was in ROTC. His son, William R. Parsons III, still has a "thank-you" letter from an Arkadelphia-area church, which paid his father, a part-time pastor, $2.50 for the "splendid service" he had conducted the previous Sunday afternoon.

In February 1942, just three months before he was to receive his degree from Southern Baptist Theological Seminary at Louisville, Kentucky, his ROTC unit was called to active duty and he entered the service as an infantry officer.

Bill met his wife-to-be, Juanita Marshall of Little Rock, when he came to the First Baptist Church, which at that time was at 12th and Louisiana. He was there to work on a Ouachita class assignment on a census of who was enrolled as members of the churches in Little Rock. They were introduced to each other on the front steps of the church by Moise Seligman, Class of 1941. Juanita, a student at East Side Junior High School in Little Rock, was fourteen and Bill was seventeen. For the next four years, Juanita said, "we were together whenever he would hitchhike to Little Rock, which was every weekend."

They had no money when he came to visit, so "we went to the zoo because it was free," she said, regretting that the only photos she had of

THE FIGHTING TIGERS

William Reed Parsons Jr., Class of 1939

those times were those they would take of each other. "Today, you can ask someone to take your picture, but that just wasn't the way you did it back then." She remembers how they would sit in the gazebo in the National

THE FIGHTING TIGERS

In England, Lieutenant Parsons operated two mess operations: one for the GIs and a second one for feeding twenty to thirty thousand POWs a day.

Cemetery near her grandparents' home in Little Rock. "One day," he once said, "I will be buried in a place like this."

Juanita also recalls the time when she chose to ride a bus to Arkadelphia to join Bill for a Ouachita ROTC party instead of taking a history exam—and not asking for an excuse because she didn't have the nerve to tell her teacher why she would be absent. As a result, she had to retake the course the following semester. But no problem. Recalling the party with obvious relish, she remembers borrowing a white lace dress for the occasion. After the military party, Bill took her back to the bus station because she had to be in school the next day.

After his graduation from Ouachita—in the First Baptist Church of Arkadelphia—Bill and Juanita were married on the night of her Central High School graduation on May 28, 1940, in the home of her grandparents, Mr. and Mrs. J. D. Chapman. The following fall, they both enrolled in the Southern Theological Seminary in Louisville, Kentucky. As she and Bill were getting ready for exams in February 1942, just two months after Pearl Harbor, he was called to

With an unidentified Ouachita building in the background, Juanita Marshall and William Reed Parsons pose for a graduation day photo in 1939. Introduced to each other by Moise Seligman (Class of 1941), Juanita and William married on May 28, 1940, the day Juanita graduated from Little Rock Central High School.

THE FIGHTING TIGERS

active duty. "If he hadn't been in ROTC," she said, "he wouldn't have had to go. But he needed the money."

After he left, Juanita lived with her grandparents, where, she said, "I lay on my bed and cried all the time. I couldn't take him going into service." Sensing Juanita's need to be with her husband, her grandparents paid her way to visit him in his stateside training camps.

According to Juanita, who now lives in Texarkana, Texas, Lieutenant Parsons was "a wonderful guy . . . cheerful all the time, very loving. A lot of girls at Ouachita were crazy about him and I can see why. But they talked about him being taken by the 'Belle of Little Rock' . . . which was me! I never got over him being killed. Even at eighty-two, it still affects my life. The last thing Bill told me, was that if he didn't get back, 'You have to get married again so someone can look after you.'"

At first, Juanita refused to remarry, but with her young son Billy and no one else to help her, she met and later married Alva Dykes Middlebrooks, from Hope, Arkansas, who had just returned home from the war. He died in 1986. They had two children.

Referring to Alva Dykes, her husband, Mrs. Middlebrooks said, "I [nick]named him 'A.D.,' but later just called him 'D.' . . . But I never forgot Bill."

## . . . and How He Died

Much of the following information received on Lieutenant Parsons was provided by Vergie Sinyard, Parsons's niece, who gathered the material from letters and newspaper clippings and sent it to me by e-mail.

> One of his army friends wrote the family after his death. He said when they arrived in England in late September of 1942, Lieutenant Parsons was an officer of Company C, 156th Infantry Regiment and at the first camp he was made Battalion Mess Officer, setting up a mess hall and kitchen to feed 2,000 GI's. He did a good job of that for which he received a commendation from their commanding officer. He was known as a quiet officer but one who could get the job done.
>
> In November of 1944, they opened up a closed British POW camp and operated the first POW camp in the ETO [European Theater of Operations] for this war. Lieutenant Parsons was assigned

the job of guard officer and post exchange officer in addition to his company duties. Later on [he was made] a finance officer. He remained at this one camp located at Bourton-on-Hill, Moneton-in-Marsh, Gloucestershire, until the spring of 1944.

In the spring of 1944 he left Bourton for Devizes, England, to establish and operate a receiving pool for all POW's captured in France on D-Day. He again received the job of operating a Mess for the GI's and one for the POW's, a monstrous task of feeding 20,000 to 30,000 prisoners a day. In September 1944, his company left for France and later was sent to Belgium and Luxembourg.

One of his friends, who was with him when he died, wrote that he was the finest lieutenant anyone could have. He was liked by every person that ever knew him, and he was the nicest, bravest and best guy you could ever hope to meet. He held services on Sundays when they were in a position that it was possible for all of the Second Platoon.

It was just before noon on March 4, 1945, when they ran into the Germans. They were making an attack and Lieutenant Parsons was looking over a fallen fir tree when a burp gun rang out with three shots. He was mortally wounded. His dying words were, "God, help me."

Lt. Parsons was awarded the Purple Heart. He is buried in the Henri-Chapelle American Cemetery and Memorial in Belgium. In this cemetery rests 7,989 of our military dead, most of whom gave their lives in the repulse of the German counter-offensive in the Ardennes, popularly known as the "Battle of the Bulge," or during the advance into and across Germany during the fall and winter of 1944 and the spring of 1945.

Although it was Juanita's decision for Bill to be buried in a military cemetery in Belgium near where he was killed, his sister, Valree Bates, who objected, had a memorial constructed to his memory in the Old Washington (Arkansas) cemetery. "They were very close and she always held it against me," Juanita said, "but since Bill and I sort of courted in the National Cemetery in Little Rock and he had told me that this was what he wanted, I felt it was the right thing to do."

Bill Parsons was survived by his parents; his widow, Juanita; one brother and five sisters; and a two-year-old son, William Reed Parsons III, whom he had never seen. Bill Parsons III, sixty, lives in Bedford, Texas, midway between Dallas and Fort Worth, where he is an associate professor of art at Collin County Community College in Plano, Texas. His wife, whose name is also Juanita, is a school counselor with some private practice.

During a visit to the Ouachita campus early in 2003, Bill said his father "was called by God to be a regular infantry soldier. But he was also called to be a minister to his men when there was no chaplain."

# Thomas Pool

Pfc. Thomas Marion Pool Jr., former student, 1941–1943
Hometown: Poplar Bluff, Missouri
Died: February 20, 1945
37 633 790, Company I, 275 Infantry Regiment, Seventieth Infantry Division, Seventh Army

## How He Lived

Pfc. Thomas Marion Pool Jr. was born on September 18, 1922, in Little Rock, Arkansas, to Thomas Marion and Elouise Hinton McGehee Pool, members of Pulaski Heights Baptist Church. When he was twenty months old, his mother died, leaving his father with three children. Marian Elouise Pool (Henderson), age five at the time of her mother's death, graduated from Ouachita in the class of 1951. Leslie Truett "Jerry" Pool, then age eight months, attended Ouachita in 1942 until he joined the paratroopers during World War II.

From 1941 until 1943, Tom Jr. attended Ouachita, where he studied for the ministry and was a member of the Life Service Band, the Ministerial Association, the Ouachita Choir, and the Ouachita Band. Daniel R. Grant, a classmate who later became president of OBU, remembers Tom as a good musician.

Tom's sister, Marian Pool Henderson, who now lives with her daughter's family in

Tom Pool, sophomore, 1943 *Ouachitonian* yearbook

THE FIGHTING TIGERS

145

Thomas Marion Pool Jr. (Photo provided by his sister, Marian Pool Henderson.)

Vancouver, Washington, said Tom Sr. was transferred by the Singer Sewing Machine Company from Little Rock to Hot Springs in 1927. Tom Jr. attended the Central Baptist Church in Hot Springs where his father met and married Pearl Orr, "who became a loving mother to the children," said Mrs. Henderson.

"Another big move for the family," she said, "came in 1940 when his dad was transferred to Poplar Bluff, Missouri." While in high school there, Tom Jr. met his future wife, Shirley Dean Frank. After he left Ouachita to join the army, they were married on May 9, 1944. Tom's unit was sent to Europe, and his daughter, Kathryn Sue, was born after his death. Kathy, who now has three sons and three grandchildren, lives in Little Rock.

"Thomas Marion Pool Jr.," she said, "was a fun-loving young man who loved God, his family, and his country."

### . . . and How He Died

In a letter dated April 17, 1945, to Mr. and Mrs. Pool, who were then living in Joplin, Missouri, Lt. Col. Loren T. Jenks, U.S. Army, division chaplain, provided details concerning Pfc. Pool's death.

> Dear Mr. and Mrs. Pool:
>
> Your son joined his company at its rear command post at Rouhling, France, on the afternoon of 19 February 1945. After a few hours, he and a number of other soldiers were sent to the company's forward Command Post at Etzling, France. This was a town which had been taken during the drive forward to the heights overlooking Saarbrucken.
>
> During the night of 19–20 February, your son was quartered in the same building with the company command post at Etzling. About 0600 on the morning of 20 February the enemy opened up with a heavy artillery and mortar barrage which turned out to be a prelude to a counterattack by three enemy Infantry companies. The counter-attack was thrown back but during the preparatory barrage one shell hit the command post in which your son and other soldiers were quartered. Those (who) were not injured immediately began to examine the others and it was found that Private Pool had been killed instantly by shell fragments . . .

An indication of the esteem in which Thomas Pool was held was a one-hundred-dollar money order sent to his wife by members of his unit in honor of their former comrade. In a letter dated April 17, 1945, Lieutenant Colonel Jenks told Mrs. Pool that with the approval of his commanding officer,

> Pfc. Kenneth L. Miller, . . . representing a group of your husband's friends who desire to remain anonymous, has requested me to act as agent for them in presenting to you an expression of sympathy in the form of a money order for $100.
>
> I am sure you will appreciate the expression of sincere sympathy which prompted this spontaneous and concrete effort on behalf of each of these friends who desired to express their sorrow in this manner. May I wish for you the sustaining comfort and strength of the spirit of God during these days of grief and loss. Few men have been honored by such an expression of loss by their friends and I know you will take great pride that your husband had such close and steadfast friends who desired to honor his memory.

Brig. Gen. G. A. Horkan, chief, Memorial Division of the Office of the Quartermaster General, War Department, Washington, D.C., sent Pool's wife, Shirley, a letter dated April 14, 1947. It included a photograph of the Epinal Cemetery, which is on a plateau overlooking a beautiful valley. "It is my sincere hope that you may gain some solace from this view of the surroundings in which your loved one rests," Horkan wrote. "As you can see, this is a place of simple dignity, neat and well cared for. Here, assured of continuous care, now rest the remains of a few of those heroic dead who fell together in the service of our country."

Details of the graveside service held for Pfc. Thomas Pool on February 28, 1945, were provided by his widow, Shirley Pool Jefferies. The information was contained in a letter from the Office of the Chaplain, Headquarters, Seventieth Infantry Division, addressed to Pool's father in Joplin:

> Dear Mr. Pool:
>
> As the Protestant Chaplain who conducted the grave side services for your son, Thomas, I wish to send you my sincere sympathy in this time of your sorrow. It may be of comfort for you to know that the service was conducted at five o'clock on the afternoon of February

28th under the warm rays of a setting sun in the United States Military Cemetery at Epinal, France.

A reverent silence prevailed, broken only by the fluttering of the National Flag in the gentle and caressing breeze as the 23rd and 121st Psalms were read, followed by the New Testament reading of I Thessalonians 5:1–11 and Revelation 14:13, 7:15–17. These words were used in closing: "We commend into the hands of the loving Father who gave it, the soul of this our comrade departed, trusting in the mercy of our Lord Jesus Christ; insure certain hope of the resurrection unto eternal life. Amen."

I am sure that you will feel, as I do, the gratefulness of the entire Nation to those who, like your son, have given their lives supremely and heroically that she might remain forever free. Only time, the solace and comfort of His spirit can minister to your sorrow, but may this verse give to you the inspiration to continue on in behalf of yet unfinished tasks:

*Turn Again to Life*

*"If I should die and leave you here awhile,*
*Be not like others, sore undone who keep*
*Long vigils by the silent dust and weep,*
*For my sake, turn again to life and smile;*
*Nerving thy heart and trembling hand to do*
*Something to comfort weaker hearts than thine,*
*Complete these dear unfinished tasks of mine*
*And I, perchance, may therein comfort you."*

May God's blessing sustain you and give you strength,
Sincerely yours

# Curtice Rankin

Maj. Curtice H. Rankin, Class of 1932
Hometown: Pottsville, Arkansas
Died: September 19, 1944
*SN 0292919, Thirty-eighth Armored Infantry Battalion, Seventh Armored Division, U.S. Army*

## How He Lived

Maj. Curtice H. Rankin was born on February 4, 1910, to Mr. and Mrs. William H. Rankin of Pottsville, Arkansas. His father was a successful farmer in the region, but because Pottsville did not have a high school, "Dad went to Russellville during his high school years," said his son, David. "The Russellville High School yearbook of the time referred to Dad as the greatest all-around athlete in the history of the school." After graduating from Russellville High School, he entered Ouachita College in the fall of 1928 where he majored in chemistry. An outstanding athlete, he lettered in football, track, and basketball. His other campus activities included membership in the Sons and Daughters organization and in the "O" Association, which he served as secretary, and he was president of his Sunday School class.

He earned a commission in the U.S. Army Reserve through the ROTC program at Ouachita. After graduation, he studied at Georgia Tech University, earning a degree in textile engineering, and later became an engineer with the Tennessee Eastman Division of Eastman Kodak in Kingsport, Tennessee.

He and his wife, the former Carolyn Simmons of Junction City, Arkansas, met while they were students at Ouachita. They had one son, David, who was two years old when his father was killed in action.

Dr. David Rankin, who was a visiting professor of business and economics and a consultant in the School of Business at OBU in 1992–93, is now serving as president of Southern Arkansas University in Magnolia. Major Rankin's granddaughter, Beth Anne Rankin, was the 1993 Miss OBU. In that same year, the Maj. Curtice H. Rankin Endowed Scholarship

Maj. Curtice H. Rankin

Fund was established by his mother, the late Mrs. Lillie Morton Rankin, in honor of her son.

As a member of the track team, Curtice was known as the fastest runner in the state. Called "the greatest all-around track and field athlete in history

Major Rankin, his wife, Carolyn Simmons Rankin, and their son, David. Dr. David Rankin now serves as president of Southern Arkansas University in Magnolia.

at Ouachita College, and a great football and basketball player," Curtice was known throughout the state as an outstanding all-around athlete. The following story was reported in the *Atkins Chronicle:*

**Curtis Rankin Achieves Fame as O.C. Athlete**
**Junior Student Turns in Two Outstanding Performances during Year of 1930**

Curtis Rankin, athlete at Ouachita college here, turned in two sensational achievements during the year 1930 that surpassed anything done by any other athlete in Arkansas and a much larger territory, it is believed.

In the spring of 1930 he sped down the 100-yard dash course at the state intercollegiate track and field meet in 9.9 seconds, breaking the 22-year-old record of 10 seconds flat made by Roy Dougan of Henderson College in 1908.

On Thanksgiving Day of the recent past football season, Rankin, a halfback, received a kickoff on his own 10-yard line and with his mates doing some good blocking, which he utilized cleverly, sped 90 yards for a touchdown, going through the state champion Henderson State College eleven, conceded unanimously as being the best college team the state has seen for five years. His speed was the big factor in this history-making run, for it has been a score of years since that feat was accomplished in Arkansas collegiate football.

Rankin, a junior, is outstanding as a track and field athlete and rates with the best standing guards in basketball in the state. He is just finding himself in a football way and his college looks forward to his playing next fall confident he will prove a powerful factor in the race for the championship.

In a separate story, an unnamed reporter used a play-by-play approach in describing Rankin's ninety-yard run: *"He's got it! He's off! He's away! He blows through the line like a storm. He sails down the field with the pack at his heels and the football under his arm."*

So impressive were his track skills that he was a major factor in the Tigers' 70-66 defeat of the University of Arkansas in 1929, as reported in a news release:

> After holding a commanding lead until the final event, the mile relay, Arkansas faltered at the finish and lost their first track meet of the season to Ouachita College by the score of 70 to 66 here today at Razorback oval. Foy Hammons [the Ouachita track coach] had a real ace to spring on the Porkers when he flashed Rankin, a one-man track team, who was entered in six events. Rankin delivered for his tutor, placing first in the 220- and 440-yard dashes, second in the 100-yard dash, third in the pole vault and was a letterman on both the winning half-mile and mile relay teams.

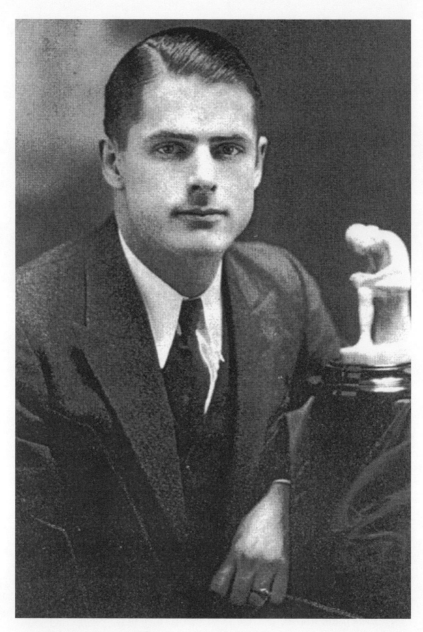

Curtice Rankin, Class of 1932

Curtice was also voted the "Best Athlete" in Ouachita *Signal*'s yearly "Who's Who" contest (circa 1931–32) and picked up virtually all of the athletic awards in the 1931 *Ouachitonian* yearbook:

**Football:** Curtice Rankin. Halfback. Weight 170. "The romping, stomping 'War Hoss' of the Tiger backfield. Curt has shown his class and speed to fans and opponents for the past two years, and it seems utterly impossible to keep him off the All-State teams for the next two years."

**Basketball:** Curtice Rankin. Guard. "'Curt' is the same fighting man on the court that he is on the gridiron. His hard work and fighting spirit was largely responsible for the defeat of the 'Red Warriors' [possibly what was later called the Henderson State University Reddies]. 'Curt' is a Sophomore and in the next season should be an All-State selection."

**Track:** Curtice Rankin. "Curt is the fastest man ever to run in Arkansas. He broke the 100-yard dash record of 22 years standing to run the distance in 9.9 seconds. Rankin won first in the 220-yard dash in the state meet, and was anchor man on two of the relay teams. In dual meets he handled the discus and shot. He is the most versatile track man in Arkansas."

He even received an award from the American Olympic Committee certifying that he had won second place in the 100-meter run during preliminary tryouts in Memphis to select a team to represent the United States in 1932 at the Tenth Olympiad in Los Angeles.

## . . . and How He Died

After earning a commission in the U.S. Army Reserves through the ROTC program at Ouachita, he continued to serve in the Reserves and held the rank of captain at the outbreak of World War II. Soon after being called to active duty, he was trained at Fort Benning, Georgia, and was later stationed at Camp Polk, Louisiana, and Desert Center, California. In June 1944, he was sent to France, and promoted to the rank of major; he served as the executive officer and occasionally as commander of the Thirty-eighth Infantry Battalion with the Seventh Armored Division of General Patton's Third Army.

Breaking out of Normandy in the summer of 1944, the Third Army "began a rapid pursuit of the Germans across France," said his son, David, in a summary of his father's military service.

According to David,

> In the race across the countryside, the Seventh Armored Division liberated numerous cities and towns, including historic Verdun, where so much of the bitter fighting of World War I transpired.
>
> However, on Sept. 1, 1944, the Third Army ran short of fuel and had to stop to wait for a fresh supply. This pause allowed the Germans to strengthen their positions and organize their defenses opposing the Third Army. By September 6, fuel was again flowing and new plans of attack were developed.
>
> One of Patton's objectives in the fall of 1944 was to capture the German stronghold at Metz, France. The Seventh Armored Division had a major role to play in the assault. In order to cross the Seille River, a number of German positions had to be eliminated, including the one at Sillegny.
>
> The assault by the Thirty-eighth AIB on Sillegny, which began on September 18, was met with a hail of artillery fire and counterattacks by German Infantry and tanks, the soldiers of the 38th fought their way to within a few yards of the nearest buildings by nightfall.

The German garrison in Sillegny was reportedly composed of the Thirty-seventh and Thirty-eighth SS Panzer Grenadier regiments, reinforced by the bulk of the division artillery of the Seventeenth SS Panzer Grenadier Division.

An insight into the fighting that took place on September 19, the day Major Rankin was killed, is provided in *The Lorraine Campaign* by H. M. Cole:

> Through the morning of 19 September, a confused and bloody battle continued at the edge of Sillegny. Col. Rosebro was mortally wounded. The executive officer of the 38th, Maj. C. H. Rankin, was killed; and when Maj. T. H. Wells, the next senior officer took command, he, too, was lost.

THE FIGHTING TIGERS

Further details are provided in Anthony Kemp's *The Unknown Battle: Metz, 1944*:

> The day on which the 38th Armored Infantry would win glory was 19 September, but it ceased to be a fighting force in the process. Throughout the day a savage battle ranged in and around Sillegny, reminiscent of some of the close-quarter fighting of the great trench battles during the First World War.

As reported in a dispatch from his division, Major Rankin "was killed . . . in heavy fighting during an attack by the Thirty-eighth on a German position near the French town of Sillegny." Citing him for directing the fighting in company with the commanding officer, the dispatch said, "Major Rankin heroically advanced to within five yards of enemy pillboxes, disregarding his own personal safety. Standing in front of his troops, he led them on in a gallant manner until he himself was killed."

"By the end of the fighting on Sept. 20," his son writes, "almost all of the officers were dead and the Battalion had suffered 75 percent casualties. The 38th was pulled back from the front to wait for replacements, and then transferred to Holland where it saw additional action. Metz did not fall until the end of November," more than two months after his father's death.

Major Rankin was posthumously awarded the Silver Star for gallantry in action during the attack on Sillegny, and he was awarded the Purple Heart. In the *Atkins Chronicle*, October 20, 1944, it was reported that:

> Maj. Curtis [*sic*] Rankin, greatest all-around track and field athlete in history at Ouachita College, and a great football and basketball player, from the fall of 1928 when he entered until 1932 when he graduated, was killed in France on September 19. . . . Rankin could win points in any state (track) meet in the shot, discus, pole vault and broad jump. He was carefully coached by Coach Foy Hammons and usually was in top condition. Rankin was a star defensive back on the football team. He played at a time when Ouachita's football fortunes were rather low. However, his ninety-yard run for a touchdown against one of Coach J. H. Rowland's great Henderson State College teams in 1930 is still remembered here. . . . His work on the basket-

ball team was good. His scholastic grades were excellent. Survivors included his widow, the former Miss Carolyn Simmons of Junction City, and one son, David; one brother, Morton Rankin, of Pottsville, also a well-known athlete at Ouachita.

"One of the interesting events to come out of the fighting across France," David Rankin said, "concerned Capt. Robert Kinoshita, the Japanese-American commander of the Thirty-eighth AIB Medical Detachment. Captain Kinoshita earned a number of combat citations during his service with the Thirty-eighth. In a 1998 letter written to a fellow veteran from the Battalion, Capt. Carl Mattox, Kinoshita said, 'I think that Major Curtice Rankin was one of the finest officers and men that I have ever met. He was to affect my life long after his death in France and long after the war was over.'

"After the war, Major Kinoshita was not able to buy a house, was not allowed to join the staffs of the local hospitals, could not get a credit card, and faced various types of discrimination. However, in 1946, he received a letter from the Presidio that he was to become a major and that many of the decorations that Curtice Rankin had recommended for him had been approved. The resulting newspaper article included Major Rankin's reports as background. [According to Kinoshita his] 'situation changed much for the better after the article appeared.'"

In recalling the life of his father, David Rankin said, "There is no question that my father has been a tremendous inspiration to me. In spite of the fact that he died shortly before my third birthday, I was very motivated by the example he set for me. My mother never remarried and is now buried next to him in the Little Rock National Cemetery."

# Thomas Reagan

Lt. Col. Thomas Hampton Reagan, Class of 1930
Hometown: Waldo, Arkansas
Died: December 18, 1944
*020415, Senior Chaplain, Seventy-eighth Infantry Division, U.S. Army*

## How He Lived

Lt. Col. Thomas Hampton Reagan was born May 17, 1909, to Dr. and Mrs. W. T. Reagan in McNeil, Arkansas. After graduating from Waldo (Arkansas) High School in 1926, he entered Ouachita that fall, where he enrolled in ROTC and earned a bachelor of arts degree in 1930. While at Ouachita, he was ordained to the ministry in June 1928 at the Central Baptist Church in Magnolia, Arkansas.

After graduating from Ouachita on June 3, 1928, during the presidency of Dr. Arthur B. Hill, Thomas Reagan entered Southwestern Baptist Theological Seminary in Fort Worth, where he received a master in theology degree in 1933.

His cousin, M/Sgt. (Ret.) Dean Reagan, who lives in Magnolia, Arkansas, remembers Thomas as a young man before he went to college. After the death of his parents, he was reared by his grandmother, Mrs. Emma Stringer, of Waldo, Arkansas.

Thomas Reagan, Class of 1930

After graduating from the seminary, Thomas Reagan returned to Arkansas hoping he could pastor rural churches. Biographical data from the National Archives show that he served several churches during this time, including

Lt. Col. Thomas Hampton Reagan

the Community Church in Garland City, Arkansas (May–August 1933); the Baptist Church in Buckner, Arkansas (July 1929–August 1930); and the Baptist Church in Bonita, Louisiana (July 1933–January 1935). Reagan did associational mission work in Hope, Arkansas, from 1928 to 1929. Because times were so hard during the Great Depression, however, his cousin said the churches "couldn't pay him enough to live on, so he asked for active duty."

After serving briefly as chaplain of a Civilian Conservation Corps (CCC) unit in Arkansas, he was appointed to the chaplaincy on January 28, 1935, and went on active duty on that date. His army assignments included the Camp Beauregard (Louisiana) CCC Camp (January 28, 1935); Fort Totten, New York (August 1936); Fort Amador, Canal Zone (May 1937); Fort Lewis, Washington (June 1939); and Camp Wheeler, Georgia (April 1941). After the outbreak of war, he was assigned to the Seventy-eighth Infantry Division on July 14, 1942.

"Thomas didn't associate with officers," Dean added, "but preferred to stick around with the enlisted men. It was while he was stationed in Panama that one of his daughters was born. He was later sent overseas, serving in England, Belgium, France, and Germany."

Of the 531 graduates of Southwestern Baptist Theological Seminary— including 425 chaplains, ninety-nine men in other branches of service, and seven women—nine lost their lives in the war. Of these nine, two were Ouachita graduates: Lt. Col. Thomas Reagan and Capt. Andrew Thigpen, Class of 1939, who suffered a fatal heart attack in Ohio the night before he was to be shipped overseas.

In a handwritten biographical summary dated in 1944, Thomas Reagan listed his dependents as his wife, Mary E. Stringer Reagan, thirty-five; and two daughters, Betty Carol Reagan, six, and Barbara Lynn Reagan, three. Efforts to contact the daughters, who, if still living, would be in their sixties, were unsuccessful. All other immediate family members are reported to have died. Colonel Reagan's wife didn't remarry until after the children had grown, Dean Reagan said, remembering that she "had a beautiful voice, always sang at church."

In a news story that appeared after his death, it was said that Reagan and his wife and children formerly lived in Jackson, Mississippi, and often visited there. His sister was Mrs. Lorraine Kinzer of Waldo, Arkansas.

Thomas Reagan's family included his wife, Mary E. Reagan, and their two daughters, Betty Carol and Barbara Lynn. Efforts to gather information on Thomas Reagan's family were unsuccessful.

## . . . and How He Died

War Department documents reported that the Seventy-eighth Infantry Division was said to have entered combat during the last stages of the Battle of the Huertgen Forest when the 311th Infantry Regiment was attached to the Eighth Division.

"The 78th was on the right or southern flank of the Bulge and it had the mission of protecting those flanks as Gen. George Patton moved the Third Army north out of France to rescue Bastogne," the report states. "The 78th heavily engaged the German flank. On December 18, 1944, the division seized a critical road junction at Monshau that prevented the Germans from expanding the bulge further south."

The following description of the events surrounding Colonel Reagan's death was written by John Lewis, an officer in G Company, 310th Infantry, Seventy-eighth Division. It was later sent to Colonel Forgy by one of the division association historians.

> There was trouble at Kesternich. A special service officer came with a truck late on the 16th. He said, "I need all of you to go help at the front to hold the line. Wear your uniform, take a weapon, canteen and a raincoat." At midnight we reached the front and were led through a cleared path in a minefield. There were dead men everywhere, ours and theirs. We moved past a burned-out tank to a quickly dug trench. Two of us were put with two of the men from the battalion who were already holding the line. Fire of every description was coming from every direction.
>
> As daytime came, it was snowing and there was a heavy fog. We had been spaced over a 3,000-yard line, within sight of each other, and were told to dig in. One boy didn't bring his rifle, and I carried the wrong digging tool. I was given the choice of a folding shovel or a two-piece mattock (hatchet). The command post was in a cellar behind us. When they could get hot food to the command post, they came and got us one at a time for a brief stay out of the weather. The sunshine on the fresh snow caused an unrelenting glare. We couldn't wear eyeshades because the light reflecting off of them gave the Germans a target. Sitting in the fox holes with wet shoes and restricted movement was rough on the feet and legs.

The firing never stopped. The big shells sounded like barrels rolling. The mortars made a swishing sound, and the German 88s made your teeth hurt. We started working on our real-estate holdings. The real doctor from our medical group was killed.

Despite being warned by superior officers to stay away from the fiercely-fought battle being waged, Lt. Col. Reagan, the Division chaplain, had come to encourage us and while he was standing near the cellar he was killed on Dec. 18, 1944, by mortar fire—the third day of the Battle of the Bulge. We were also receiving sniper fire from behind. It turned out to be a German hiding in the burned-out tank.

We still had men in Kesternich so could not call heavy fire on the town. After German tank personnel had captured several of the American GI's, others were still inside houses at the edge of town.

We thought they were still there and therefore we could not call in heavy shelling. Carrying parties finally helped rescue them. Most had to be sent to hospitals. They all suffered from trench foot and were weak because they had had nothing to eat for several days.

We felt sure that [the] main part of [the] German's Bulge had already moved on, so we couldn't figure why we kept getting so much shelling from Kesterich. December 23rd, the sun started shining again and our planes could fly. We thought we could see where some of the enemy artillery fire was located. The field artillery observer came to our foxhole to see and agreed. Starting at the bottom of the hill, we walked our artillery fire up the hill and back down. It must have worked, because the deadly 88's fire stopped.

A news clipping from Waldo, Arkansas, dated February 12, 1945, thought to have been published in the *Arkansas Gazette,* is included in a Reagan-family scrapbook. The story reports that "In the heat of combat, Chaplain Reagan was constantly at the front, bringing courage and inspiration when it was greatly needed. His contributions were a pronounced factor in the highly efficient role the chaplains played in combat. His fearlessness and devotion to duty are in accordance with the highest military traditions."

Chaplain Reagan is buried in the American Cemetery at Henri-Chapelle, Belgium. He was awarded the Bronze Star posthumously for meritorious service in Germany from December 13, 1944, to December

18, 1944; the European Theater of Operations ribbon, the Presidential Citation, and the Purple Heart. Although not noted in his military records, he would also have been entitled to the American Campaign Medal, the American Defense Medal, the European-African-Middle Eastern Campaign Medal, and the WWII Victory Medal.

# John Reed

2nd Lt. John Franklin Reed Jr., Class of 1941
Hometown: Pine Bluff, Arkansas
Died: April 10, 1943
0-410533, U.S. Army Air Corps

Lt. John Franklin Reed Jr. was born November 12, 1916, to John F. and Vera Parnell Reed in Pine Bluff, Arkansas. With plans to pursue a medical career, he graduated in 1941 with a bachelor of arts degree in biology. His extracurricular activities at Ouachita included serving as president of the sophomore and junior classes and as president of the Sigma Alpha Sigma social club. He was also the captain of the football team for one season, served as an assistant coach, and was a quarterback on the All-Southern team.

In addition, Frank was a member of the "O" Association and the Chemistry Club, served as ROTC cadet captain, was named to Who's Who, and was voted "Most Handsome" and "Most Popular." His yearbook caption:

John Franklin Reed, senior, 1941
*Ouachitonian* yearbook

"An all-around man, liked all around." His sister, Rosemary Reed, graduated in the Class of 1937.

**How He Lived**

H. B. "Hunk" Anderson, Class of 1942, of Parkville, Maryland, remembers "Rock" Reed as "a fine football athlete. He was my opponent when playing against each other in high school (North Little Rock High School v. Pine Bluff High School) and again in the Arkansas Tech/Ouachita series. He also was an excellent leader and liked by everyone."

Lynn Jones, Lieutenant Reed's niece, remembers her mother saying, "When Uncle Buddy's coach at Ouachita Baptist College was inducted into the Hall of Fame, he was asked who was the greatest players he had coached and he named two. Uncle Buddy was one of them."

He had signed up with the University of Alabama to play football, she said, and had attended practice before the season started. But a short time later, said Lynn Jones, "My grandmother looked out the door and saw Uncle Buddy coming up the walk. He told her that he was coming home. When asked why, he said that the other football players or at least one of them had stolen his razor, watch, and personal items. All the football players lived in a separate dorm. He could not tolerate that type of behavior. The University of Alabama coach came all the way to Pine Bluff to try and talk him into coming back to play. He told them 'No' and went to Ouachita to play. Later one of our cousins—Bear Bryant—became coach of the University of Alabama."

Also noting that Frank was "a star football player," Jim Shaw, a classmate, wrote that Frank followed him as Sigma Alpha Sigma president. "The main thing I remember about the S.A.S.," he said, "was how many times I was called into President J. R. Grant's office to try to explain why the S.A.S. had an orchestra at their last party if it was true that the S.A.S. had forbidden dancing at their parties. I was never successful in just telling a Ouachita president that we just liked to listen to good music. I hope Frank had better luck."

A friend of Frank since they were in grade school, the late Gen. (Ret.) Herman Hankins, of Arkadelphia, remembered him as "a real fine person. He was a natural-born leader. He was small to be a football player but he had all the guts in the world. He was offered a scholarship to Alabama, but came here because his sister was the secretary to the business manager. He had the integrity of George Washington."

Before leaving for military service, Frank married his college sweetheart, Rose Lee Sanders, a piano major from Forrest City, Arkansas, in 1942. After graduating in 1940, "Rosie," who died a year after she had remarried, is remembered by Marjorie Allen Bishop, Class of 1942, of Bradley, Arkansas,

THE FIGHTING TIGERS

Second Lt. John Franklin Reed served as ROTC cadet captain at Ouachita.

as "a wonderful pianist" who later taught in a state college in Huntington, West Virginia.

"Frank took his first flight training in the Civilian Pilots' program," Bishop said. "He and Virgil Benson were best friends. He played football at Pine Bluff High School and they were in the flying class together. Both married talented musicians. They both played football together at OBC. Frank had training in the Air Force in California, later at Westover Field in Massachusetts. He was killed in a training flight there. Both were wonderful young fellows and their wives were both great girls."

After graduating from Ouachita, Frank was transferred to the U.S. Air Corps. He received preflight training at Santa Ana, primary training at Visalia, and basic training at Merced, all in California. He received his wings and commission at Luke Field, Arizona.

### . . . and How He Died

In an interview a few months before her death in 2002, Rosemary R. Hamner, Frank's sister who was living in Monroe, Louisiana, said he was killed in an aircraft accident on April 10, 1943. "He was teaching pilots how to fly in formation," she said. "The planes had been grounded for a month because of fears of sabotage. But in this case, he and another pilot were working with the others on formation flying when his plane suddenly lost all of its fuel. He radioed his partner to say that because planes were so scarce at that time, he was going to stay with the plane to save it. His partner reported later that he saw Reed's plane go into a slow spiral from a high altitude. Rather than jump, however, Reed evidently chose to stay with the plane until the last minute, but he waited too late. When he jumped, his plane was at treetop level, and his chute never opened."

Lynn Jones, Mrs. Hamner's daughter, pointed out that Frank "remained in his plane to steer it away from a residential area. His chute did open, and was caught in a tree. But when he dropped to the ground, he fell on a tree stump, breaking his back and dying. Before medical help could reach him, someone had stripped him of all his valuables." At the time of his death, he was stationed at Westover Field, Chicopee Falls, Massachusetts.

# Wallace Robinson

Lt. J.G. (USN) Wallace Rufus Robinson, former student, 1941–1942
Hometown: England, Arkansas
Died: January 2, 1945
*299133, U.S. Navy, Bombing Squadron 116, Fleet Air Wing 14, Pacific Fleet*

The youngest of five children, Lt. Wallace Rufus Robinson was born on June 25, 1922, to John D. and Jennie Seaton Robinson in Humnoke, Arkansas. His father was a merchant, his mother a homemaker. He had two older brothers, one sister, and a fifth sibling who was unknown to Wallace's widow, Lillian Robinson of Little Rock. After his father died when Wallace was six years old, he and his mother lived with his aunt in England, Arkansas.

While attending England High School, where he graduated in May 1940, "Wally" worked for the local Kroger store after school and later became assistant manager of a Kroger store in El Dorado, Arkansas. In high school, Wallace worked on the school newspaper. His widow, Lillian Robinson of Little Rock, remembers that during his senior year at England, all students had to attend school in the local American Legion's log cabin Legion Hut because a severe tornado had blown away the top of the school just after the close of the 1939 spring semester.

Wallace Robinson, freshman, 1942
*Ouachitonian* yearbook

When war was declared in December 1941, he applied for and was accepted into the U.S. Naval Air Corps program. After basic training at the University of Georgia in Athens and flight training in Olathe, Kansas, he was sent to the base at Corpus Christi, Texas, where he received his pilot's wings in July 1943.

## How He Lived

Asked how she and Wally met, Lillian answered, "We went to high school together. During the summer there was a group of friends who got together often. Our home seemed to be a gathering place, especially after movies, and so forth, especially on the large screened porch where we three sisters had a record player and a well-stocked kitchen nearby. Our going together just evolved gradually."

"He often tried to remind me that we had been lab partners in biology in high school and that he had to do all the dissecting of frogs, etc., because I was too squeamish. To this day, I don't remember this! But he liked to tease me about it." Gradually, Lillian and Wallace began to "pair-off. We became engaged during the time Wallace worked at the Kroger grocery store in El Dorado. He proposed to me in the back of the store. How's that for unromantic?" she added with a giggle.

Wedding plans had to be postponed for three weeks, because he was stationed in Corpus Christi, Texas, and his orders hadn't come through. When they did come through, however, Wallace and Lillian were married in her parents' home on July 16, 1943.

"Wally was mischievous, a big tease; he loved people and people loved him. He never met anyone he didn't like and he *loved* flying!" Lillian

Lillian and Wallace Robinson on their wedding day, June 16, 1943, at her parents' home in England, Arkansas. Lillian, who never remarried, graduated from Ouachita in 1943.

THE FIGHTING TIGERS

remembered with a smile as she shared dozens of her photographs with me. "He was the youngest of four or five children. With two older brothers and a sister who was eight or nine years older than he, Wally must have been a menopause baby." She still recalls with amusement the time when he entered the navy and had to get a birth certificate for the first time. "All his life, he thought his name was Rufus Wallace. But it turned out to be Wallace Rufus! Friends called him Robbie."

While he finished his flight training, Lillian remained at Ouachita College, graduating with a bachelor of science degree in home economics in 1943. When Wallace was ordered overseas, Lillian went to England, Arkansas, to be with her parents, Mr. and Mrs. James Edward Swaim Sr., in the spring of 1944.

After she and Wallace were married, they traveled by train to Hollywood Beach, Florida, where, "to his dismay," she said, he was sent for further navigation training since there weren't enough planes for all the pilots at the time of his commission. After further flight training at Escondido, California, in the Ventura aircraft and then to Oakland, California, to "check out" the four-engine B-24s, he was transferred to the Marianas Islands in the South Pacific in the spring of 1944, where he began flying missions as a copilot.

Although Wallace Robinson had returned to the South Pacific before his daughter was born, he received this photograph of his wife, Lillian, with their new daughter, Jean, just two days before he was killed in action.

His last time to be with Lillian was in the fall of 1944 when his crew flew to California to return airplanes for repair and to pick up new ones. While waiting for his new aircraft, he caught a flight to Little Rock to spend several days with Lillian, who was pregnant with their daughter, Jean Marie. Although he had returned to the South Pacific before his daughter was born on November 6, 1944, he received a photo of his wife and child two days before he was killed.

## . . . and How He Died

Wallace was copilot of a PB4Y-1 patrol bomber, the navy version of the Army Air Force's B-24D. Said Jack Forgy: "The navy adopted the B-24/PB4Y-1 because it had four engines, was heavily armed, could carry bombs, depth charges, and mines, and fly great distances. The four engines gave them far more range than the two-engine PBY Catalina."

In a U.S. Navy Casualty Report, the circumstances of his death are reported in dispassionate military terms that are chilling in their detail:

> On 2 January 1945, Lieutenant Robinson flew co-pilot on a patrol mission from Tinian to the Bonin Islands area, a distance of nearly 1,000 miles. Just as they turned to come home they observed a 4,000-ton Japanese freighter. Not having any bombs on this mission, the pilot decided to attempt a sinking with low-level strafing runs, using his forward, top and rear machine guns. Four times he dove out of the sun to 150 feet and the crew raked the freighter with all the .50 caliber machine guns they could bring to bear.
>
> At the end of four runs, the freighter was burning and some of her defensive guns had been knocked out, but there were still two guns left and their firing became more accurate with each run. On the fifth run, one of the Japanese gunners succeeded in penetrating Lieutenant Robinson's windshield with a .20mm bomb, hitting him in the head and killing him instantly.
>
> The explosion threw shrapnel and skull fragments into the right eye of the pilot, Lt. Elwin A. Petersen. Stunned by the wound, the pilot lost control of the aircraft momentarily but the trim tabs were set in the slightly up position, giving the navigator time to remove Robinson from his seat to the flight deck and grab control of the plane and climb to altitude.
>
> Lieutenant Peterson recovered sufficiently to take over from the

Lt. JG Wallace Rufus Robinson. "He loved flying," said his wife, Lillian.

Wallace Robinson *(front row, second from right)* was copilot of a PB4Y-1 patrol bomber, the navy's version of the Army Air Force's B-24D. Robinson was twenty-two at the time of his death.

navigator and the crew chief came forward and took the co-pilot's seat, while the navigator administered first aid to the pilot. They then headed for home with the auto-pilot engaged.

Additional details were provided in an Aircraft Action Report:

> Three .20mm explosives struck the plane. In addition to the one that killed Robinson, a second one hit the underside fuselage forward starboard side through the port bomb bay tank and doors, damaging the hydraulic line and bomb bay doors and causing a leak in the bomb bay tank; the third one struck, penetrated the starboard side tail turret, damaging the booster pump. The crew chief continued to monitor the controls and the Navigator insured they stayed on course. When they arrived over Tinian, the pilot took the controls and made a perfect landing. So perfect was the landing that not a drop was spilled from a cup of water placed on the console for the pilot.

Almost sixty years later, as he reflected on the heroic actions taken by Wallace Robinson's flight crew after he was killed, Jack Forgy said, "A lot of uncommon valor was displayed that day."

A much more emotional account of Wallace's final flight is provided in a Tactical and Operational Data report that was initially classified as secret but later declassified.

> At 0615 2 January 1945, Lt. E. A. Petersen, USNR, slipped his Blue Raider off the deck at West Field, Tinian, on an epic search flight into the Nanpo Shoto area.
>
> The cross leg of the sector was completed and course set for home. Ten minutes later at 1430, 975 miles from home and 300 from Tokyo, Lt. j.g. W. R. Robinson, USNR, co-pilot warily scanning for the enemy, shouted "enemy ship below at 2 o'clock on course 230°." Pulling hard right on course 176°, the pilot looked below to see an enemy Fox Tare Charlie (a 4,000-ton heavily armed Japanese freighter) plunging through heavy swells toward Chichi Jima.
>
> Lacking bombs, it was decided to strafe. All stations were alerted and steadied for the attack with the terse command, "Man your battle stations, we're goin' in." Immediately thereafter Lieutenant Petersen banked sharply to the left, dropped from 4,000 to 2,000 feet and headed for the quarry down wind out of the sun. Just off the Japs starboard bow the Blue Raider was nosed over in a 50° dive. The order was passed to rake gun positions. At 2,000 feet, bow and deck turrets opened with a hail of armor piercers, incendiaries and tracers. . . . Although S-turning on the run to avoid enemy fire, the nose of the Blue Raider was kept on the length of the enemy with a vicious tenacity. The ship was cleared at 150 feet altitude. There was no apparent damage other than a complete absence of enemy anti-aircraft fire.
>
> Wrapping his plane up in a sharp climbing turn to port, Petersen prepared for a second strafing dive from 2,000 feet. This time, the gunners were ordered to riddle the superstructure and riddle it they did, bow, deck, port waist and tail turrets poured in a lethal stream of fire. Passing the dumbfounded Nips at 150 feet altitude just off their bow, black smoke was seen oozing from the superstructure. For the first time moderate and inaccurate anti-aircraft fire was noted.

Duplicating his retiring-and-approach maneuver of the second run, Petersen positioned for the third and ruinous attack. Boring in over the quarry's starboard quarter, all gunners were directed to aim for the bases of the stack. The Japs, somewhat recovered from a stupor induced by the audacity of the relentless Blue Raider, opened with intense AA from forecastle, poop, atop superstructures and along sides of the same on the deck. The caliber was believed to be .25-mm and .20-mm.

Jamming the yoke forward, the Blue Raider again assumed the attitude of a dive bomber. The air-speed indicator shot up to 270 knots. Van Pool in the bow turret and J. P. Richardson, manning the deck guns, poured a deadly accurate fire into the base of the stack from 2,000 feet on in. Return fire by the Jap was erratic and inaccurate. Ensign F. G. Jaussi, USNR, Navigator, observing the show between the pilot and co-pilot, remarked at interrogation that he had never seen such gunnery—he estimated that 90 percent of all rounds fired were on the point of aim. At 1,000 feet from the ship, there was a violent explosion. Petersen twisted over on his left wing to avoid flying debris. The whole superstructure became a brilliant red-orange inferno. Flames leaped 100 feet in the air. Dense, gray smoke billowed upward to be carried away on a stiff breeze. Petersen yelled, "We got 'em, we got 'em" as he pulled up out of the dive at 150 feet altitude. Both bow and deck turret gunners remarked at interrogation, "It seemed like we were headed straight through a wall of flame."

To survey the extent of damage inflicted, Lt. Petersen climbed to 2,000 feet and circled the enemy twice.

The sight that met all hands' eyes was gratifying. Dead in the water, wallowing helplessly in the heavy swells, the Japs presented a picture of utter desolation. Fiercely burning fires had spread over three quarters of the ship. From point just forward of the superstructure aft to the fantail the freighter was a mass of seething flame and gray to black smoke. The only distinguishable feature of the vessel was the typical Jap bow and gun installation on the poop deck which continued firing. From a point amidships below the water line on the starboard side, heavy oil oozed from a rupture in the ship's hull. Fanning out on the windward side of the ship to an estimated 1,500 feet, the slick calmed the turbulent seas to disclose quantities of debris, crates, planks and drums. A definite list to starboard and decks awash gave further evidence of sprung plates. All hands agreed the Jap [ship] was settling and were impatient to deliver another punch.

The eagerness of the crew prevailed and runs four and five were made in quick succession. Both were similar to those preceding—down wind, out of the sun, terrific speed and deadly accurate fire concentrated on the only exposed portions of the victim—the gun position on the poop deck and a forward hatch. All else was blanketed by a mixture of steam and black smoke spewing from the ship's vitals.

On the last run, the only active gun was knocked out—seconds after the bandy-legged fanatics had obtained lucky but near fatal hits on the Blue Raider.

Seconds before the pull out on the last air-splitting dive a .20-mm explosive holed the starboard windshield exploding on impact with [Lt. Robinson's] forehead. Fragments of skull and steel entered the pilot's right cheek lodging in and destroying his right eye. [Because Lt. Petersen had been rendered] momentarily unconscious, the plane continued its dive toward the sea. A precautionary pre-attack setting of back tab by Petersen worked against the precipitous descent. Stunned by the 20-mm explosion, blinded in his right eye, with depth perception impaired in a supreme and heroic effort, Lt. Petersen struggled back to consciousness, pulled back the yoke, avoiding disaster by a bare 50 feet.

Ensign F. G. Jaussi, USNR, navigator, taking in the situation at a glance went to the cockpit, pulled the dead co-pilot away from the yoke and assisted the pilot in steadying the plane. Martin, the plane captain, ordered forward by the pilot, helped remove Robinson's body from the cockpit to the flight deck and on orders from Petersen took over in the co-pilot's seat.

The foregoing transferred in a matter of seconds. With amazing lucidity and self control in one so seriously wounded, with his crew and plane so near disaster, Lt. Petersen took command of the situation and formulated a plan of action which brought the plane safely to base.

The esteem in which Lieutenant Robinson was held was apparent in the letters Lillian received after his death. Two of these letters follow, the first from F. N. Anderson, chaplain, U.S. Navy Fleet Post Office, dated January 5, 1945.

> By the time you read this letter you will know the deepest sorrow that any young woman can know. It is, unfortunately, the same sorrow that many others like you have yet to bear. As a Minister of God, I want to help you with that grief if I can.
>
> [Your husband] came to my attention when word came to us that one of our planes was returning with dead and wounded aboard. The squadron officers asked me to meet the plane and I was glad to do so. Lt. Robinson had met an instantaneous death. We took him from the plane and tenderly as only comrades can do. We wanted to do something but that was all we could do for either of you.
>
> Yesterday, January 5th, 1945, we laid his body to rest in the American Cemetery. His shipmates were there. A detail of Marines fired the salute which was his due. A bugler blew Taps and then another bugler echoed them from a distance. May I assure you that everything possible was done. His funeral was dignified and with full honor to the sacrifice which he had made.
>
> It is my hope and prayer that you will be able to find solace in your God. The question of "why" will plague you. But we only know that we have a task to do and we do not care to live unless we can achieve a victory over all forms of evil. We owe an overwhelming debt to these men who have died. We owe you a debt, too.

A second letter was dated January 4, 1945, from Donald G. Gumz, commander, USN, Commanding VPB 116:

> It was with deepest regret that I found it necessary to notify the Navy Department of the loss of your husband. He had been with the squadron long enough for all of us to know him and like him very much. We admired his ability and courage.
>
> On the morning of the second of January he left his base as copilot with his regular crew on a routine patrol. When well out near the extremity of his sector, your husband spotted an enemy merchant ship of good size. He called Lt. Petersen's attention to the target and the boys dove their plane in at low-level strafing attack with all guns.

THE FIGHTING TIGERS

There was also considerable return fire from the enemy, but they continued their strafing runs until, on the third pass, the enemy freighter exploded amidships and started burning furiously. To be sure of their kill, they came in low for a fourth and a fifth run [when] sporadic enemy return fire from a single automatic weapon placed an explosive bullet in the cockpit. Your husband was killed instantly and Lieutenant Petersen was wounded as was another crewman. The remainder of the crew was able to get the plane back to base. The enemy ship never reached port.

We were a depressed and saddened squadron that evening, for though we had scored heavily against the Japs, we had paid with the life of a fine officer. We buried him with full military honors and the services were conducted by the chaplain of the local air base. . . . The entire squadron joins me in extending to you our deepest sympathy.

In recognition of his valor, Wallace Robinson was posthumously awarded the Distinguished Flying Cross, the Purple Heart, the American Campaign Medal, the Asiatic-Pacific Campaign Medal, the World War II Medal, and the Air Medal. Had he lived, Wallace would have been promoted to captain. In fact, he had already purchased his new insignia. Lieutenant Robinson is buried in the National Cemetery of the Pacific in Honolulu.

After his death, Lillian remained in England, Arkansas, with her parents. When her daughter, Jean, was two, Lillian began teaching in a local school system. Three years later, she moved to Little Rock where she worked until her retirement in 1986.

Lillian Robinson in 2002

# Carmon Rucker

1st Lt. Carmon B. Rucker, Class of 1941
Hometown: Grand Saline, Texas
Died: April 15, 1943
*410534, 883rd Bomb Squadron, 500th Group, Twentieth Air Force, U.S. Army Air Force*

## How He Lived

First Lt. Carmon B. Rucker was born to Grover and Alice Sharp Rucker on January 17, 1918, in Grand Saline, Texas. "Jack" was one of seven children—five boys and two girls, whose mother died of "heart problems" at the age of forty-five. Entering Ouachita in 1937, he majored in chemistry and minored in education; and he graduated in 1941. He was a member of the Rifle Club, the Red Shirts social club, the Chemistry Society, the Arkadelphia company of the Arkansas National Guard, and he was enrolled in ROTC. His yearbook caption reads: *"I don't say anything I can't back up."*

1st Lt. Carmon B. Rucker in flight suit

He worked on the construction of the football stadium at Ouachita to help pay his tuition, said Jean Davis, his sister, and worked in the dining hall to pay his rent. "He was a pretty good talker!" she said, referring to his yearbook caption. For example, she said, in the middle of the Great Depression, in 1937, when Carmon was doing the best he could to earn enough money to stay in college, the college's business manager, Leonard Price, called him in and said, "Carmon, we are just going to have to have some money."

Carmon's reply: "I sure am glad because I sure do need some."

His earlier plans to play football were ended when he almost cut off his finger in a dining hall accident. The accident led to the discovery that he was a borderline hemophiliac, which led him to become the football team's manager instead of a player. A classmate, "Hunk" Anderson, recalls that "Carmon was our football manager when I came to Ouachita in 1940. He was a most likable fellow—had to be to take care of a bunch of football jocks—always helpful and accommodating."

The diagnosis may have been enough to stop him from playing football but it didn't prevent him from going into active duty. At graduation, he received his commission in the infantry in June 1941, transferred to the Air Corps in March 1943, and was sent overseas in December 1944. His wife was Helen Lucy Rucker of Arkadelphia, Arkansas, described by his sister as "a lovely lady," who died in 1990 in California.

Helen Lucy Rucker and Carmon B. Rucker in 1942 or 1943 in Hays, Kansas

Carmon Rucker *(back row, second from left)* with members of his crew. Rucker was declared missing in action after his B-29 was forced to ditch during a bombing mission to attack an aircraft plant near Tokyo.

## ... and How He Died

Lieutenant Rucker was copilot of Aircraft 45, one of eighteen B-29s that took off from Isley Field No. 1, Saipan, on January 9, 1945, on a bombing mission to attack the Musashino aircraft plant near Tokyo. Air Historical Group Records report what happened:

> Takeoff time was from 0746 to 0805. As a result of poor weather, assemblies of the two squadrons was not accomplished according to plan. Some planes joined the squadrons from other groups. Other planes, after not being able to locate the formation, turned back. Poor weather with several fronts persisted along the entire route. The planes still in formation did not break out into the clear until the mainland of Japan had been reached. In the first squadron only four planes

THE FIGHTING TIGERS

broke out of the overcast together. A fifth plane of this formation which lost the formation en route bombed the city of Kamimsake on Cape Omae.

On the way back, aircraft No. 45 ["Mustn't Touch," Carmon's plane] was forced to ditch. It is believed that his plane did not reach the mainland of Japan, but was forced to turn back early. The causes of the ditching were not given by the ship in distress, but one plane's report was that the ditched aircraft's No.1 engine was feathered or observed to be feathered, when the plane turned back. A ditching message was received from this plane at 1410. No further position was given, and no one saw the plane ditch.

Laverne Rucker Hood, one of his two sisters, said that of the eleven-man crew, Carmon was the only crew member listed as missing in action. The others were listed as having been killed in action. "This [was] the only report his wife and our family received until the report of his death was declared officially one year later," Laverne said.

Jean Davis, his other sister, of Sulphur Springs, Texas, said that before Carmon's widow died, she requested that her ashes be scattered from the Golden Gate Bridge in San Francisco, because the last time she saw him was in nearby Oakland where they were living at the time.

"She always felt bad because she didn't tell him good-bye," said Mrs. Davis, "but now understands what happened: Because of tight security, Carmon could not tell her that his squadron was leaving for the South Pacific at midnight. When Carmon's father, Grover Rucker, was told that his son was missing in action, he said that now he knew why his mother 'had been taken because she couldn't have taken the loss.'"

After Jack's death, Laverne enlisted in the U.S. Navy Waves and later married a sailor while in the service, and wound up in Amarillo. Although Carmon's body was never recovered, Jean Davis had a monument to him erected by their parents' graves. Had he been taken prisoner by the Japanese, she said, his health would not have let him survive because of his borderline hemophilia.

"Of the five boys, all five served in military," Mrs. Davis said. "We had a lot of stars in our window. Dad didn't marry again until all the kids were married. He kept us all together at home. He was a good Baptist."

Lieutenant Rucker's military awards included the Air Medal and the Purple Heart. He is memorialized on the Tablets of the Missing in the Military Cemetery in Honolulu.

# Gaston Shofner

1st Lt. Don Gaston Shofner, former student, 1939–1941
Hometown: Morrilton, Arkansas
Died: April 15, 1943
0-728752, 328th Fighter Squadron, First Air Force, 352nd Fighter Group, U.S. Air Corps

**How He Lived**

Lt. Don Gaston Shofner was born on September 17, 1921, to P. M. and Ina Thomason Shofner in Damascus, Arkansas. He attended Ouachita from 1939 until 1941 where he played saxophone in the band. His father, described by a family friend as "a very religious fellow," was a retired section foreman for the Missouri Pacific Railroad who took care of the track between Conway and Russellville, Arkansas.

A classmate at Ouachita, Frank Cochran, remembers him as "one of the quietest students on campus, who studied hard, was one of those folks who always wanted to fly." He was in the first class of civilian private training at Ouachita, Frank said, and "must have gotten through on a scholarship on football."

Gaston Shofner, sophomore, 1942 *Ouachitonian* yearbook

**. . . and How He Died**

Lila R. Montgomery of Conway, Arkansas, Gaston's widow, whom he married on August 16, 1941, said her husband enlisted in the Air Corps in January 1942, and was stationed at Mitchell Air Force Base at the time of his death.

"He was a quiet, gentle person," she said. "We were together for such a short time; he didn't get to come back very often. His ambition? He really wanted to fly. That was his great ambition. He had been offered a job

THE FIGHTING TIGERS

1st Lt. Don Gaston Shofner

teaching school. He would have been a teacher if he had not gone into service. He was a good-looking man." After he died, Lila went into the Navy Waves in 1943.

An Air Corps Accident Report stated that Lieutenant Shofner died on

April 15, 1943, when his P-47 "Thunderbolt" exploded in midair off the coast of Long Island, New York. The wreckage was not found at the time of the report. Records indicate that the plane exploded from a gas leak. He either did not have time to bail or was overcome by the explosion. He had logged 425 hours of flying time in P-47s. The report continued,

> Up to the present time, it is impossible to arrive at any definite conclusion as to what caused this accident. The wreckage has not been recovered, after more than a week of search by dragging with boats and the use of divers. . . . It would appear that in some way a gasoline leak developed between the fuel pump and carburetor allowing gasoline to collect forward of the fire wall in such a manner that it was ignited by the hot exhaust manifold. The resulting explosion apparently was great enough to rupture the gasoline tank and cause the forward section of the fuselage to catch fire. Another possibility is that the propeller may have thrown a blade, thereby tearing the engine from the ship and the leaking of fuel lines caused the resulting fire.
>
> The Accident Committee believes that there is more probability of a gasoline explosion than propeller failure since Lt. Schlagel states that he heard a "muffled explosion" and Lt. Shofner made no attempt to jump. Since the explosion was great enough to blow the engine clear of the airplane, in all probability Shofner was either killed instantly or stunned to the point that he was unable to use his parachute. There was ample room to jump from the altitude that the explosion occurred (4,000 feet).

News of Gaston's death was understandably "devastating" to his family, said John Ward, seventy, a family friend. His and Gaston's family "were members of the church my father pastored—Bethel Baptist Church (now called Calvary Baptist Church) in Morrilton, Arkansas. . . . P.M., Gaston's father, called my dad one night and asked to meet him out on a country road near Morrilton. They were very good friends. When my dad got there, P.M. was walking around and around his car, saying. 'Oh, my God! Oh, my God!' He didn't know how to tell Mrs. Shofner the news. She absolutely idolized Gaston."

"His mother never got over his death," said Jane Paladino, a family friend who still lives in Morrilton. "She was a loner, wanted to be by herself. When Shofner's body was returned, she didn't think it was her son."

A memorial service was held at the church. "I remember it vaguely," Ward said, "and a picture of Gaston was on the table up front. Gaston was quite a hero to the folks in Morrilton, of course. My older sister remembers him as blond, really quite handsome, and says his sister was just beautiful, also blonde—naturally!"

Although J. D. Huddleston didn't know Gaston, he did know his parents and his sister, Jane Shofner Warrington. After Gaston's plane went down at sea, Huddleston said, the story goes that his parents made several trips to the crash site. On one trip they were praying and the body floated to the surface.

Recalling essentially the same story, Dennis Gaston Moore, of Morrilton, said his father, Roy Moore, and P.M., Don Shofner's father, were Baptist preachers. "They preached revivals together and were real good friends. When Gaston died, his parents went out there (to Long Island Sound) and prayed and his body rose up by the boat and that's how they retrieved him." Dennis's dad named him Gaston after Gaston Shofner "because it was a miracle that that happened."

Lieutenant Shofner was buried beside his parents in Elmwood Cemetery in Morrilton, with full military honors. His gravestone bears an image of the P-47 in which he died.

# Joseph Simpson

Pfc. Joseph Thomas Simpson, former student, 1941–1943
Hometown: Russellville, Arkansas
Died: December 12, 1943
*18067158, C Company, First Battalion, 143rd Infantry Regiment, Thirty-sixth Infantry Division*

## How He Lived

Pfc. Joseph Thomas Simpson was born on August 20, 1920, to John T. and Mollie Simpson in Russellville, Arkansas. "Smokey Joe," as he was nicknamed by his teammates, was a graduate of Russellville High School. At 5'9" and 160 pounds, he was described by his high school coach, Wallace Bailey, as "the best all-around player Russellville ever had." He was also recognized as "an outstanding football player" at Ouachita College, where he attended from 1941 to 1943.

Milton Howell of Russellville, one of Joe's classmates and one of his best friends, noted that Joe was twenty-one when he entered Ouachita. "The probable explanation for his late entry into college," Howell said, "is that Joe probably had to drop out of high school to help earn money for his financially strapped family."

On Joe's birth certificate, his father's occupation is listed as "coal miner" and his mother's occupation as "housewife." Mary Frances Taylor of Russellville, one of Joe's classmates in both junior high school and high school, said, however, that "Joe's mother was known as Mollie Simpson and was a beauty operator. I never knew anything about his father and Joe was Mollie's pride and joy. Everybody liked Joe. He was a rather quiet, easy-going, friendly-to-everyone guy. Not only that, I thought [he was] very good looking. I believe he had black, wavy hair and a very personable way about him."

Howell, Joe's childhood buddy, said they did a lot of "double dating" during their high school years, and that Joe did have "a way with the women." Recalling that Joe won a first-place award in a state boy's voice

Joe Simpson is remembered by his Russellville High School classmates as "a free spirit."

contest in Fayetteville, Howell said Joe's favorite song was, *"Are the stars out tonight? I can't tell if it's cloudy or bright, for I only have eyes for you."*

"I remember that one," Mrs. Taylor said. "The songs were more romantic back then. He even sang when we had programs at school. I don't

Joe Simpson (No. 35 on third row), described by his coach as "the best all-around player Russellville ever had," poses for the Russellville High School team photograph, circa 1940.

remember the songs but then there was this special 'reading' that he performed about his imaginary friend 'Arley.' Joe was quite solemn about 'Arley' as he reeled off a story about the time they were walking down the railroad tracks on their way home. One day, Joe told his audience, he heard the train going *tooooot! toooot!* After the train passed on through, Joe walked down the track looking for Arley. 'Well,' Joe said, 'there was an arm there and a leg over there and . . . something musta happened to Arley!'" Obviously recognizing the story wasn't nearly as amusing as it had been sixty years ago, she said—almost apologetically it seemed, "The way he told the story was very amusing to the junior high crowd."

Joe was "a sweet friend of long ago," she said. "I was quite saddened to learn of his death so young. And Mollie never got over it! I never knew who Joe's dad was but I am so proud of what he accomplished in his short lifetime and that he attended Ouachita College."

Another friend, Mercedes Ball Wheeler, who was a Ouachita freshman in 1941–43, remembers the time when "a lot of the boys were leaving the campus to go to war. I can't remember when [Joe] left, probably during my sophomore year, but they were leaving in droves." Mercedes recalls Joe as being "a happy-go-lucky guy with a lot of personality. A typical Ouachita student: We were all high-quality people! We felt we were above the run-of-the-mill college kids. The kind of kids who go to war with a spirit that made that group of people 'The Greatest Generation.'"

Joe "was typical," she continued. "The boys were anxious to get into action. I was a friend but didn't date him. He was a nice-looking black-haired boy. A lot of the girls would have liked to date him. He did a lot of joking around by the Old Bookstore and under the trees. When he was getting ready to leave, we were at the bookstore drinking Cokes (if we had enough money). We were standing around in a group. He came up to me and said, 'Mercedes, I'm going off to war. I won't see you soon. But there is just one thing I want to tell you before I leave. I just wish the best for you and I hope that all of your babies are born naked.'"

"That's the last thing I remember about him," she said.

## ... and How He Died

In an obituary published in the Russellville *Courier-Democrat* on February 4, 1944, it is reported that Pfc. Joseph Simpson was inducted into the army on February 23, 1943, and sent to Camp Robinson (in North Little Rock, Arkansas). He received his basic training at Fort McClellan, Alabama, then was assigned to Camp Shenango, Pennsylvania. On August 10, he arrived in North Africa, and he was sent to the Italian front on October 8. The last letter from him received by his mother, Mrs. Mollie Ashmore Simpson Howell of Russellville, was dated November 29, and received December 18. (The obituary listed Pfc. Joseph Simpson's maternal grandmother as Mrs. R. M. Willis of Russellville.)

"I still have hope the report is a mistaken one," Mrs. Howell is quoted as saying in the story. "There have been so many cases of boys reported killed who have later turned up alive. I can't help but hope Joe will turn out to be one of them."

Sadly, however, his mother's hopes were not fulfilled. Pfc. Joseph Simpson was killed in action on December 12, 1943, during the Battle of San Pietro, Italy, just four days after the battle started on December 8. Military records reported that "The most serious obstacle impeding the capture of San Pietro . . . was the 4,000-foot Mt. Sammucro, known militarily as Hill 1205. In what was to become one of the hardest-fought battles in the Italian Campaign, Simpson's Battalion was given the mission of attacking its summit."

Mt. Sammucro, "one of the steepest heights scaled by Allied troops during the war, descends to the village of San Pietro on its southern slope," according to the Thirty-sixth Infantry Division's web site. "Along its icy trails and treacherous cliffs the Germans had craftily organized a formidable chain of mutually supporting pillboxes."

The following description of the battle is also taken from the Thirty-sixth Division History:

> It has been said by military men of wide experience that the physical discomforts of Washington's Army at Valley Forge could not have been compared to those suffered by the foot soldier in the Italian mountains. Hill 1205 substantiated that opinion. For ten days at an abnormal altitude the men fought on without blankets, overcoats or raincoats. Under these conditions, freezing temperatures made sleeping dangerous. Even for those who stayed awake, frozen feet were common. Then, too, for the first three days, food and water were inadequate—only a single K ration unit per man during the period and a single veedon (flask) of water for a squad. It was difficult to bring up supplies . . . it was also difficult to take down the wounded. To negotiate Sammucro required considerable stamina even without packs or rifles. To climb it carrying a box of rations or to come down it with a litter demanded maximum effort.

A documentary, *The Battle of San Pietro,* which was made by the legendary Hollywood director John Houston, won a number of awards. "In addition," writes Jack Forgy, "famed war correspondent Ernie Pyle wrote a story called *Dead Men,* which was about the Battle of San Pietro. I think Robert Mitchum played the part of Captain Wasko, and Burgess Meredith was Ernie Pyle, in a movie called *The Story of G.I. Joe.*"

Mollie Simpson Howell, Joe's mother, died in 1992 at the age of ninety-one. Nine years earlier, in 1983, she had purchased a memorial marker for her grave and had even written her own epitaph. A tombstone rubbing of her grave marker in Rest Haven Cemetery in Russellville, reads: "Mary E. Ashmore Simpson Howell, beloved wife and mother in memory of Joe Simpson, my son. March 1, 1901–1992." No mention is made of her husband nor is there a day and month of her death. Pfc. Joseph Simpson, however, is buried in the Sicily-Rome American Military Cemetery in Nettuno, Italy.

"Up to the day Mrs. Howell died," said her foster daughter, Terry Bradberry of Conway, Arkansas, "she would sit in her chair and weep for her lost son."

# Edwin Smith

2nd Lt. Edwin Wadley Smith, former student, 1938–1941
Hometown: Arkadelphia, Arkansas
Died: October 9, 1942
SN 41-9186, 339th Bomb Squadron, Ninety-sixth Bomb Group

**How He Lived**

Second Lt. Edwin Wadley Smith was born on July 24, 1920, in Arkadelphia, Arkansas, the second son of Steve Edwin Smith of Princeton, Arkansas, and Beulah Sanders Gresham Smith of Arkadelphia. After graduating from Arkadelphia High School in 1937, he entered Ouachita where he majored in English and received military training in the ROTC program. To pick up some extra money, he worked after school at the Royal Theater in Arkadelphia. Eddie Smith dropped out of Ouachita during his senior year in 1941 to enlist in the U.S. Army Air Corps.

Eddie Smith, junior, 1941 *Ouachitonian* yearbook. Smith dropped out of Ouachita during his senior year to enlist in the U.S. Air Force.

Frank Cochran, one of his classmates at Ouachita, remembered him as being "a little bitty fellow." Dan Grant, also a classmate, recalled Eddie as being "Johnny Hall's tennis partner in Arkadelphia High School and in Ouachita. His brother, the late Faunt Smith, was editor of the Ouachita *Signal*, the student newspaper, as I recall or perhaps the *Ouachitonian* yearbook, and painted a Ouachita Bluff scene for Jane Ross." (The late Miss Ross was a civic leader in Clark County and a generous philanthropist through the Ross Foundation.) Eddie's niece, Melissa Smith of Little Rock, said he was also a gifted portrait painter and worked at the Royal Theater in Arkadelphia.

Second Lt. Edwin Wadley Smith, remembered as "a gifted portrait painter," was killed during a night-flying exercise in South Dakota.

Eddie Smith *(second from left)* was a member of the Ouachita Tigers track team in 1940–41.

In a family history she prepared for this project, Melissa wrote:

> Eddie's grandparents were William Wadley Gresham from Mississippi and Arkadelphia and Eudocia Speakes Gresham, an Arkadelphia native. W. W. was owner and founder of the Gresham Mercantile Co., and the Gresham Opera House, both located in the Gresham Building, built in 1894.
>
> Eddie's great-grandparents were William Lewis Anderson and Eudocia Moore Hill Anderson. In about 1845 they moved from Social Circle, Georgia, to the Richwoods community south of Arkadelphia, where they established a plantation called "Ashland." They brought with them a square rosewood piano, which was the first piano in the area. Anderson was a Baptist minister as well as a planter. Four of their sons were killed in the War Between the States. William

Lewis Anderson's father, William Anderson, was a Revolutionary War veteran.

Eddie's family was related to several families in Arkadelphia, including the Andersons, the Heards, the Triggs, the Greshams and the Biscoes. Nancy Gresham Biscoe, who taught at Ouachita and in the Arkadelphia public school system, was a first cousin of W. W. Gresham. Her great-granddaughter, Caroline Cagle Luck, is currently a professor at Ouachita.

Eddie and his older brother, Faunt Biscoe Smith, were born in the family home at 1018 Caddo Street, in Arkadelphia, as were their mother and their aunt, Elizabeth Gresham. The house was constructed around 1858 by their great grandfather, Samuel Speakes, a carpenter from Virginia.

From boyhood, Eddie was fascinated with airplanes and flying. He read magazines on the subject and constructed model planes from balsa wood and tissue paper; in fact, years after his death, examples could still be found in the attic of his mother's home.

The boys attended the Arkadelphia public schools, and after graduation, entered Ouachita. Eddie was interested in physical fitness and was on the tennis and track teams in college and high school. He was a senior in high school when his mother was widowed due to his father's death from complications from injuries received in an auto accident. Widowhood was especially difficult for Eddie's mother, who had an unusually strong devotion to her family.

Eddie's many ties to Ouachita included his mother, his aunt, his sister and his brother, the late Faunt Smith of Camden, a magna cum laude graduate in 1939. Faunt and his future wife, Anna Bess Stegall, met while attending Ouachita. Anna Bess's aunt, Patricia Irby Gunn, was head of the Home Economics Department at Ouachita during this time. Later Faunt was commissioned to paint a portrait of Dr. J. W. Conger, Ouachita's first president. In lieu of payment, he established the Beulah Gresham Smith memorial scholarship for music students in honor of his mother.

## . . . and How He Died

After completing navigator-bombadier training at Ellington Field, Texas, and Seabring Field, Florida, Lieutenant Smith was transferred to Rapid

City, South Dakota, for B-17 transition. "To Eddie," Melissa Smith said, "becoming a navigator in the U.S. Army Air Corps was a dream come true. Unfortunately, its fulfillment was short-lived, as it led to his death at age twenty-two. He had just recently arrived at the air base at Rapid City, South Dakota, where on October 9, 1942, he was participating in a training exercise. During the mission, the bomber crashed, killing three and injuring five of those on board."

In a statement from a surviving crewman, an Accident Report dated October 8, 1942, described the crash:

> At 11:59 p.m., just a minute before midnight on October 8, 1942, the pilot had been cleared to land. His approach was extremely poor. In this approach he was offside. This course took him over the hills near the airport. This particular approach was long with a minimum airspeed of 110–112 mph.
>
> Suddenly the lights on the field blacked out, but the town lights were still visible. As these lights blacked out, the pilot applied throttle and pulled back hard on the control column. At the same moment the right wing tip struck about 20 feet below the top of the ridge. Then the right outboard engine, right inboard, and right wheel struck in that order. This contact severed the plane so that the left wheel and nose ended on the top of the ridge. The fuselage snapped in two at the bomb bay. The ship began burning instantly. The crew tried to release another member of the crew whose leg was pinned under the wreckage. The fire prevented this from being completed and the other crew were compelled to leave him behind.

According to a War Department Aircraft Accident Report, "Although the approach to the runway meets the minimum requirement of a 40-1 glide angle, action was being taken to place red obstruction lights on the ridge to prevent future accidents."

"At the time of his death," Melissa said, "Eddie was engaged to be married to a girl named Louise but the family never knew her last name." He was buried on October 14, 1942, in the Gresham family plot in Rose Hill Cemetery in Arkadelphia. Dr. R. E. Naylor, pastor of the First Baptist Church of Arkadelphia, officiated the service.

"The tragedy of Eddie's death devastated his mother, who never recovered," Melissa said. "His future sister-in-law, Anna Bess Stegall Smith, who was with her during the time before, during and after the funeral, said she was the most distraught of anyone she ever saw. For the rest of her life, his mother could not say Eddie was killed or had died. The subject was taboo in her presence. On the infrequent occasions it was mentioned, she referred to the incident as 'when Eddie was hurt.'"

The following poem was written in memory of Eddie by his brother, the late Faunt Smith:

### For Eddie

He needs no lines to show him straight and clean
From anyone, and least of all from me.
The tree that he was always will be green,
Nor axe nor time shall desecrate that tree.

To show him tragic, garbed in sober glory,
There is no need—no need to sigh and say
The stark and sober melancholy story
That led him to that last October day.

All I can say is that he was my brother.
Other than that, I don't know what to say.
And I can add, I would have had no other.
I will not soil him with a saccharine lay.

And though I hope to hide my loss in years,
I will not drown his memory with tears.

# William Stell

1st Lt. William Cone Stell, former student, 1937–1941
Hometown: Warren, Arkansas
Died: April 22, 1944
SN 0727937, 336th Bomber Group, 480th Bomb Squadron, Third Air Force, U.S. Army Air Corps

## How He Lived

First Lt. William Cone Stell was born on November 15, 1916, to L. B. and Beadie McFarland Stell in Banks, Arkansas. After graduating from Tinsman (Arkansas) High School, he entered Ouachita in 1937, where he majored in ministerial studies and minored in English. His yearbook caption referred to him as "a born business man." His activities at Ouachita included membership in the Baptist Student Union Council, the Tennis Club, the Dramatic Club, and the Life Service Band. He also served as president of the Baptist Student Union and was a member of the ROTC cadet staff in 1941. Cone received a bachelor of arts degree posthumously in 1944. His younger brother, Harley Stell, who now lives in Tacoma, Washington, attended Ouachita in 1939–1940.

William Cone Stell, junior, 1940 *Ouachitonian* yearbook

Remembering Cone as being "lively and friendly," Madelyn Ewbank, a classmate, recalls the time that "Cone asked me to drive and care for his car while he went to summer camp. I had it serviced so he could just drive on home. They didn't add water and he had trouble driving home. I regretted it so much. The other ones (who also died in the war) as I recall were mighty fine young men. It is so sad thinking about them again."

First Lt. William Cone Stell, home on leave in his undated photo after flying forty missions in the European theater, was dubbed the "Flying Parson" in a "Terry and the Pirates" comic strip published during the war.

Another classmate, Floyd J. Taylor, of El Dorado, Arkansas, said, "Cone was from a business-type family, grocer and farming. His father was living in Tinsman, Arkansas when I met him. He had a small store and farm. Mr. Stell was on the heavy side, flesh-wise, so was Cone. Both had black hair. Cone was a young man on the go with a bright future. He was a planner and had purpose."

Robert L. Newton, of Warren, Arkansas, who served with Cone's niece, Susie Green Hartsfield of Searcy, on the Arkansas State Board of Education for several years. (Mrs. Harstfield is the mother of Julie Hartsfield Knight, wife of OBU football coach Todd Knight.) Newton was pastor of the Tinsman First Baptist Church in 1942 and 1943. "I traveled by train to and from Arkadelphia to minister on the weekends," Newton said. "One weekend I needed a ride to Tinsman. At the time, Cone had his parents' new Chrysler Imperial and let me ride to Tinsman with him. He was a really nice Christian young man. Soon after Cone was called up to military duty, as I recall, he was either in military pilot training or training other would-be pilots, when one day he went out over the Gulf of Mexico and was never heard from thereafter. What happened that day remains a secret known only to God."

William Cone Stell, senior, 1942 *Ouachitonian* yearbook

An insight into Cone's compassion for his fellow students was provided by classmate Louise Morris Davis of Texarkana, Arkansas. "He was hating it because so many people were feeling left out because they weren't invited into social clubs," she said. "As BSU president, he was just wishing that more had been asked, that there had been more opportunities. He was very friendly."

## ... and How He Died

Although Lieutenant Stell entered military service with the 153rd Infantry, Arkansas National Guard, he transferred to the Army Air Corps in 1942. After forty missions as a combat pilot, he earned the nickname of the "Flying Parson" and even appeared as such in the old "Terry and the Pirates" comic strip.

An interview with Cone was published in the *Arkansas Gazette* on January 9, 1944, under the following headline:

### "Flying Parson" Finds War not Righteous after 40 Missions

Arkansas' "Flying Parson," Lt. William Cone Stell of Little Rock, believes World War II is not a righteous war but "something we got into and something we have to end."

A ministerial student at Ouachita College and pastor of the Baptist church at Banks (near Arkadelphia), Lieutenant Stell left his work to get that job done with the Arkadelphia unit of the National Guard in December 1940. Anxious for more active participation in the big task, he volunteered as an aviation cadet in January 1942, and now, after forty flight missions (over North Africa and Italy), is respected by fellow airmen as one of the best medium bomber pilots of that area.

Back home for reassignment, he said yesterday the Caserta raid near Naples was the most dangerous for his plane—a B-26 Martin Marauder bomber. His group was jumped by German ME-109 fighters over their bomb run and had a running fight for seven minutes.

Four other American bombers were shot down but Lt. Stell's crew kept the fight going.

During Lieutenant Stell's forty combat flights, his gunners downed four enemy aircraft and were credited with two probables. The fighting minister was not injured but three members of his crew won Purple Hearts when they flew through "flak valley" over Salerno beachhead when the invasion of Italy began. A burst of flak struck his Marauder as it was covering advancing ground troops on that flight and knocked out its hydraulic system. Lieutenant Stell was able to get the wheels down coming in but the nose wheel had been damaged and gave way. The plane skidded to a stop with such damage it was "washed out."

On another occasion a German fighter put a 20-mm cannon shell in his plane but it did not explode and the damage wasn't great. Among the Flying Parson's missions was a raid on Rome. He described the flak as "pretty accurate," but with no direct hits. On the way home, however, the American plane behind him went out of control and was forced down. Two of its crewmen have been heard from since that time, reporting that they were safe as prisoners of war.

He had a close decision with fate during his final raid, which was over Italy. This time his group again was attacked by fighters and had to put up a running fight for five minutes. The turret gunner on one of the planes was killed by a cannon shell . . .

Of religion, Lieutenant Stell said he had learned from combat experience that most men under fire "nearly always show some religious affiliation and a strong faith in God." Some of the most inspiring services in my experience have been out in the field with men under field conditions.

Wearer of the Air Medal with nine Oak-Leaf Clusters, the modest parson is awaiting assignment with the Army Transport Command or as an instructor within the United States. He was married to Miss Bonnie Williamson of Lakeland, Florida on January 2, 1944. She plans to join him at his new post. The couple met when Lt. Stell was training in Florida before gong to North Africa.

Lt. Stell spent his boyhood in Bradley and Calhoun counties. He entered Ouachita College in 1937 and was in his senior year when he left for Army service. He plans to finish his college work and return to the ministry at the close of the war.

THE FIGHTING TIGERS

The story of Cone's appearance in "Terry and the Pirates" attracted considerable attention in Little Rock. Under the headline, "Local Boy Pilot Crashes Front Page of a Comic," the *Arkansas Gazette* ran the following story:

> When a hometown boy gets good enough to crash the pages of a comic magazine, he is really going places. To Lt. William Cone Stell, son of Mr. and Mrs. L. B. Stell, formerly of Warren, it is this distinction. One page of *Military Comics, Secret War News*, in a recent edition, carried the story of the flying Parson under the heading *"The Atlantic Patrol."* It is the sketch of Lt. Stell "The Flying Parson" on a bombing raid as pilot on a B-26 Marauder.
>
> First is a picture of the big bomber and there is written above: "Lt. William Cone Stell, The Flying Parson, gave up his peaceful pastorate and enlisted in the Army as a private. After switching to the Air Corps, he became one of their best B-26 Marauder pilots." Next there is the nose of the big bomber with Stell in the pilot's seat saying to the Sarge in the front behind the gun, "Let him have it, Sarge," to which is the reply: "An ME-109 attacking." From an American base in Algeria, they are on a flying mission over Sardinia.
>
> The next picture shows the gunner Sergeant yelling back, "He's right in my sights." The next view shows the Flying Parson passing back: "Good work, Sergeant Farr. You raked him from the nose to the fuselage—you must have killed the pilot—the plane's out of control."
>
> In sequence is the picture of the American bomber on its way back to its base with the pilot saying: "There is one less Nazi to worry about," and the Sarge replying: "But Lieutenant, why did you give up preaching for fighting?"
>
> The answer of Stell cinches the proof of his loyalty to his country and his old home town: "Well, I want to get this war over with so I can go back to Warren, Arkansas, and preach the peaceful settlement of disputes."
>
> Some true story is this about another great kid from this country!

Unfortunately, however, he would never get the chance to return to Warren. A USAAF Accident Report, dated May 8, 1944, details what little is known about the accident that took his life.

> 1st Lt. William C. Stell (the instructor pilot) and crew departed Lake Charles (Louisiana) Army Air field on a navigation training mission to Miami, Florida, at 1100 CWT on 22 April 1944, in airplane No. 41-18244, a B-26. They remained overnight at 36th Street Airport, Miami, Florida. At 1200 CWT on 23 April 1944, the student pilot, Lt. Paul H. Arnold, contacted his home base prior to clearance, in compliance with AAF Memorandum 55-8 dated 6 March 1944, and Captain Ballinger B. Moore, who was emergency operations officer for the 336th Bomb Group, cleared him for take-off. The pilot actually took off from the 36th Street Airport, Miami, Florida, at 1312 CWT. No radio contact was made. He was declared missing one hour after the expiration of his estimated time en route. An extensive search of the entire route and all possible routes and surrounding area was made, beginning on 23 April 1944 and ending on 30 April 1944, with no results.

The search was abandoned on May 2, 1944. All seven crew members were officially declared dead by the War Department. Because the bodies were never recovered, his parents placed a memorial to him in the Oakland Cemetery in Warren, Arkansas, on which is engraved, William Cone Stell, *"The Flying Parson."*

*Author's note: Requests to the syndicate that produced the "Terry and the Pirates" comic strips for copies of the episodes containing Cone's story have thus far gone unanswered.*

# Ralph Stockemer

Lt. Ralph "Bo" William Stockemer, former student, 1938–1941
Hometown: Huttig, Arkansas
Died: November 27, 1943
*145982, VC-28, United States Naval Reserve Air Force*

## How He Lived

Lt. Ralph "Bo" William Stockemer was born on November 6, 1918, in Monroe, Louisiana, the first son and second child of Ralph William and Mamie Opal Shaw Stockemer. He had one sister, Molly Dawson Stockemer, born in 1915, and a younger brother, Paul Gene Wallace Stockemer, born in 1927. He attended public schools in Broken Bow, Oklahoma, Dierks, Arkansas, and Huttig, Arkansas, before his family moved to El Dorado—so he could play high school football. After graduating from high school in 1938, he enrolled at Ouachita that fall on a football scholarship, intending to pursue a medical career.

In response to my request for information on his brother, Paul, a retired pastor of Hilltop Baptist Church who with his wife, Gwen, lives in Burleson, Texas, prepared a remarkable and loving tribute to Bo titled "Reflections on Ralph William Stockemer Jr.," dated June 24, 2002.

> Bo—actually "Bo Diddle," as our family nicknamed him—was one of those individuals that God just seems to bless wherever they are, in whatever occupation they are engaged.
>
> I remember him as my hero and friend. It made me feel invincible to be in his company. I hung on every word and marveled at his ability to find favor with people of all ages. As his younger brother [Bo was nine years older], I respected him so much that I never thought about fighting or even disagreeing with him on anything. I liked hitchhiking with him, for I felt that he was my protector and we would only have good adventures. He played football and I played football. I was not the talented athlete that he was. When we went fishing, he excelled at that, too.

Lt. Ralph Stockemer, U.S. Navy aviator, 1942–43

Our dad, Ralph William Stockemer Sr., worked as a sawyer for lumber companies in Arkansas, Oklahoma and Louisiana. During Bo's last two high school years, Dad worked in Huttig. Since Huttig was a typical mill town, the entire industry was owned by the Frost Lumber Company. We lived in a company house and bought groceries and necessities at the company store. This caused a dilemma for all the employees. Since the lumber company owned everything, you were beholden to the company for your job; thus it allowed you the privilege of having that job, and then allowed you to pay the company what they paid you for the privilege of supplying your needs, thus perpetuating your indebtedness forever. There was some train and bus service. If you were in the better-skilled labor force and were able to save for a car, or had friends with one, you could shop elsewhere. El Dorado, a larger town, was 35 miles away. If you were young and carefree, you could hitchhike.

Bo graduated from the eighth grade at Broken Bow, Oklahoma, where he first played football. Then he played at Dierks, Arkansas. We moved to Huttig for Dad to work for Frost Lumber Company. Huttig High School was too small to have a football team; therefore, our mother, Bo and I moved to El Dorado to allow him to play football. We lived with a lady named Miss Aleda Richmond, who dearly loved Bo.

During the summers, he worked for the lumber company in various jobs. He would be assigned almost impossible jobs for a young student, but he did them with a willingness and determination to succeed.

One summer he delivered ice, driving a horse-drawn wagon, with a cab built over the wagon with a tarp which covered the ice blocks. He delivered ice to the company hotel, store, service station and homes. Cards were placed in windows indicating whether he should deliver a 25-, 50- or 100-lb block. He had to break the ice blocks apart in the correct groove. He covered his shoulder with leather to insulate it from the ice; then picked up the block of ice with tongs, lifted it to his shoulder and carried the ice and deposited it in the ice box. It took most of each day to deliver the ice. Customers were constantly telling our parents about his courtesy to them. No Sunday deliveries. No stores open. Churches were. The community house was open on

Lt. Ralph Stockemer *(back row, second from right)* with his fellow navy dive-bomber pilots in a photo dated March 1, 1943

Sunday afternoons to purchase soda pop. Some people played pool in the back room.

Another summer he worked in a very dangerous place called "the power house," where the sawdust was ground up and dropped into a big room below. People in this room were assigned to shovel sawdust into the furnaces to keep the whole city running with electricity. This powered the mills and furnished DC lighting for the occupants of the city of Huttig. DC electricity was very unpredictable. Refrigerators could not operate on DC. His job was usually given to unskilled and unschooled black men. Since Bo was willing to take any job, was strong and our family was pressed for money, he accepted it. A black man had suffocated one day, because the mountain of sawdust shifted and covered him. This saddened our parents and caused them to worry about Bo's safety.

One day he worked over twelve hours, two hours past the usual ten-hour day. Our mom sent dad and me to the mill to check on him. We met him coming out of the mill. They had simply needed him to work longer.

Smackover and El Dorado were archrivals and fights would break out between the teams. During Bo's two high-school years, 1936–38, El Dorado, being a larger town, had a better chance of securing better players, thus making it easier for Smackover to lose.

When one game got beyond their reach, about three-fourths into the game, the Smackover players started a fight. One of Bo's friends hit the referee. All the players were told to go to the clubhouse. The officials called the game off. Then the spectators in the stands started to fight, and continued fighting on the field. Our mom sent Dad and me to the dressing room to check on Bo. He had heard that the fight had continued and was on his way back out to the field to fight. Out of respect for Dad, he did not go back even though he said, "They need me." Dad replied, "The adults are fighting now. They don't need any students fighting." On the school bus on the way home, the students chanted, *"Chew tobacco, Chew tobacco! Spit on the wall! Smackover, Smackover can't play ball."*

He loved our mother and spent time with her in the kitchen making chocolate fudge and learning to cook. I copied him in his gift giving and courtesy to our mother. When he went on a trip, he would bring her back a gift. I also copied his courtesy toward other women. Our dad had this same respect for women. He showed me respect of our Father, which I also emulated. He was always concerned about the family's need for money. He told me that he would see that I was college educated. When I entered Southwestern Baptist Theological Seminary, my parents sent me the $59 a month that they were receiving from the U.S. government because of his death to help pay my way. I felt like he could do or be anything. Our sister, Molly D., planned to be a nurse and served in Panama with the Civil Service. Later, she became a nurse anesthetist. She and I wondered if they might have served together in a hospital. I admired him as a young Christian who was truly an All-American boy.

His football athletic skills earned him All-State and All-Southern honors at El Dorado High School and scholarship offers to Alabama and Louisiana State University. However, in a strange twist of events, he accepted a scholarship to Ouachita College, where he truly found a home, many wonderful friends and teachers who apparently loved and respected him. He played end, guard, tackle and was also the place kicker. Earning All-College honors, he was a star tackle on the 1941 State Championship Ouachita Tigers football team.

It was in Huttig that Bo met his future wife, Ruth Evelyn Johnson. "Her dad, Fred Johnson, editor and publisher of the *Huttig News,*" Paul wrote, "drove a 12-cylinder Lincoln, was postmaster and was treasurer at the First Baptist Church." Asked during a telephone interview in June 2002 to recall their romance, Mrs. Johnson replied quickly, "He was wonderful, very friendly, most affable, very popular." And at six feet tall and 182 pounds, with brown hair streaked with blond from time spent in the sun, Bo was "some combination," Ruth said with a giggle.

When the Japanese attacked Pearl Harbor on December 7, 1941, she and Bo were in Little Rock where she was working. Upon learning of the attack, she recalled, Bo told her that he was not going to finish school that year because he didn't like what the Japanese had done.

### . . . and How He Died

True to his word, Bo joined the Naval Air Corps on December 8, 1941, leaving his college career behind. Following his flight training at New Orleans, Pensacola, Corpus Christi, and Miami, he received the Navy Wings of Gold at Corpus Christi.

After being sent into combat duty in the South Pacific, "his assignment," said his sister-in-law, Gwen Stockemer, "was to fly low over a ship, release a bomb, then fly back to the carrier," which was regarded as "very dangerous flying for the Naval Air Corps." After surviving fifteen torpedo-bomber missions during furious fighting in the Solomon Islands—earning for him the Air Medal and recommendation for the Distinguished Flying Cross by Admiral Halsey—Bo was placed on thirty-day leave and sent to the Salton Sea Naval Air Base in California to instruct other navy flyers who would later be assigned to the South Pacific on completion of their training. Bo himself was also scheduled to return to combat duty in the Atlantic.

Following the completion of additional training in Fort Lauderdale and Norfolk, he took advantage of his stateside assignment to return to Arkansas and marry his childhood sweetheart, "Fette," as Bo called Ruth Evelyn, on March 25, 1943, in the First Baptist Church, Huttig. After a quick honeymoon in Hot Springs, Arkansas, the newlyweds moved to California where he did more training on takeoffs and landings on a carrier.

THE FIGHTING TIGERS

Soon after, he was sent to the Solomon Islands in June and July of 1943, where he served on the USS *Chenango.*

In a lighthearted letter to his parents and his brother, "Buddy," dated June 3, 1943, from somewhere in the South Pacific, he writes, "Cigars are scarce as hen's teeth here. You can hardly even get any at all, but an enlisted man that I have been giving hops (free flights) to gave me a whole box of Robert Burns panatillos yesterday. Didn't know there were any of them within a thousand miles. I'm having to sleep with them under my pillow."

Later, in the same letter, he writes, "A new bunch of Englishmen just came in yesterday. I'm beginning to understand them a little better now and like them much more. I find they are just a bunch of fellows that want to go home, too."

After his composite Squadron 8 rotated back to the United States, allowing him to spend a thirty-day leave in Arkansas, he and Fette returned to the West Coast where he prepared new squadrons for air combat in Oregon and California.

"When our family said goodbye to Bo and his pretty new bride, Ruth Evelyn, more than fifty-nine years ago," Paul wrote, "it was the last chapter of a young man's earthly life that was lived well for his Lord and Savior." Bo was killed on November 27, 1943, when the plane in which he and a cadet were carrying out a routine low-level night-bombing training exercise went down into forty feet of water in the Salton Sea. Although the aircraft was recovered, Bo's body was never found nor were any articles of his clothing or his parachute. "Searches were made in the water and in the desert," Paul said. "They searched for several days, then called off the search. Our family received notes of commendation and sorrow from government officials and officers who had known him in the navy."

In a report of Bo's death published in the *Huttig News* on December 30, 1943, it was said that only a few days before he died, he had been awarded the U.S. Navy's Air Medal. The citation accompanying the recommendation for the medal was signed by Adm. W. F. Halsey of the Pacific Fleet, and read as follows:

> For meritorious achievement while participating in attacks against the enemy while serving as a dive bomber pilot attached to a composite squadron operating in the Solomon Islands area during the period from June 27 to July 23, 1943. Ensign Stockemer took part in

numerous missions against enemy shore installations, airfields and shipping, many of which were pressed home in the face of heavy concentrations of anti-aircraft fire or determined fighter opposition. He participated in two artillery spotting missions over enemy positions on New Georgia Island, during which he successfully spotted the fire (for) our unit and furnished them with valuable information.

His courageous conduct contributed materially to the damage inflicted upon the enemy by his squadron and was in keeping with the highest traditions of the United States Naval Service.

(Signed) W. F. Halsey, Admiral, U.S. Navy

Just prior to this, the commanding officer of the squadron of which young Stockemer was a member, forwarded his recommendation to the commander of the South Pacific Forces for the Distinguished Flying Cross. The citation accompanying this recommendation read in part as follows:

Ensign Stockemer, during a tour of duty at Henderson Field, Guadalcanal, as a combat pilot has participated in numerous and extended raids on enemy territory; has crowded in five raids on Munda; one on Bila; a long night shipping patrol into the Kahili-Shortland-Fauro area; a shipping strike near Kahili; a raid on Bairoko Harbor, New Georgia. For conspicuous gallantry and intrepidity in action while participating in eleven bombing missions against heavily defended enemy positions, the successful accomplishment of such missions being carried out in the face of heavy anti-aircraft fire and severe enemy fighter opposition. Stockemer was promoted from Ensign to Lieutenant before his death.

Only a few months before Bo was killed, he received a poignant letter from his father-in-law, Pop Johnson, in Huttig, Arkansas. A copy of the letter was forwarded to me by the Stockemer family. Johnson wrote,

Would like to ask you a lot of questions, Son, but they will just have to wait until you come home, for since censorship is so strict, you might become embarrassed in trying to answer them. All America is anxiously awaiting that cherished day though when victory is completely won and you and all the other boys can come home. Then

THE FIGHTING TIGERS

we will sit silently and with mouths wide open, listening with pride and admiration as each of you tells us of the epic struggles you went through each day in order that decency and liberty might be preserved. You are doing a magnificent job . . . doing it well . . . and we pray each day that God will ride the skyways with you and all the other mothers' sons, to keep you safe, to give you courage, strength and determination to carry on. And may you remember each day, too, Ralph, to ask Him for that divine guidance . . . He'll do it if you ask Him.

Pop Johnson ended the letter with two requests: "Write me when you can and remember what I told you when you left Huttig—Get one of those ***** Japs for me."

During our 2002 interview, Ruth Evelyn provided additional information from naval records concerning her husband's death. "When he got to the altitude at which he was supposed to release the bombs," she said, "he did, but the force of gravity pulled him into the Salton Sea." The navy told her that Lieutenant Stockemer "almost surely got out of the plane because he was wearing a Mae West vest. As a result of the accident, the navy established new regulations that required a minimum altitude before bombs could be released."

In a letter dated December 29, 1943, addressed to Bo's parents after his death, Lt. Cmdr. Gordon "G.E." Schecter, Composite Squadron Eight, San Francisco, California, said:

> It seems too illogical to believe that Ralph got out of his parachute and sea harness after his plane came to rest in the water then subsequently drowned or became lost in the desert surrounding the sea. We know definitely that Ralph had on a life jacket when he departed for the flight; and the Salton Sea Air Station is located directly on the shore line about five miles south of the point where Ralph's plane crashed. A rotating beacon light operates all night on a tower located at the station. This light can be seen from any spot on the Salton Sea and should have been a perfect landmark for Ralph were he in any condition to make use of it. As you know, we haven't found a single trace of Ralph; no life jacket, flight gear or article of clothing has turned up. . . .

I can't say enough for Ralph's work while he was with us. He was the exemplification of calm assurance and ability. All of us felt that Ralph was, by way of experience, much older than his actual years. He was always most agreeable and cheerful—an ideal shipmate. It made me so proud to be able to award him the Air Medal for work he did in the South Pacific—and he was so modest about it.

In recalling Bo's death sixty years later, Paul said, "My brother's favorite hymn while serving in the South Pacific was 'Day Is Dying in the West.' On leave, after combat missions in the Solomon Islands, he was asked by his church to give a testimony. He stated the hymn was sung on his aircraft carrier each evening as the sun was setting over the Pacific Ocean. The majesty of God and His Power took on a new meaning as he listened in a far-away place, many miles from a little town in Arkansas, separated from his family who loved him dearly.

"Our comfort through the years has been his statement to all of us, particularly to our mother, 'Please don't worry about me. I am ready to go at any time.' When uncertainty was all around him, he found certainty in our Lord Jesus Christ."

As a footnote to his *"Reflections"* on his brother's life and lasting influence, Paul said, "Our oldest son, Ralph William Stockemer III, whom we named after 'Bo' and my dad, resembles my brother in many ways. He, too, is a Christian and was a great athlete (All-State tailback) in Alma (Arkansas) High School, Baylor University (All-Conference), and in the NFL for the San Diego Chargers and Kansas City Chiefs. He and Bo have divine favor to make people feel better for having known them."

# Andrew Thigpen

Capt. Andrew C. Thigpen, Class of 1939
Hometown: Hosston, Louisiana
Died: February 13, 1944
*0-501837, Forty-seventh Ordnance Battalion, U.S. Army, Fort Dix, New Jersey*

## How He Lived

Capt. Andrew C. Thigpen was born December 19, 1911, in Mira, Louisiana, to Ashley and Margaret Betterton Thigpen, one of thirteen children—four boys and nine girls. Four of his sisters were homemakers, one was a registered nurse, one was a nurse's aide, and three were teachers. One brother died early in life, and the other two became Baptist pastors.

After spending two years at Decatur Baptist College (the forerunner of Dallas Baptist University in Dallas, Texas), Thigpen transferred to Ouachita College in 1937, where he played basketball and was a member of the Life Service Band and president of the Ministerial Alliance. To earn extra money, a family member said, he ironed white dress shirts for his fellow students. In the 1939 *Ouachitonian* yearbook, he was said to be "Wise, steadfast in the strength of God, and true." Andrew graduated from Ouachita in 1939 with a bachelor of arts degree in Bible.

He spent the next two years and nine months at Southwestern Baptist Theological Seminary. Of the 531 graduates of Southwestern Baptist Theological Seminary—including 425 chaplains, 99 men in other branches of service, and 7 women—9 of them had lost their lives in the war. Two of those nine were Ouachita graduates: Capt. Andrew Thigpen, Class of 1939, and

Andrew Thigpen, Class of 1939, *Ouachitonian* yearbook

Andrew Thigpen, photograph dated "before 1939"

Capt. Andrew Thigpen with his wife, Gertrude, and Martha Ann, one of their three daughters

Lt. Col. Thomas Reagan, Class of 1928, who was killed in action during the Battle of the Bulge.

While attending the Seminary, Andrew served churches in Vivian, Louisiana; Ida, Louisiana; Bloomburg, Texas; Mira, Louisiana; and McLeod, Texas. A stained-glass window in the Parkview Baptist Church in

Shreveport, Louisiana, purchased by his widow, the late Gertrude Yates Thigpen, is dedicated to Captain Thigpen. During a recent visit to the Ouachita campus, his granddaughter, Joanna Ballard, remembered how as a child, "a big thing was to sit by granddaddy's window."

Andrew and Gertrude had three daughters, Martha Ann Thigpen Holemon of Shreveport; Lois Nell Thigpen Hevelone, who lives in the Greater Boston (Massachusetts) area; and Wanda Sue Thigpen Wittman of Urbana, Illinois.

Recalling a story her mother had told her, Martha Ann said recently, "Serving churches in rural east Texas and northwest Louisiana, while attending Seminary in Fort Worth, required a good deal of traveling [through] hill country. At the time, funds and possibly gasoline were limited. When the gas tank was low, Andrew would tease his wife by asking, 'Where's your faith? Where's your faith?' as he coasted downhill to conserve fuel."

After being appointed to the chaplaincy on October 24, 1942, he left the Seminary on November 25, 1942, to volunteer for active duty in Shreveport. Before his death on February 13, 1944, he served as a chaplain at Camp Pickette, Virginia.

"About eight years ago," Martha Ann said, "I met a lady, now deceased, who was saved as a child under Andrew's ministry. My oldest daughter, Joanna, was present and asked a question that I'd never thought about before. 'Was Andrew a hell fire and damnation preacher?' she asked. The response was, 'No. He read the Scripture and then explained it.'"

## ... and How He Died

On February 13, 1944, the day before he was to be sent overseas, possibly to a combat area, Captain Thigpen had complained to friends that he was not feeling well and was returning to his room in the Tygant Hotel in Elkins, West Virginia, to rest. When he didn't show up for a scheduled event, he was found dead in his room, the victim of a heart attack.

On what was surely just hours before she was notified of her husband's death, Mrs. Thigpen, pregnant with her third child, Sue, was "in a restless mood one day" and was evidently looking for something to do. Confident that Captain Thigpen would be returning home soon and seeing no reason to keep all of his letters, she burned them. "Shortly after that," Martha wrote, her mother received word that her husband had died.

Andrew Thigpen *(right)* with two unidentified fellow chaplains

"The repeated thought that was expressed," Martha said, "was that Andrew died of a broken heart because he was leaving his wife and children. This in spite of the fact he had to volunteer to be in the service because preachers were not drafted."

Mrs. Thigpen, who had completed nurse's training before she and Andrew married, "never complained about being left alone with two children and one on the way," Martha continued. "She always felt that God had given her daughters, because He knew that she would have to raise them alone." Choosing never to date again after her husband's death was an easy decision for Mrs. Thigpen: "When you've had the best," she said, "why would you want anyone else?" Later, as the three daughters grew older, their mother told them that she had seen many men be nice to a widow's children before they married, but that they changed after they were married.

In response to a letter requesting additional details on how Captain

Thigpen lived and died, Martha Ann said he was "a big tease" but it was always done in love. She remembered, too, that her father loved baseball and basketball and had "a fondness" for motorcycles. A typical date, her mother once said, involved "attending baseball games and putting peanuts into their bottles of Coca Cola." Noting that her extended family seldom mentioned her father, she said, "I think that generation did not freely discuss their emotions. I believe Andrew's family felt his death as such a strong and painful loss that it was especially hard to discuss."

In a letter dated May 16, 1944, to Captain Thigpen's widow, William R. Arnold, chief of chaplains, extended "the deepest sympathies of the Chaplain Corps which shares with you this loss. It will be comforting to you to know that your husband served both his Country and his Church in an exemplary manner. The men with whom he served held him in the highest esteem and respect because of his work and conduct as a minister of God. It is our prayer that Almighty God will grant you Divine consolation in your bereavement."

Captain Thigpen, who was advanced to the rank of captain posthumously, is buried in the Enon Cemetery, Enon Baptist Church, in Doddridge, Arkansas, on "the south-most corner of the Texas/Arkansas border," according to his daughter, Martha. "At one time," she said, "Andrew had remarked on how peaceful and beautiful the place was. It is on top a hill surrounded by woods full of dogwood trees." His wife, Gertrude, both of his parents, and his parents-in-law are also buried in the Enon Cemetery.

"I never once heard Grandmother complain," Joanna Ballard said. "And the only time I ever saw her cry was not all that long before she died. I came into the kitchen one day and saw her standing by the sink crying.

"'What's wrong, Grandmother?'" I asked. "'Why are you crying?'"

"'I miss Andrew,'" she sobbed softly. "'I want to go home to be with my Andrew.'"

# James Flanagin Turner

1st Lt. James Flanagin Turner, former student, 1933–1934, 1936
Hometown: Arkadelphia, Arkansas
Died: January 21, 1945
SN 0-1287967, Company F, Second Battalion, 143rd Infantry Regiment, Thirty-sixth Division*

## How He Lived

One of seven children, 1st Lt. James Turner was born on December 13, 1915, to Cleve and Laura Eva Flanagin Turner in Arkadelphia, Arkansas. After graduating from Arkadelphia High School in 1934, he attended Henderson State Teachers College (now Henderson State University in Arkadelphia) and later entered Ouachita.

His brothers were Cleve Turner Jr., a CPA; Humphreys Turner, who taught engineering at Louisiana State University; and Otis Turner, a prominent attorney in Arkadelphia, who later became an associate justice on the Arkansas Supreme Court. His sisters were Ann Turner Wardlaw, Martha Turner Mitchell, and Laura Eva Maurer of Houston, Texas.

James entered the army in 1942 and trained at Camp Wolters, Texas; Camp Maxey, Texas; Fort Benning, Georgia; Camp Blanding, Florida; and Camp McCall, North Carolina. After three years as a parachute-school instructor, he served in Italy

In the 1934 *Ouachitonian* yearbook, James Flanagin Turner was listed as a member of the "Sons and Daughters Club" sponsored by Estelle McMillan Blake.

---

*"The Thirty-sixth Division was a Texas National Guard Division that saw much fighting in Italy and southern France," said Jack Forgy. "While in Italy in 1943, they were involved in a serious incident at the Rapido River that caused them many casualties. The Texas press claimed that the 'Rapido River ran red with the blood of valiant Texans.' It was claimed that General Mark Clark, the Fifth Army commander, bungled their deployment and that he would never visit Texas after the War."

1st Lt. James Flanagin Turner

and France. Frank Mitchell of Arkadelphia, his nephew, said James "entered the army as a private, went to Officer Candidate School (OCS), ended up a second lieutenant and was promoted to first lieutenant after his death."

In a summary of the correspondence between James and his mother, Laura Eva Turner, from the late 1930s until he was killed in action in 1945, Frank said the early letters during this period "seem to be upbeat and full of adventure from a young man set out to challenge, if not conquer life." It was not the best of times, however. Frank said he could "only imagine" what it must have been like for a teen to grow up in the midst of the Great Depression "when there was not only no money to be made but no way to make any. Frighteningly, there were no government-sponsored programs in place to protect anyone from the harsh realities of the basics of survival. People were on their own in an ocean of despair but swimming with all their neighbors and friends.

"It was a time," Frank said, "that 'steeled a nation' for the hardships that were soon to come. . . . The story begins with James going west to find work. His first report was about visiting his sister, Ann, and her husband, Andy, in southern California. James seemed to be a precocious young man, fearless and full of life. He wrote that he and a friend from home had gotten jobs with a grocery supplier in Arizona, the friend a truck driver and he in the warehouse."

Continuing his memories, Frank wrote:

> Farsighted, James guessed that the drivers, who made more money, were stuck in their jobs. His foresight was rewarded when he was promoted, at the age of twenty-four, to warehouse foreman and later assigned to oversee the stocking of a new warehouse and managing it. He wrote his father to tell him that he was required to wear a tie "but it was nice to be called Mr. Turner."
>
> The Turners were a large and close-knit family; a frame from the Spencer family of the movie, *Spencer's Mountain,* as one sibling prospered or became educated, he pulled up the next sibling. There was Cleve Jr., Ann, James, Humphreys, Martha, Otis and little Laura Eva, a family already reflecting a long pedigree of high achievement and the overcoming of adversity.
>
> The news was full of war and the challenges that faced Americans, the old and especially the young. James volunteered for the Army and

was assigned to an Arizona area for his initial duties. One early military letter contained a photograph of James in uniform and an unidentified W.A.C. It seems James was shopping in Arizona for the new bicycle he never had and later sent to his younger brother and sister. A very handsome young man, he had been asked while shopping to pose with the W.A.C. for a staged military photo that ran in a local Phoenix newspaper.

James applied for and was accepted into the paratroopers. Very quickly, he became a sergeant and later applied for Officer Candidate School (O.C.S.). When the United States entered the war, he was assigned to a unit that was to be dropped behind enemy lines during the invasion of France. James's temper, however—the incident was never explained—got him assigned instead to a support and replacement brigade that came up through Italy and the back door of France to a point that brought him to be assigned to the 101st Airborne unit as a replacement officer. He was promoted to first lieutenant but never got to wear his silver bars.

Lt. Turner, as was true of all his siblings, was very loving of his mother, Laura Eva. His father, Cleve Sr., died on October 1, 1939, leaving Laura Eva to take care of Martha, Otis and little Laura Eva alone. By 1941 or 1942, Laura Eva was operating a small grocery store on the northeast corner of the present Regions Bank parking lot. She was struggling to make ends meet. Humphreys by this time was a sergeant serving in the Army in Alaska.

Over a six-month period at the end of 1944, James and Humphreys conspired to get their mother out of the long, unproductive hours she was enduring at the store. The plot was to convince her that being a widowed mother with dependent children and "loaned-to-the-cause" children, she was eligible for some assistance from her government. In truth, James would have $100 and Humphreys $50 per month deducted from their pay and sent to their mother. She bought it and closed her door. She received her first check in January 1945, the month James was killed. Because James was on the front lines of battle, he wasn't receiving his mother's letters nor was she receiving his, communication became increasingly confusing. In fact, Laura Eva once wrote that she suspected that there was no government program and that the government was on to them. James never received that letter. . . .

James began his journey as a playful and rebellious kid, almost having been pushed out to make his way because he did not conform to the achievement goals and paths set by his hopeful and ambitious parents (probably demanded because of the harshness of the times). Neither hard-hearted nor vindictive, however, he continued to correspond, almost boastfully, that he could make it on his own. When his father died, James' position changed to protector of his family so far away from his stateside training area, sending money gifts and advice to his mother and siblings.

He offered to put Martha through Ouachita if she would conform to the rules he had earlier sidestepped, offering paternal advice to his brother, Otis, as he wove his way through high school. He seemed to be stepping up to the "father" role as he prepared to leave the United States for Europe. His letters were full of sage and selfless encouragement while at the same time, I know he was enduring the hardships of training and the pressures of facing a formidable enemy. His training as a paratrooper almost guaranteed action in a hazardous area under unusual conditions.

## . . . and How He Died

Details of the circumstances surrounding Lieutenant Turner's death during heavy fighting in the Battle of Bowden's Woods in southern France on January 21, 1945, are contained in a Regimental Unit History for that month. On January 4, the report states, "all battalions bivouacked in the vicinity of Montbronn, France. The cold was bitter and the snow heavy on the ground. There was an inadequate supply of houses to billet the troops. The battalions vigorously dug shelters for the men in the hard, snow-covered ground. Morale was high and good health was evidenced by the small number of personnel evacuated because of respiratory diseases and exposure."

In his earlier letters sent back home, Frank said, "James wrote of the adventure, telling Otis of Salerno, Rome and the Vatican but most of all, the adventure. It's eerie how youth is so oblivious to danger." But trying to survive the cold and a ferocious enemy, his sense of "adventure" began to fade. James's letters became "more suggestive of hardship and fatigue," Frank continued. "Yet there were always the selfless 'How's little Laura Eva?' or 'Tell Otis not to get hurt playing football.'"

Up to a point, said Mitchell, his uncle's "letters to his mother were upbeat." But toward the end, when Europe was suffering the harshest winter in decades, Frank said, "The tone of [James's] letters became more desperate, as he asked his mother to send him warm clothing. Anything—gloves, a scarf, a knit hat, which was essentially a ski mask." In time, such scarce items were sent but they were never received. "I sense from his letters that James wished that he had made other choices and that he desired so deeply to be home," said Mitchell.

According to the Regimental Unit history,

> Early in the morning of the day that James was killed in action, military documents reported that the enemy, trying to gain cover by the darkness, infiltrated our positions in the "Bowden's Woods."
>
> Cannon Company mounts were brought up and fired at the Germans. The enemy was not cleared of the woods. Later, the entire Second Battalion was engaged by enemy Infantry trying to penetrate the Second Battalion positions. Enemy tanks were brought up to reinforce the German Infantry. The Second Battalion fought fiercely and nobly to clear the woods. At the same time, enemy tanks overran the left flank of the Third Battalion in Company L position. A total of eight enemy tanks penetrated the position and fired directly into them. The enemy was trying hard to break our line . . .
>
> As Companies F and G continued their valiant fight to hold their positions and clear the woods, Company E was ordered to attack and relieve the pressure in their battalion sector. By mid-afternoon on 21 January 1945, Companies F and G sectors were reported clear of the enemy and Company E continued the attack to the north.

In an Operations Report for that day, made available by Jack Forgy, it is reported that in the Battle of Bowden's Woods in southern France,

> Lt. Turner's unit was attempting to clear a heavily defended stand of woods. The Germans resisted fiercely and many casualties were

THE FIGHTING TIGERS

incurred on both sides. At one point in the afternoon, E Company had to mount an attack against the German force in its sector.

James, his uncle, was killed, Mitchell said, when he was sent on a "strength probe" to locate the enemy. Frank added that he had been told by Otis Turner, James's brother, that "because of the blizzard-like conditions and the horrific battle being fought," Lieutenant Turner "may have been killed by friendly fire."

The result of the Second Battalion engagement in "Bowden's Woods" netted 163 prisoners, 60 known dead in front of their positions, and the capture of numerous valuable documents of enemy orders, strength, and general information.

Lieutenant Turner's awards included the European-African-Middle East Area Campaign Medal with four Bronze Stars, the American Defense Medal, and the Purple Heart. A Chaplain's Report states that graveside services were conducted on January 26, 1945, by Chaplain Goldman S. Drury, a Southern Baptist chaplain, at the U.S. Military Cemetery, Epinal, France.

In the conclusion to his tribute to his uncle, Frank Mitchell wrote that regardless of the horrific conditions in which he found himself toward the end of his life, James was "never complaining about his station in life. He answered his country's calls, as did scores of thousands in all forms of unity to rid the world of the tyranny that plagued the time. Such is the curious harmony, yet complete solitude, war yields. Everyone seems to be alone together. Peace has never been easy."

# William West

Tech 5 William Ellis West, former student, 1941–1942
Hometown: Princeton, Arkansas
Died: April 20, 1945
SN 38511597, 594th JASCO (Joint Assault Signal Company), U.S. Army

**How He Lived**

Tech 5 William Ellis West was born on March 28, 1924, in Little Rock to W. E. and Zella Ridens West. Ellis lived in the Princeton and Holly Springs area in Dallas County (Arkansas) and was a 1941 graduate of Princeton High School. His father, who was pastor of the Methodist Church in Princeton, received a telegram notifying him of his son's death as he was preaching a sermon.

After leaving Ouachita, Ellis taught at the New Hope (Arkansas) School, located in the Cooterneck community in 1943–44, where he boarded with the Fenniston family. Pamela Waldrop of the *Fordyce* (Arkansas) *News-Advocate* said the school consisted of two rooms and employed two teachers. Mr. West also served as the principal. "After teaching for one school term, " she said, "West was called into service. He was well liked by his students and the entire community."

William West, freshman, 1942 *Ouachitonian* yearbook

Nell Clark, also of Fordyce, and one of Ellis's childhood friends, wrote that he was "a very dear friend to our family who was a regular guest in our home. When the school bus stopped in front of their country home, Ellis and Nell's brother [who were classmates] threw their books and whatever on the dining table and headed for the peanut barn."

"I made peanut brittle for them. One day I was studying for an exam. I saw his black diary on the table. I opened it at random. The only thing I

William West and Nell Clark, a Princeton (Arkansas) High School classmate, during a school picnic in 1940

read was very striking to me. He wrote, 'The most wonderful thing that has happened to me is when Melvin Hickman accepted Christ through my witnessing to him,' I closed the book, because I knew a diary was personal," a lesson she had learned from her mother.

Although both of his parents, his two brothers—Oren West of St. Louis, Missouri, and Kenneth West—and a sister, Joyce Ann West Hearne of Holly Springs, Arkansas, were still living when Ellis was killed in action, all are now deceased, said Mrs. Clark.

"Ellis was a good person. Smart, witty, had personality plus and was an artist. I was the class poet and he was the artist. I was in the eleventh grade and he was a senior. I never dated Ellis. He was a good friend—like a brother—and teased me when he could." She remembers him as having thick, black hair, black oriental eyes, an olive complexion, and "no fat!"

He was also a tease. "When I had a tonsillectomy and talked through my nose," Nell said, "I sounded terrible. He mocked me and teased me. My throat was too sore to yell at him, so he won the battle." She remembers how during class periods he would draw caricatures of the teachers. "Ellis could draw you to look like yourself or he could make you look like a chipmunk." He was so funny, she said, "that he could make you laugh during your mother's funeral!"

Mrs. Clark also remembers Ellis's father. "At my church at Mount Olivet (Arkansas), he sprinkled me," she said. "I learned after age fifteen that a sprinkle was not enough for me. I am and have been a Missionary Baptist for sixty years."

## ... and How He Died

For whatever the reason, records for the Joint Assault Signal Company units were not as carefully kept as they were for most other military units. Yet knowing their function and the dangerous missions to which they were assigned, it is reasonably safe to speculate on how Tech 5 William Ellis West died.

As described by Jack Forgy, the JASCOs were special signal units set up to establish and maintain communications of the navy, the marines, and the army during landing operations. One of the missions of the units was to provide forward air controllers on shore, which was the most dangerous assignment. "Unless he was aboard a ship hit by kamikazes," he said, "that was probably where he was killed."

Further insights into the dangers of a JASCO assignment is provided in the following Signal Corps document:

> After costly experiences in Tarawa and Guadalcanal, Maj. Gen. Alexander A. Vandergrift directed that "communications for air liaison, naval fire control and shore parties all be pooled in one organization. The addition of shore fire control and air liaison parties to the special signal companies, which had been organized a year earlier,

resulted in the JASCO (Joint Assault Signal Companies). JASCO had both air liaison and shore-fire control parties.

Shore fire control teams were doubled, from 5 to 10 officers and men. The air liaison parties were nearly doubled, from 3 to 5 members. Five (men) were needed—to operate three radio sets; to drive a jeep; to keep informed on the air support needs of the troops; and to maintain control over air-ground communications.

One of the Signal Corps members of one of the JASCO units received a Silver Star for gallantry in action on Guam. A radio operator serving with a naval gunfire team attached to an Infantry battalion of the 27th Division, he was caught in an enemy counterattack, which killed many officers of the unit. Organizing a new defense line, he helped fight off the Japanese, looked after the wounded, and heartened the defenders. He refused to withdraw when he himself received a wound and fought on until fatally hit.

An obituary published in the *Fordyce News-Advocate,* dated June 28, 1945, reported that

> News has been received by Mr. and Mrs. W. E. West of Holly Springs of the death April 20 (1945) on Okinawa of their son, Cpl. William Ellis West, 21 years old. He was killed in action. Corporal West was graduated from Princeton High School and attended Ouachita College at Arkadelphia. He taught school one year at New Hope, near Fordyce, and entered the service Aug. 10, 1943. Corporal West took training as a radio operator at Camp Adair, Oregon, and San Luis Obispo, California, with the Joint Assault Signal Company.

Pamela Waldrop reports further that Tech 5 West was buried in Oakland Cemetery at Fordyce in a burial plot that is near that of his good friend, Buck Raney, who was also killed in WWII. "Buck Raney was my father's uncle," she said. "This burial request was Ellis's wish and was honored by his father."

THE FIGHTING TIGERS

# Earl Whiteley

Capt. Earl Bunch Whiteley, former student, 1937–1941
Hometown: Manila, Arkansas
Died: December 1, 1943
SN 0-011931, Scout Bombing Squadron 236, Marine Aircraft Group 21, First Marine Aircraft Wing, FMF, USMC

**How He Lived**

Capt. Earl Bunch Whiteley was born on August 14, 1918, to the Reverend Fielden Andrew Whiteley (Class of 1907) and Coralee Earle Whiteley in Slayton, Texas. After graduating from Ironton (Missouri) High School, on May 14, 1936, he attended the University of Missouri. He later transferred to Ouachita Baptist College in the spring of 1937, remaining there until the end of the 1941 spring semester.

On May 6, 1941, he entered the U.S. Naval Air Station at Miami, Florida, graduating as a second lieutenant. In April 1942 he accepted the appointment as first lieutenant in the U.S. Marine Corps Reserve for temporary service.

Earl married Madeline Jewell East, Hattiesburg, Mississippi, in January 1943, while stationed at Yuma, Arizona. At the time he was reported missing in action, Mrs. Whiteley was a military nurse—probably army—assigned to the 39th General Hospital c/o FPO San Francisco, California.

Earl Bunch Whiteley, undated class photo in the *Ouachitonian* yearbook

**. . . and How He Died**

Earl's sister, Mrs. Walter "Jiggs" Ramsey (former student, 1941–1942) of Hot Springs Village, Arkansas, said that soon after his marriage, he was

Capt. Earl Bunch Whiteley

ordered to the South Pacific and assigned to a Marine Scout Dive Bombing Squadron in September 1943, and was stationed in the Solomon Islands.

A previously classified USMC War Diary dated December 1, 1943, found in the National Archives, revealed that Lieutenant Whiteley was one of sixteen pilots who participated in a dive bombing and strafing attack on Japanese antiaircraft guns and installations in the vicinity of Ballale and the Kara airfields in Bougainville. When their aircraft was hit by antiaircraft fire while diving on AA positions on Ballale Island, Lieutenant Whiteley and his gunner, Tech. Sgt. Charles A. Gotchling, were observed to bail out. One person, thought to be Lieutenant Whiteley, was observed to land on the Japanese airstrip he had hit during the strafing attack, which prevented any rescue attempt.

In a letter from the Marine Corps informing his parents that Earl was missing in action, it was said that he "bravely and courageously served his country, participating in its defense at the time of its greatest need. He contributed toward the future of a better world."

The fact that Lieutenant Whiteley was carried in a "missing in action" status until January 11, 1946, when he was declared dead, indicates that the navy apparently had hopes that he and Tech. Sgt. Gotchling would be found in a camp somewhere, but apparently they never were. Jack Forgy said his research of Pacific Operations indicated that "the Japanese were not kind to our aviators when they caught them. My guess is they were executed."

Two years after Lieutenant Whiteley was reported missing, his parents received a letter dated January 18, 1946, from the Commandant's Office of the U.S. Marine Corps.

> The termination of hostilities has afforded an opportunity to conduct an extensive search for all Japanese prisoner of war camps and records, and to question returned prisoners of war, but all efforts to locate your son have been unsuccessful.
>
> In view of the circumstances surrounding your son's disappearance and the length of time which has elapsed without word of his whereabouts, the conclusion is inescapable that he lost his life at Bougainville, British Solomon Islands.

It is with deep regret that I inform you that an official declaration of presumptive death has been made by the Navy Department in the case of your son. The date of death for administrative purposes is deemed to be 11 January 1946, which is the date of the final review of his case.

I realize that there is nothing I can say to comfort you, but I hope you will find consolation and pride in the fact that your son did his part in helping to bring this war to a successful conclusion, and that the knowledge of his patriotism and unselfish contribution toward a better world in the future will sustain you in your grief.

Lieutenant Whiteley was awarded the Purple Heart, the Asiatic-Pacific Campaign Medal, the American Campaign Medal, and the Victory Medal World War II. Later in December 1943, he was posthumously advanced to the rank of captain in the U.S. Marine Corps Reserve.

Since his remains were never recovered, his name is inscribed on the Wall of the Missing in the Manila American cemetery.

# APPENDIX

*Alumni Survey*

October 20, 2001

Dear [former student's name],

I need your help in a project that I should have tackled long ago: Telling the stories of the 36 Ouachitonians who were killed in action during World War II.

During the 35 years that I have been on the OBU faculty, I must have passed by the granite monument bearing their names thousands of times. But my interest in actually writing about these fallen heroes wasn't aroused until recently when my good friend, Dr. Daniel R. Grant, the former president of OBU, recalled the life of his brother, Maj. George Shell Grant, a paratrooper who lost his life during the D-Day invasion—and whose name is among those on the monument erected by the Class of 1946.

Thanks to a university research grant I received this spring, I now have the opportunity to tell the stories of these fallen heroes. To do so, I am turning to you—graduates, former students and friends—who I hope can provide me with any memories you may have of these 36 men whose names appear on the attached pages. I wish I could provide you with more information, but our alumni office has reported that whatever records there may have been have either been lost or destroyed. The information the office does have, however, is included with the names. As you will notice, in most cases we don't even know in which branches of service these men served. I have made contact with the Office of Veterans Affairs in Washington, D.C. in hopes that some of the information I seek can be supplied by the military archives.

What I ask you to do, then, is simply this: Look over the list, share any stories you may recall that will help readers today to better know these valiant men, correct mistakes, suggest other sources of information, i.e., names of other people or offices that I can contact.

As I stated in my research proposal, "I want to make every effort possible to resurrect memories of these men so that those of us who have benefited so much from their gallantry can gain a deeper appreciation of who they were, what they wanted in life, the things that made them laugh and cry, the persons they love and whatever else I can find that puts faces and stories with these names carved in granite."

A return envelope is enclosed for your convenience. You may also call me at 245-5207 or send me an e-mail message at the following address: downsb@obu.edu. Thank you for any help you can give me.

Sincerely,

William D. Downs Jr.
Chair

## Ouachitonians Killed in Action during World War II

The following names of Ouachitonians killed in action during World War II are carved on the campus monument given to Ouachita by the Class of 1946. In the space below each name, please share (1) any information you can provide concerning your memories of these Ouachitonians *(letters, photographs, anecdotes, etc.)* or (2) suggestions concerning how we can gather additional background on them so that the stories of their lives can be made known to those who enjoy the freedom made possible through the sacrifices of these 36 men. There are almost surely many mistakes and even misinformation in the following list but that's part of the process: Sifting what is correct from that which is incorrect and ultimately publishing an account that will appropriately honor these fallen heroes.

• Virgil Benson, Class of 1941 *(no record of rank), Pine Bluff, Ark. Born March 21, 1917 in Harrell, Ark. to Mr. and Mrs. C. A. Benson. Married Frances Tow (Class of '41). B.A. in Bible, minor in speech. Activities: Ministerial Association, SAS, Alpha Psi Omega, Ouachita Players, Student Senate, captain of the football team, "O" Association, ROTC Cadet Captain,* Who's Who in American Colleges and Universities. *Hobbies: Hunting. Yearbook caption: "I still believe two can live as cheaply as one."*

• Maj. Robert Elmo Chaney, Class of 1937 and 1938. *Brinkley, Ark. Born Jan. 20, 1914 in Brinkley to Elmo and Laura Hurst Chaney. Father was mayor of Brinkley. B.A. in English and history. Activities: Football (All-State halfback and fullback, team captain) baseball and track. Killed in action in April 1945.*

• Capt. Merrill Cole, Class of 1933. *Harrisburg, Ark. B.A. Cum Laude. Attended Valley Springs (Ark.) High School. Killed in action in Germany on Nov. 29, 1944.*

• Pfc. Ralph L. Croswell. *Attended Ouachita only in the Fall of 1941. Crossett, Ark. Activities: Ouachita Band. Killed in action on Guadalcanal in 1943. Ralph was the first Ouachitonian killed overseas. The caption under his yearbook photo: "I am not afraid of tomorrow, for I have seen yesterday and I love today."*

---

THE FIGHTING TIGERS

243

• Lt. Edward Ecil Douthit, Class of 1936. *B.A. Magazine, Ark. Transferred to Ouachita from Arkansas Polytechnic College in Russellville, Ark. Went by the name Ecil. May have had two children: Sue Douthit and Joe Carl Douthit. Killed in action on March 1, 1945.*

• John M. Duffie *(no record of rank), Hope, Ark. Reported to have been a businessman in Hope. Wife's name: Opal. One son, Richard Rankin Duffie, Class of 1956.*

• Pfc. Jarold Duke, *Strong, Ark. No records.*

• Lt. Paul Beverly Garrett, *Okolona, Ark. No records.*

• Maj. George Shell Grant, Arkadelphia, Ark. *No records.*

• Lt. John Milton Hall, Class of 1943. *Arkadelphia,, Ark. B.A. in English and Math. Born June 15, 1921, in Arkadelphia to R. C. and Hattie Jordan Hall. Activities: SAS (vice president), Rifle Club, Math Honor Society, Tennis team (state singles champion during freshman year); ROTC Cadet Captain, "O" Association; went by the name of Johnny; killed in action in France, July 4, 1941.* Yearbook caption: "His mien distinguished any crowd."

• John Calvin Halsell *(no record of rank).* Attended Ouachita in Fall of 1938 and 1939. *Born Dec. 8, 1917 in Bradley, Ark., to W. C. and Marie Marbury Halsell. A native of Little Rock but graduated from Arkadelphia High School. Reporting missing in action.*

• Thomas Royce Johnson *(no record of rank).* Attended Ouachita 1941–1943. *Born Dec. 5, 1923 in Amity, Ark., to Thomas Henry and Blanche Talleson Johnson. Hometown was Texarkana, Texas, but graduated from Nashville (Ark.) High School. Killed in action in 1945.*

• Pvt. Paul Brantley Lambert, *Hayti, Mo. Listed as Paul Rambert in the 1946 yearbook (Ouachita men killed in action). No other records.*

• William C. Lawrence, *(no record of rank), Little Rock, Ark. No other records.*

• Lt. Cmdr. Ralph Mann, *Judsonia, Ark. No other records.*

• Lt. Dan Joseph Mathews, *Little Rock, Ark. No other records.*

• Pfc. David Neil Matlock, *Arkadelphia, Ark. Enrolled at Ouachita in Fall 1942 but no record of how long he was here. Two sisters: Madge Evelyn (former student 1937–38) and Merle. Was his wife's name Mary Stueart of Dallas? Was his son Neil Stueart Matlock, Class of 1964? May have served in the U.S. Army. Killed in action in January 1945.*

• Lt. Leo Winfred Mattox, Class of 1943, *Shawnee, Okla. Born in Poteau, Okla., to Robie Lester and Bernice King Mattox. After his father died, his mother remarried to Shelby Coffey of Shawnee, Okla. B.S. in Math, B.A. in Economics; graduated Magna Cum Laude. Activities: Math Honor Society, Math Lab Assistant, ROTC Cadet Captain, 12th in class of 100; married Elizabeth, who transferred from Oklahoma Baptist University and graduated in 1943 with as B.A. in English. One son: William Harrell Mattox, Class of 1966, B.A. in accounting. Lt. Mattox died of burns on Sept. 26, 1944, at O'Reilly Hospital in Springfield, Mo.*

• Pfc. Clyde Vernon McCalman, *Bradley, Ark. Born June 13, 1923 in Bradley, Ark., to R. O. and Gertrude Cupp McCalman. Attended Ouachita from Fall 1941 to Fall 1943. Wife's name may have been Sarah Jean (Sally) Allen, Class of 1950. Activities: Beta Beta, Symphonic Choir, Ministerial Association, Signal.*

• Capt. Francis Allen Norton, *Arkadelphia, Ark., later Washington, D.C. Activities: Band, Glee Club, Dramatic Club, Yell leader. Yearbook caption: "to love one maiden only, cleave to her and worship her by years of noble deeds." Killed in action in the Pacific in June 1944.*

• Lt. William Reed Parsons Jr., Class of 1939 *(B.A.), Louann, Ark. Killed in action in the Pacific in June 1944. No other records.*

• Pfc. Thomas Marion Pool, *Poplar Bluff, Mo. Born Sept. 18, 1922 in Little Rock to T. M. and Elouise McGhee Pool. Attended Ouachita from 1941 until*

*1943. Activities: Life Service Band, Ministerial Association, Symphonic Choir, OBU band.*

• Maj. Curtice H. Rankin, *Pottsville, Ark. Contrary to the listing of his name, a note in the alumni records indicates that his first name was Morton. Killed in action in September 1944. Activities: Football, basketball, track, Sons and Daughters, "O" Association (secretary), president of his Sunday School class.*

• Lt. Col. Thomas Reagan, *Waldo, Ark. No other records.*

• Lt. John Franklin Reed Jr., Class of 1941, *Pine Bluff, Ark. B.A. in biology, planned to enter the medical profession. Born Nov. 12, 1916 to John F. and Vera Parnel Reed. Activities: SAS (president), "O" Association, Chemistry Club, All-State football (Captain), sophomore and junior class president, ROTC cadet captain, Who's Who, Assistant Coach; voted "Most handsome," "Most popular." Hobbies: Hunting and fishing. Killed in a plane crash. Yearbook caption: "An all-around man, liked all around."*

• Ensign Rufus Wallace Robinson, *England, Ark. Attended Ouachita in the Fall of 1941. Born June 25, 1922, in Hummock (?), Ark., to John and Virginia Seaton Robinson. Went by the name of Wallace. Served in the Navy.*

• Lt. Carmon B. Rucker. *Born in Grand Saline, Texas, Jan. 17, 1918, to Grover and Alice Sharp Rucker. Attended Ouachita from 1937 until 1940. Majored in chemistry, minored in education. Activities: Rifle Club, Chemistry Society, Red Shirts. Yearbook caption: "I don't say anything I can't back up." Member of 883rd Squadron, 500th Bomb Group. Reported missing in action.*

• Lt. Don Gaston Shofner, *Morrilton, Ark. Attended Ouachita from 1939 until 1941. Born Sept. 17, 1921, in Damascus, Ark., to P. M. and Ina Thomason Shofner. Father was a sectional foreman in Morrilton, Ark.*

• Pfc. Joe Simpson, *Russellville, Ark. Born in 1920. Father deceased, mother was Mary Howell. Killed in action in December 1943.*

• Lt. Edwin Wadley Smith. *Attended Ouachita from 1938 until 1941. Born*

THE FIGHTING TIGERS

*July 24, 1920, in Arkadelphia, Ark., to Steve and Beulah Gresham Smith. Killed in action on Oct. 8, 1942.*

• Lt. William Cone Stell *(no record of rank). Born Nov. 15, 1916, in Banks, Ark., to L. B. and Beadie McFarland Stell. Hometown was Warren, Ark., graduated from Tinsman High School. Brother: Harley Stell, former student 1939–1940, majored in Bible, minored in English. Called "a born business man." Activities: BSU council, Tennis Club, Dramatic Club, Life Service Band, President of the BSU, Cadet staff in 1941. Called to active duty in the National Guard. Received a B.A. posthumously in 1944.*

• Lt. Ralph William Stockemer, *Hutting, Ark. Attended Ouachita from the Fall of 1938 to Spring 1941. Born Nov. 16, 1918, in Monroe, La., to R. W. and Opal Shaw Stockemer. Graduated from El Dorado High School. Played football.*

• Capt. Andrew C. Thigpen, Class of 1939, *B.A. in Bible. Houston, La. Born Dec. 19, 1911, in Mixa, La., to Ashley and Margaret Bettenton Thigpen. Activities: Life Service Band, Ministerial Alliance (President), basketball. Served as a chaplain at Camp Pickett, Va. Died in March 1944.*

Lt. James Flanagin Turner, *Arkadelphia, Ark. Parents were Cleve and Laura Eva Flanagin Turner. Sister: Eva Turner. Attended Ouachita in 1933–1934 and the fall semester, 1936.*

• William Ellis West *(no record of rank), Princeton, Ark. Born March 28, 1924 in Little Rock, parents were W. E. and Zella Ridens West. Attended Ouachita in 1941–1942. Killed on April 20, 1945 in Okinawa.*

• Earle Bunch Whiteley *(no record of rank), Ironton, Mo. Born August 12, 1918, in Sleton, Texas, to Rev. R. A. and Coralee Earle Whiteley. Transferred from the University of Missouri in the spring of 1937 and remained until the summer of 1941.*

Other comments, suggestions, etc.

THE FIGHTING TIGERS

So that we may stay in contact, please provide the following information:

Name_____Year graduated / last attended_____

Address_____City_____
State_____ZIP_____

Telephone number_____/_____

E-mail address_____

Please tell us something about yourself and your memories of Ouachita.

"A Band of Brothers," a front-page article in the *Hot Springs Sentinel-Record*, caught the attention of Jack Forgy, a native Arkansan and the chief researcher for the American WWII Orphans Network.

# ACKNOWLEDGMENTS

So much of the success of this project can be credited to the following people and organizations who took the time to reply to my inquiries through mail, e-mail, telephone conversations, fax transmissions, and in some particularly memorable cases, through face-to-face meetings. Thank you for your invaluable assistance in keeping alive the memories of these thirty-six brave young men, the "Fighting Tigers" of Ouachita Baptist University. If I have failed to acknowledge anyone who was kind enough to respond to my request for information, I sincerely apologize.

Mamie Ruth Stranburg Abernathy, H. B. "Hunk" Anderson, Arkansas Historical Society, H. B. Arnold, Jr., Bernice Ashcraft.

Dr. Billie Bagby, Dr. John Bagby, Tom Bagby, Frances Tow Benson Barnes, Tiffany Thomas Beck, Lurline Birkhead, Marjorie Allen Bishop, W. N. "Wink" Bledsoe, Judith Grant-Botter, Terry Bradberry, Norma King Bradley, James Walter Brandon, Edna Mae (Pugsley) Brantley, Harvey M. Braswell, Mary Brent, Lucille Brislan, Helen Smith Bruening, Jim Bullington.

Elizabeth Johnson Carroll, Ernest Cashion, Hattie Castleberry, Central Delta (Arkansas) Historical Society, Mark Chapel, Chris Christensen, Clark County (Arkansas) Historical Society, Nell Clark, John Cloud, Frank Cochran, Lt. Col. (Ret.) Bill Cole, Hubert Cone, Bob Coulson, Lamar Crawford.

Jean Davis, H. Franklin Dearing, Thomas DeBlack, Millie J. Dees, Brandi Dodson, Robert Douglas, Harold "Bud" Duke, Joseph E. Du Pont, Jr.

Ann M. Early, Nelson Eubank, Alma Hope Elledge, Madelyn Ewbank.

Neno Flaig, Lt. Col. (Ret.) Jack O. Forgy.

Rodney A. Geno, Robert Gladden, Smith D. Gooch, Dr. Daniel R. Grant.

Andrew Hall, Rosemary R. Hamner, Jeral L. Hampton, Maj. Gen. Herman H. Hankins, Bill Hargis, Susie Hartsfield, Nancy Harris, Marian Henderson, Dorothy Hickingbotham, Evelyn Johnson, James Henley, Maurice Hitt, Katherine Hobgood, Martha Ann Thigpen Holeman, LaVerne Rucker Hood, Beverly Hopkins, Charla Hopkins., Milton Howell, J. D. Huddleston.

Shirley Pool Jefferies, Lynn Jones, Margaret Haynes Jordan, Lynn H. Jones.

James V. Kelley, Norma Jean Maddox Kramer.

Ray Y. Langley, Gerald Laux, Steven and Brenda Leonard, W.T. Little, Archie Lyons.

Van Malcomb, Thomas L. Mann, Gene C. Martin, Ferrel Mason, Billie McCalman, Glynn McCalman, Alice Gardner Meek, Emily Kathryn Michael, Juanita Parsons Middlebrook, Les Minor, Anna Beth Mitchell, Frank Mitchell, Lila R. Montgomery, Dennis Gaston Moore, David Moyers.

Marilyn Nations, Mary D. Ponder Nelson, Bill Newberry, Robert L. Newton, Dolores Nunnally.

Jane Paladino, Marguerite Bowers Palmer, Gladys McManus Parham, Raymond E. and Bonnie B. Peeples, Don Pennington, John V. Pennington, Ken Phelps, Martha Phelps, Dr. Charles Pope, Dr. Norton A. Pope, Pope County (Arkansas) Historical Society, James L. Powers.

Virginia Queen.

Martha Whiteley Ramsey, Dr. David Rankin, Dean Reagan, Doris Reagan, Beth Reed, Lois Rice, Donna Riddle, Paul Roberson, Lillian Robinson, Mrs. James Rogers, Jeff Root.

Dale Sandlin, Mrs. C.H. Seaton, Lynda Sawyer, John Schirmer, Billie Jeanne Blackshare Scroggin, Jim Shaw, Jean Shepard, Billie Lou Shofner,

Johnnie Shofner, Laura L. Shull, Vergie Sinyard, Mac Sisson, E. M. Sleeker, Anna B. Smith, Melissa Smith, Robert W. Smith, Larry B. Stell, Paul and Gwen Stockemer, Zenia Sullivan, June Mathews Stuckey, Rebecca Syphers.

Floyd Taylor, Sr., Mary Frances Taylor, Mary Nell Turner, Molly Turner.

John and Rhonda Ward, Ray Ward, Al Wheeler, Pam Waldrop, Mercedes Ball Wheeler, Jerry Whiting, Jordan and Miller Williams.

Betty Young.

# ABOUT OUACHITA BAPTIST UNIVERSITY

Ouachita Baptist University (pronounced WASH-ah-tah) in Arkadelphia, Arkansas, was founded by the Arkansas Baptist State Convention on April 8, 1886. In 2003, with an enrollment of 1,538 undergraduate students, the university was ranked for the third consecutive year by *U.S. News & World Report* in the top-five regional comprehensive colleges and universities in the South: fifth in academics and fourth in "best value."

Strongly committed to the liberal arts with emphasis on both academic and Christian excellence, the university is divided into nine schools: the School of Interdisciplinary Studies, the Frank Hickingbotham School of Business, the Chesley and Elizabeth Pruet School of Christian Studies, the School of Education, the Bernice Young Jones School of Fine Arts, the School of Humanities, the J. D. Patterson School of Natural Sciences, and the School of Social Sciences.

In a university publication, *A Common Bond in an Uncommon Place,* it is said that the school's "uncommon approach to higher education is marked by a commitment to educate the whole person. While striving for and achieving prominence in its academic program, a Ouachita education also addresses the students' spiritual, social, and physical development.

"On a campus where students study together, worship together and live together, and where the faculty members know and care for their students, a sense of common purpose pervades. These are the elements that attract uncommon men and women to Ouachita. And it's that common bond that extends the Ouachita experience beyond the college years by nurturing lifelong relationships."

Ouachita maintained a military department continuously from its founding in 1886 until 1990. After World War I, the school was selected as one of only two Reserve Officers Training Corps (ROTC) programs in Arkansas, the other being the University of Arkansas in Fayetteville. During World War II, Mitchell Hall, an auditorium and classroom building that was under construction, was used by the Army Air Corps for housing air cadets. Among the residents was the late George Wallace, the former governor of Alabama.

# ABOUT THE AUTHOR

Dr. William D. Downs Jr., who is chair of the Department of Mass Communications at Ouachita Baptist University, joined the faculty in 1966 after a professional career in public relations and the news media. He received his B.A. degree in English and journalism from the University of Arkansas in Fayetteville, and his M.A. and Ph.D. degrees from the University of Missouri. In addition to his teaching responsibilities at OBU, he serves as the adviser of the university's American Advertising Federation's National Student Advertising Competition.

His recognitions include the Pioneer Award from the National Scholastic Press Association; two awards (1987 and 1989) as the OBU Student Senate's Outstanding Faculty Member; the national Distinguished Yearbook Adviser Award from the College Media Advisers; the Outstanding Journalism Educator Award from the Arkansas Press Association; Outstanding Advertising Educator awards from both the American Advertising Federation's Tenth District (Arkansas, Oklahoma, Texas, and Louisiana) and from the Arkansas AAF Chapter.

As the executive secretary of the Arkansas High School Press Association from 1969 until 1995, he led a successful effort through the Arkansas state legislature and the Arkansas Press Association to gain passage of a new Student Press Law for Arkansas's high schools, one of only six such state laws at that time in the nation.

In 1998, he was appointed by Arkansas governor Mike Huckabee to a six-year term as a commissioner for the Arkansas Educational Television Network, which he now serves as chairman. He has also been recognized as one of the founders of the Hot Springs (Arkansas) Documentary Film Institute.

Dr. Downs's civic activities include membership in the Rotary Club of Arkadelphia, serving as president of the Arkadelphia-area Chamber of Commerce, and as director and president of the Clark County United Way. He is a deacon and Sunday School teacher at the First Baptist Church of Arkadelphia. In addition, he and his wife, Vera, coordinate the church's ministry to the city's three nursing homes.

He has three sons, Bill III (wife, Susan), Bob (wife, Kathy), and Ben (wife, Sharon); and two grandchildren, Emily and Harrison. Bill and Vera were married in June 1990. Vera has one daughter, Tammy Lambert (husband, Steve), and two grandchildren, Chase and Cash.

# PRAYER ON WORLD WAR II MEMORIAL

Senior Class 1945, Ouachita Baptist University

Almighty God, merciful father of all mankind, Hear my dying petition. Inspire those who shall live in the world to see the futility and tragedy of war, fill their hearts with love of Thee and their fellow men, grant unto them courage and wisdom to guide our world into a lasting peace. May my supreme sacrifice help those who shall come after to remember the terrible cost of war and then I shall not have died in vain but in the service of Thy Son, the Prince of Peace.
—By Raymond Rauch

# INDEX

Allen, Wade, Jr., 95
Alpha Psi Omega,1
Ambrose, Stephen, xv
American Battle Monuments Commission (ABMC), xvii
American Military Cemetery, St. Avold, France, 30
American Military Cemetery, Luxembourg, 115
American WWII Orphans Network, xi, xvi, 66–67, 248
Anderson, Eudocia Moore Hill, 198
Anderson, F. N., 179
Anderson, H. B. "Hunk," 3, 166, 182
Anderson, William Lewis, 198
*Arkadelphia* (Arkansas) *Daily Siftings Herald,* 7, 113
*Arkansas Gazette,* 82, 89, 116, 118, 164, 205, 207
Arnold, William R., 224
Atchley, Mary, 82
*Atkins* (Arkansas) *Chronicle,* 152, 157
Auschwitz (Oswiecim), 90, 96

Bagby, Billie, xviii, xix
Bagby, John, xviii
Bailey, Wallace, 190
Ballard, Joanna, 222, 224
*Band of Brothers,* xv
Baptist Student Union Council, 202
Barnes, Frances Tow Benson, 4–5
Barnes, William, 4
Bataan Death March, 101, 103–7
Battle of Bowden's Woods, 229, 230, 231
*Battle of San Pietro,* 194
Battle of the Bulge, 9, 23, 88, 114, 143, 221
Bates, Valree, 143
Beck, Tiffany Thomas, xviii
Bennett, Sydney, 66
Benson, Mr. and Mrs. C. A., 1
Benson, Virgil "Nub," 1–5, 169, 243
Berry, Trey, xviii
Beta Beta social club, 126, 129
Billibad Prison, Manila, 104
Bird, R. Harland, 129
Biscoe, Nancy Gresham, 199
Bishop, Marjorie Allen, 126, 128, 129, 167, 169
Blair, Mrs. Milton W., Jr., 85
Blake, Estelle McMillan, 225

Bledsoe, W. N. "Wink," 111
Blish, Ruby Sue, 81
Blitz Doughs, 9, 10
Blue Raider, 176, 177, 178
*Booneville* (Arkansas) *Democrat,* 37
Bradberry, Terry, 195
Bradley, Lester, 82, 83–84
Brandon, James Walter, 7
*Breaching the Mariannas: The Battle for Saipan,* 137
Brokaw, Tom, xv, xvii
"Brother, The," 117, 119–21
Bryant, Bear, 167
Bryant, Jessica, xviii
*By God, We Made It!,* 92

Cabanatuan Prison Camp, 104–10
Campolieta, Patsy, 90
Carroll, Elizabeth Johnson, 81, 82, 83
Castleberry, Mrs. Neil, 33
Cauby, O. D., xvi
Chaney, Carter, 7
Chaney, Elmo, 6
Chaney, Laura Hurst, 6
Chaney, Marsha Hannah, 6, 8
Chaney, Robert Elmo "Modie," 6–10, 243
Chapel, Mark, 7, 9
Chapin, John C., 137
Chapman, Mr. and Mrs. J. D., 141
Chemistry Club, 166, 181
Chennault, Gen. Claire, 76, 79
"Chicken Chatter," 13
Christensen, Vern, 90, 91, 92, 93, 94, 97, 98–99
Clark, Hosea, Jr., 58
Clark, J. F., 58
Clark, Nell, 232, 233, 234
Cloud, John, xviii
Cochran, Frank, 186, 196
Cole, Bill, xviii, 11, 12, 13, 15, 19, 20, 21, 22, 26, 27, 29, 30
Cole, Carolyn Yvonne, 18
Cole, Cassie, 13, 14, 18
Cole, Elaine, 29
Cole, H. M., 156
Cole, Helen Marie White, 15–16, 17, 18, 19, 27
Cole, Ida Francis Moore, 11, 13
Cole, Lex, 13
Cole, Lonnie, 13

Cole, Merrill, xx, 11–30, 243
Cole, Orin, 11, 13, 14, 18
Conger, J. W., 199
Cookson, F. E., 50
Cowling, Dr. Dale, xx
Cox, Loyd F., 58
Croswell, Ralph, 31–34, 243
Croswell, Mr. and Mrs. Will E., 31

Daniel, Mary Stueart Matlock, 111
Davis, Jean, 182, 184
Davis, Louise Morris, 205
*D-Day with the Screaming Eagles,* 64
Dearing, George, 15
Dearing, H. Frank, 86, 88
Dearing, Jane, 15
Decatur Baptist College, 219
Dillingen, France, 30
Dillon, Mrs. Mike Lawrence, 89
Disheroon, Homer, 90, 92
Dobervich, Mike, 103
Dodson, Brandi, xviii
Douthit, Asa, 35
Douthit, Doyle, 35
Douthit, Edward Ecil, 35–40, 244
Douthit, George Albert, 35
Douthit, Glynn, 35
Douthit, Opal, 35
Douthit, Retha, 35
Douthit, Ruby, 35
Douthit, Ruth M., 35, 39
Downs, Vera, xviii
Downs, Bennett, Sharon and Harrison, 255
Downs, Robert, Kathy and Emily, 255
Downs, William III and Susan, 255
Doyle, Maude Johnson, 81
Dramatic Club, 130, 202
Duffie, Anna McDonald, 41
Duffie, Jerome, 41, 45
Duffie, John, 41–45, 244
Duffie, Richard, 41, 44, 45
Duke, Bettie, xvi
Duke, Harold Morgan, 46, 47
Duke, Jarold, 46–53, 244
Duke, John Harold, 46, 48
Duke, Sula Ida Brillhart, 46, 47, 50, 51, 52, 53
Dupont, Joseph, 101

Epinal (France) Military Cemetery, 149
Ewbank, Madelyn, 202

*Fighting Men of Arkansas, The,* xviii
Floyd, John, 8, 9
"Flying Parson," 203, 205–6, 207, 208
"For Eddie," 201
*Fordyce* (Arkansas) *News-Advocate,* 232, 235
Forgy, Jack, xiv, xiv, xvi, xvii, xviii, 34, 39, 83, 84, 107, 163, 173, 176, 194, 225, 230, 234, 238, 348
Forgy, Percy O., xvii
Fowler, Madge Matlock, 111
Fowler, Paul L., 9
Frederick, Robert T., 52

Gajosowna, Marja, 96
Garner, Richard, 90
Garrett, Beverly, 54
Garrett, George M., 54
Garrett, Matilda, 54
Garrett, Paul Beverly, 54–59, 244
Garrett, Rufus, 54
Garrett, Theenie, 54, 58
Gathright, Felix W., 58
*Ghost Soldiers,* 108
Glee Club, 130
Gotchling, Charles A., 238
Grant, Daniel R., xv, xviii, 7, 60, 61, 62, 63, 65, 68, 100, 111, 129, 145, 196, 241
Grant, Elizabeth, 60, 61
Grant, George Shell, xv, 60–67, 241, 244
Grant, George Shell, Jr., 60
Grant, Harriett, 60, 61, 64
Grant, J. R., 17, 47, 60, 61, 63, 64, 129, 167, 196
Grant, Mrs. J. R., 60, 61
Grant, Melba Smith, 60
Grant, Richard, 60, 61
Grant-Botter, Judith, 60, 62, 66
*Greatest Generation, The,* xv
Gresham, Elizabeth, 199
Gresham, Eudocia Speakes, 198
Gresham, William Wadley, 198
*Gripsholm,* 102
Gumz, Donald G., 179
Gunn, Patricia Irby, 199

Halaby, Raouf, xviii
Hall, Andrew, 63
Hall, Ellen Frances Johnson, 69
Hall, Harry, 71
Hall, Hattie Jordan, 71
Hall, John Milton, xxi, 68–74, 196, 244
Hall, Mathew W., 94

THE FIGHTING TIGERS

Hall, R. C., 68
Halliburton, W. H., 7
Halsell, Aubrey C., 75
Halsell, John Calvin, 75–80, 244
Halsell, Marie Annette Marbury, 75
Halsell, Mary Elizabeth, 75, 77, 79, 80
Halsell, Thomas E., 75
Halsell, William Calvin, 75
Halsell, William Howard, 75
Halsey, Adm. W. F., 214, 215, 216
Hamilton, Thelma Wallace, 122
Hamner, Rosemary R., 169
Hampton, Betty Lou Standfill, 72
Hampton, Jeral, xxi, 69, 72–73
Hankins, Herman, 11, 167
Hannah, Marsha, 6, 8
Hargis, William C. "Bill," 3, 8, 9
Hartsfield, Susie Green, 204
Hawkins, Jack, 101, 103, 105, 106–7, 108
Hays, Brooks, 12
Hearne, Joyce Ann West, 233
Henderson, Marian Elouise Pool, 145, 146, 147
Henderson, Pearl Orr, 147
Henri-Chapelle American Military Cemetery, Belgium, 40, 143, 164
Hevelone, Lois Nell Thigpen, 222
Hickingbotham, Dorothy, 33
Hickman, Marvin, 233
Hill, Arthur B., 159
*History of the Pine Bluff First Baptist Church from 1853–1978,* 1
Hitt, Maurice, xviii
Hobgood, Katherine, 132
Hoebreck, C. J., 134, 136
Holemon, Martha Ann Thigpen, 221
Hood, Laverne Rucker, 184
Horkan, Gen. G. A., 148
*Hot Springs* (Arkansas) *Sentinel-Record,* xvi, xvii, 248
"How Vern Christensen Handled Fear," 98–99
Howell, Milton, 190, 191
Howell, Mary E. "Mollie" Ashmore Simpson, 190, 193, 194, 195
Huckabee, Mike, 255
Huddleston, J. D., 189
Hudson, Catherine "Granny," 27
*Huttig* (Arkansas) *News,* 214, 215

International Club, 6
Isaacs, Gahlia Lee, 36

Jackson, W. E., 53
JASCO (Joint Assault Signal Company), 234–35
Jaussi, F. G., 177, 178
Jefferies, Shirley Pool, 147, 148
Jenks, Loren T., 147
Jennings, Morley, 43
Johnson, Anne, 81
Johnson, Blanche Tolleson, 81
Johnson, Ellen Frances, 69
Johnson, Hubert, 81
Johnson, Jim, 31
Johnson, John Charles, 81
Johnson, Nina, 81
Johnson, Pop, 216
Johnson, Thomas Henry, 81
Johnson, Thomas Royce, 81–84, 244
Jolley, Kathleen, 128
Jones, Lynn, 167, 169
Jordan, Juanita, 77

Kelley, Ellen Johnson Hall, 69
Kelley, James, 69
Kelley, Jim, 69
Kemp, Anthony, 157
Kinoshita, Robert, 158
Kinzer, Lorraine, 161
Knight, Julie Harstfield, 204
Knight, Todd, 204
Koskimaki, George E., 64
Kramer, Norma Jean Mattox, 122

Lambert, Lawrence "Larry," 85
Lambert, Lola M., 85, 88
Lambert, Ollie D., 85, 88
Lambert, Paul, 85–88, 244
Lambert, Steve, Tammy, Chase and Cash, 255
Langley, Ray, 38
Lawrence, Clara C., 89
Lawrence, Roland W., 89
Lawrence, William, 89–98, 244
Lawson, Joe, 90
Lewis, John, 163
Life Service Band, 145, 202, 219
Littleton, J. W. "Daddy Lit," 22, 27
*Lorraine Campaign, The,* 156
Luck, Carolyn Cagle, 199
Lyons, Archie, 82

MacDonald, Everett, 90
Malone, Edsel, 58
Manila American Cemetery, 80, 239

THE FIGHTING TIGERS

Mann, Jessie Catherine Brown, 101, 102, 103, 107
Mann, Ralph C., 100
Mann, Ralph Carlton, 100–110, 245
Mann, Thomas, 1, 100, 102
Mann, Winnie, 100
Math Honor Society, 60, 68
Mathews, Dan Joseph, 116–21, 245
Mathews, Mr. and Mrs. George, 116
Mattox, Bernice King, 122
Mattox, Carl, 158
Matlock, David Neil, 111–15, 245
Matlock, Hallie, 111, 114
Matlock, John Dayton, 111, 115
Matlock, Mary Nancy Salter, 111
Matlock, Owen, 111, 114
Matlock, Tom, 111
Mattox, Bernice King, 122
Mattox, Harrell King, 122, 123
Mattox, Leo Winfred "Fit," 122–25, 245
Mattox, Margie, 124
Mattox, Robie Lester, 122
Mattox, Thelma Wallace, 122, 123, 124
Mattox, William Harrell, 123, 124
Maurer, Laura Eva, 225
May, Jarine Mathews, 117
May, William "W. L.," 117
McCallum, T. D., 130
McCalman, Byrd, 126
McCalman, Clyde Vernon, 126–29, 245
McCalman, Gertrude Cupp, 126
McCalman, Glynn, 126, 128, 129
McCalman, J. Willie, 129
McCalman, Mariah, 129
McCalman, Marvin, 126
McCalman, R. O., 126
McClain, Merle Matlock, 111
McDaniels, Errin O., 51
Meek, Alice Gardner, 116
*Memphis Commercial Appeal,* 88
Memphis National Cemetery, 88
*Men of the Thirty-sixth Armored Infantry Regiment,* 10
Michael, Emily Kathryn, 117
Michel, Theodore J., 78
Middlebrooks, Alva Dykes, 142
Mill, John Stuart, xx
Miller, Kenneth L., 148
Mills, Mrs. Henry, 85
Ministerial Alliance, 219
Ministerial Association, 1, 126, 145
Mitchell, Frank, 227, 229, 230, 231
Mitchell, Harvey "Pro," 87

Mitchell, Martha Turner, 225
Mix, Ann Bennett, 66
Moffett, Al, 107
Montbronn, France, 229
Montgomery, Lila R., 186
Moore, Dennis Gaston, 189
Moore, Roy, 189
Moore, "Uncle" Willie, 24
Morris, W. H. H., Jr., 56
Mount Sammucro, 193
"My Son," 27, 28–30

National Cemetery, Little Rock, Ark., 143, 158
National Cemetery of the Pacific, 34, 136, 185
National Personnel Records Center, xvi
Naylor, R. E., 200
Nelson, Mary D. Ponder, 82
Newton, Robert L., 8, 204
Nichols, Dick, 58
Nichols, James O., 58
Nitsche, Arthur, 90
Normandy American Cemetery, St. Laurent-Sur-Mer, 74
Norton, Elizabeth, 130, 133
Norton, Francis Allen, 130–37, 245
Norton, Madison M., 132, 136
Norton, Marion, 130
Norton, Mildred Carter, 130, 133, 136
Norton, Virginia Beal "Ginny," 132, 133, 134, 136
Nowlin, Sara Warner Norton, 130, 136

O Association, 1, 68, 100, 150, 166
*Once in a Hundred Years,* 87
Opalinski, Mary, 94
Osborn, Leighton, 58
Ouachita Players, 1

Palidino, Jane, 188
Panzer Grenadier Regiment, 156
Parsons, Juanita Marshall, 138–39, 141, 142, 143
Parsons, William Reed, Jr., 138–44, 245
Parsons, William, III, 138, 144
Parsons, Mr. and Mrs. W. R., 138
Pasteum American Cemetery, Mt. Soprano, Italy, 53
Patton, Gen. George, 22, 163
Pennington, John, xvi
Pershing Rifle Brigade, 9
Petersen, Elwin A., 173, 176, 177, 178, 180

Phelps, Ken, 54
Pi Kappa Tau scholarship society, 60
Pollack, Andrew J., 52
Pool, Elouise Hinton McGehee, 145
Pool, Kathryn Sue, 147
Pool, Leslie Truett "Jerry," 145
Pool, Shirley Dean Frank, 147, 148
Pool, Thomas Marion, Jr., 145–49, 245
Pool, Thomas Marion, Sr., 145, 146
Pool, Van, 177
Pope, Crawford, 133
Pope, Floy, 132, 133, 134
Pope, Isabel Norton, 132, 133, 136
Pope, Norton A., 132, 133
Prayer, World War II Memorial, 257
Price, Leonard, 182

Queen, Virginia, 128

Rams, Antoni, 97
Ramsey, Mrs. Walter "Jiggs," 236
Raney, Buck, 235
Rankin, Beth Anne, 150
Rankin, Carolyn Simmons, 150, 152, 158
Rankin, Curtice H., 150–58, 246
Rankin, David, 150, 152, 156, 157, 158
Rankin, Lillie Morton, 150, 151
Rankin, William H., 150
Rauch, Raymond, xx, 257
Reagan, Barbara Lynn, 161
Reagan, Betty Carol, 161, 162
Reagan, Dean, 159, 161
Reagan, Dr. and Mrs. W. T., 159
Reagan, Mary E. Stringer, 161, 162
Reagan, Thomas H., 159–65, 219, 246
Red Shirts social club, 6, 7, 9, 100, 181
Reed, John Franklin "Rock," Jr., 1, 166–69, 246
Reed, John Franklin, Sr., 166
Reed, Rosemary Lee Sanders, 166, 167
Reed, Vera Parnell, 166
Regimental Combat Team (RCT), 49
Richardson, J. P., 177
Richmond, Aleda, 211
Richter, Wendy, xviii
Riddle, Donna, 35, 36, 37
Rifle Club, 68, 181
Roberson, Paul, 58
Robinson, Jean, 172, 173, 180
Robinson, Jennie Seaton, 170
Robinson, John D., 170
Robinson, Lillian, 170, 171, 172, 173, 174, 178, 180

Robinson, Wallace Rufus, 170–80, 246
Root, Deborah, xviii
Ross Foundation, 196
Ross, Jane, 196
ROTC, 1, 9, 17, 43, 60, 63, 68, 69, 126, 138, 150, 155, 159, 181, 196, 253
Roth, George, 9
Rucker, Alice Sharp, 181
Rucker, Carmon "Jack," 181–85, 246
Rucker, Grover, 181, 184
Rucker, Helen Lucy, 182
Rudolph, Mrs. Gene, 2
Russell, Carlton P., 9
*Russellville* (Arkansas) *Courier-Democrat,* 193

Sandlin, Dale, 37, 38
Scabbard & Blade Brigade, 9
Schecter, Gordon "G.E.," 217
Seaton, C. H., 87
Seaton, Mary Jernigan, 86, 87
Seligman, Moise, 138, 141
Shackelford, Richard, 58
Shaw, Jim, 8, 167
Shofner, Austin, 101
Shofner, Don Gaston, 186–89, 246
Shofner, Ina Thomason, 186
Shofner, P. M., 186, 188, 189
Sides, Hampton, 108
Sigma Alpha Sigma social club, 1, 60, 68, 166, 167
Sigma Chi fraternity, 132
*Signal* newspaper, 126, 155, 196
Sillegny, France, 157
Simpson, Carter, 107
Simpson, John T., 190
Simpson, Joseph, 190–95, 246
Simpson, Mollie, 190
Sinyard, Vergie, 142
Sisson, Mac, xvi, xviii
Sjodin, Dan, 91, 92
Skrzynska, Janina, 96
Skrzynska, Marja, 96
Smith, Beulah Sanders Gresham, 196
Smith, Cherry Virginia Mathews, 117
Smith, Edwin, 196–201, 246
Smith, Faunt Biscoe, 196, 199, 201
Smith, Holland M., 136
Smith, Melissa, 196
Smith, Robert W., 7
Smith, Steve Edwin, 196
Sons and Daughters Club, 6, 150, 225
*Southern Poetry Review,* 121
*Southern Standard,* 54

THE FIGHTING TIGERS

263

Spanish Club, 100
Speakes, Samuel, 199
Spradlin, Bert, 58
Stegall, Anna Bess, 199
Stell, Beadie McFarland, 202
Stell, Harley, 202
Stell, L. B., 202
Stell, William Cone, 202–8, 247
Stockemer, Gwen, 209, 214
Stockemer, Mamie Opal Shaw, 209
Stockemer, Molly Dawson, 209
Stockemer, Paul, 209, 215, 218
Stockemer, Ralph "Bo" William, Jr., 209–18, 247
Stockemer, Ralph William, III, 218
Stockemer, Ralph William, Sr., 211
Stockemer, Ruth Evelyn Johnson, 214, 215, 217
*Story of G.I. Joe, The,* 194
Stringer, Emma, 159
Stuckey, June Mathews, 117, 121
Student Senate, 1
Swaim, Mr. and Mrs. James Edward, 172
Symphonic Choir, 126

Taylor, Floyd J., 204
Taylor, Mary Frances, 190, 191, 192, 193
Tennis Club, 202
"Terry and the Pirates," 203, 205, 207, 208
*Texarkana Gazette,* 81, 115
Thigpen, Andrew, 161, 219–24, 247
Thigpen, Ashley, 219
Thigpen, Gertrude Yates, 221, 222, 223, 224
Thigpen, Margaret Betterton, 219
Thigpen, Martha Ann, 221, 222, 223, 224
Thomas, Tiffany, xviii
Thompson, Mrs. Ewell, 6
Thurmond, Mrs. Frank R., 6
Tolleson, Mr. and Mrs. V. J., 81
Tough Ombres, 22
Tow, Frances, 1
Tucker, Dennis, xviii
Tucker, Theodocia, 81
Turner, Ann, 225, 227
Turner, Cleve, Jr., 225, 227
Turner, Cleve, Sr., 225, 228
Turner, Humphreys, 225, 227
Turner, James Flanagin, 225–31, 247

Turner, Laura Eva Flanagin, 225, 227, 228, 230
Turner, Martha, 225, 227, 228, 229
Turner, Otis, 225, 227, 228, 229, 230, 231

U.S. Military Cemetery, Epinal, France, 149, 231
*Unknown Battle, The,* 157

Vail, Mrs. William Lawrence, 89
Vandergrift, Maj. Gen. Alexander A., 234
Van Fleet, Maj. Gen. James, 22

WAC (Women's Army Corps), 228
Waldrop, Pamela, 232, 235
Wall of the Missing, Manila, 4, 66, 237
Wallace, William "Bill," 123, 124
Wallace, Jessie Leigh Iber, 122
Wallace, L. T., 122
Walton, Bill, 4, 8, 9
Ward, John, 188
Ward, Wayne, 63, 126
Wardlow, Ann Turner, 225
Warrington, Jane Shofner, 189
Watson, Sidney E., 58
Weatherly, Allen, xviii
West, Kenneth, 233
West, Oren, 233
West, W. E., 232
West, William, 232–35, 247
West, Zella Ridens, 232
Westmoreland, Andrew, viv, xviii
Wheeler, Mercedes Ball, 192, 193
Whiteley, Coralee Earle, 236
Whiteley, Earl, 236–39, 247
Whiteley, Fielden Andrew, 236
Whiteley, Madeline Jewell East, 236
Whiting, Jerry, 91
Wichmann, Arthur, 90
Wight, Randall, xviii
Williams, Jordan Hall, 74
Williams, Miller, 74
Willis, Mrs. R. M., 193
Wingfield, William Stewart, 58
Wittman, Wanda Sue Thigpen, 222
Wolverton, Robert, 64

Young, Betty, 54